NATIONAL
GEOGRAPHIC

TRAVELER

LONDON

NATIONAL GEOGRAPHIC
TRAVELER

LONDON

by Louise Nicholson
photography by Alison Wright

National Geographic
Washington, D.C.

CONTENTS

Pages 2–3: The Changing of the Guard at Buckingham Palace
Opposite: Henry VII's Lady Chapel at Westminster Abbey

TRAVELING WITH EYES OPEN

Alert travelers go with a purpose and leave with a benefit. If you travel responsibly, you can help support wildlife conservation, historic preservation, and cultural enrichment in the places you visit. You can enrich your own travel experience as well.

To be a geo-savvy traveler:

- Recognize that your presence has an impact on the places you visit.

- Spend your time and money in ways that sustain local character. (Besides, it's more interesting that way.)

- Value the destination's natural and cultural heritage.

- Respect the local customs and traditions.

- Express appreciation to local people about things you find interesting and unique to the place: its nature and scenery, music and food, historic villages and buildings.

- Vote with your wallet: Support the people who support the place, patronizing businesses that make an effort to celebrate and protect what's special there. Seek out local shops, restaurants, and inns. Use tour operators who love their home—who love taking care of it and showing it off. Avoid businesses that detract from the character of the place.

- Enrich yourself, taking home memories and stories to tell, knowing that you have contributed to the preservation and enhancement of the destination.

That is the type of travel now called geotourism, defined as "tourism that sustains or enhances the geographical character of a place—its environment, culture, aesthetics, heritage, and the well-being of its residents." To learn more, visit National Geographic's Center for Sustainable Destinations at *nationalgeographic.com/maps/geotourism.*

NATIONAL GEOGRAPHIC
TRAVELER

LONDON

ABOUT THE AUTHORS & THE PHOTOGRAPHER

Louise Nicholson, a London resident for 25 years, considers the English capital the world's most exciting city. She is an art historian, conservationist, and journalist, and her more than 25 books mostly concern London and India. She won the London Tourist Board's "best book of the decade" award and was a finalist for the Thomas Cook Travel award. She is also author of *National Geographic Traveler: India.* In 2001 she moved to New York, gaining valuable new perspectives on the expectations of visitors to London. She received the 2010 Woman of the Year award from the National Association of Professional Women of America. Her website is *louisenicholsonindia.com.*

Alison Wright, a New York–based documentary photographer, has spent a career capturing the human spirit through her photographs, traveling to all corners of the globe photographing endangered cultures and people. Her photography is represented by the National Geographic Image collection and is published in a number of National Geographic books and publications. Wright is a recipient of the Dorothea Lange Award in Documentary Photography and a two-time winner of the Lowell Thomas Travel Journalism Award. Her memoir, *Learning to Breathe: One Woman's Journey of Spirit and Survival,* was published in 2008.

Larry Porges updated and wrote new features and sidebars for the 2011 and 2016 editions. He lived in London for five years. Along with Tim Jepson, he co-wrote *National Geographic London Book of Lists.* He misses London, especially the *London Evening Standard,* Little Venice, and being surrounded by people who know the lyrics to "Blue Is the Colour."

British-born **Tim Jepson,** who updated the Travelwise section for the 2011 and 2016 editions, is widely traveled and has written several titles for National Geographic, but home is Notting Hill, in west London.

CHARTING YOUR TRIP

This sprawling, charming city of over 8 million souls, spread over 610 square miles (1,580 sq km), is not something you're going to conquer in a few days. The city bursts at the seams with relics and reminders of its 2,000 years of rich history, including some of the world's most celebrated architecture and repositories of art and culture. London is a destination to tackle with a sense of humility.

Getting Around

By any standards, the London public transportation system is excellent. The subway system (the Tube) and London's famous red buses can take you to every corner of the city, while the Docklands Light Railway (DLR) to the east and the overground suburban train service fill in gaps. Even Thames riverboat commuting is possible; services are frequent and varied (see sidebar p. 53). The Tube is in the process of a major (and needed) upgrade, and delays and temporary closures, especially on weekends, are common. (That said, Tube service is expanding: Weekend overnight service on select lines started in September 2015.) The Transport for London website (tfl.gov.uk) is a comprehensive resource for maps and information on routes, services, and Travelcards.

Black taxis are plentiful and convenient, but pricey—they can be hailed anytime on the street. (The cab is free if the rooftop light is illuminated.) Radio cabs are also available, but need to be called in advance. (See Travelwise p. 237 for a list of companies.) Meanwhile, the app-based rideshare service Uber (uber.com) is also an option.

Don't even consider renting a car to tour central London. Traffic congestion is a major issue, plus construction for Crossrail (Elizabeth Line)—a new rail line being built from east to west London—will mean temporary street closures in some of the city's busiest districts for several years. Crossrail main service is scheduled to begin in 2020.

If You Have Only a Week

Begin your week where London began: the original City, the Square Mile that the Romans first called home. First stop on **Day 1** can be Sir Christopher Wren's 17th-century masterpiece, St. Paul's Cathedral, located on Ludgate Hill. From here, it's a short walk north to the fascinating exhibits of the Museum of London. Backtrack south across the Thames on the pedestrian-only Millennium Bridge to the Tate Modern, one of the world's leading modern art exhibition

The imperial state crown in the Tower of London

spaces. From the Tate, walk east along the riverbank to the re-creation of Shakespeare's famous Globe Theatre in atmospheric Southwark. Then cross London Bridge back to the north side of the Thames. One Tube stop east brings you to the Tower of London, where Beefeaters, crown jewels, and tales of beheadings will fill the rest of your day. A Thames boat ride from the tower or St. Katharine's Wharf is a relaxing way to head home.

Day 2 takes you to Westminster, the royal and political center of the capital. Begin at Westminster Abbey, home to Poets' Corner, beautiful cloisters, and tombs of English monarchs. It's a short walk across the street to the neo-Gothic Houses of Parliament. A loop north and west takes in Downing Street, the expanse of the Horse Guards Parade, lovely St. James's Park, and the queen's London house at Buckingham Palace. Head back to Westminster Bridge and walk over the

Thames—the views back to Parliament are the stuff of picture postcards. Across on the lively and ofttimes tourist-heavy South Bank you'll find the towering London Eye observation wheel, the Sea Life London Aquarium, and the Southbank collection of art, film, and concert venues. The excellent Imperial War Museum stands a ten-minute walk farther south.

The bustling West End, London's main entertainment district, can be the focus of **Day 3.** Start out with a stroll around Trafalgar Square, the epicenter of the action—the treasures of the National Gallery and the National Portrait Gallery are only steps away. Wander north into Leicester Square, where a booth provides reasonably priced theater tickets to West End shows. Piccadilly Circus, Soho, and Chinatown round out your roamings farther north, while electric Covent Garden to the east beckons with shops, restaurants, and street entertainers.

Visitor Information

Both the excellent **Visit London** *(visitlondon.com)* and **London Town** *(londontown.com)* websites provide a wealth of online information on hotels, restaurants, shopping, and all you need to know about visiting London, including the location of several information centers within the city. See Travelwise p. 239 for a list of other useful websites.

Be sure to check out *Time Out,* a free weekly magazine with the latest information on movies, theater, museum exhibits, events, restaurants, and clubs around the city.

Visit Bloomsbury and the British Museum's massive collection to start **Day 4.** Just south, at the north end of Lincoln's Inn Fields, is the Sir John Soane's Museum, crammed full of fine art and quirky artifacts. From there, an eclectic range of sites are all within walking distance: the Charles Dickens Museum to the northeast, the quiet lanes and courtyards of the Inns of Court to the south, and the renowned Courtauld Institute art collection (closed until 2021) south along the Thames at Somerset House.

Start **Day 5** at royal Kensington Palace and its exhibits, gardens, and grounds. A short walk southeast through

Climate

In general, London enjoys defined seasons. Winter (Nov.–March) is cold with frosts and sometimes snow. Spring (April–May) warms up. Summer (June–Aug.) can be warm enough to eat dinner outside and may even become humid and sticky. And fall's (Sept.–Oct.) chilly mornings can be the prelude to warm sunny days. See Travelwise p. 236 for more information.

Fun fact: London's famous fogs of the last centuries were not functions of climate but were actually blankets of heavy industrial pollution. They were eliminated by the Clean Air Act of 1956.

Kensington Gardens takes you to the ornate Albert Memorial, while the impressive Victoria and Albert, Natural History, and Science museums are all nearby, a short walk south on Cromwell Road. From here, the siren call of Harrods and Harvey Nichols department stores lures shoppers a half mile (1 km) east on Brompton Road.

Devote **Day 6** to touring east London, one of the city's fastest growing areas. A weekend visit is best to take in the markets at Brick Lane, Spitalfields, and Petticoat Lane, but any day is good to explore the neighborhood's South Asian culture and food. Be sure to leave time to take the DLR to Canary Wharf and the excellent Museum of London Docklands, as well as a few hours to explore lovely Greenwich a couple miles south, across the Thames.

Day 7 can be your chance to buy all those last-minute gifts for yourself and others, with some refined culture mixed in. Start on Oxford Street, one of the world's busiest retail strips. Head west from Oxford Circus to stately Selfridges department store and dozens of other retailers. A detour north a quarter mile (0.4 km) or so brings you to the art and armor of the Wallace Collection. Before Marble Arch, turn south to walk through Mayfair backstreets to indulge in a traditional afternoon tea at one of the great hotels—perhaps Claridge's, Grosvenor House, or the Dorchester.

If You Have More Time

There's so much to see and do in London, a week really won't cut it. A venture to northern London takes in **Regent's Park** and its beautiful garden, **Madame Tussauds's** kitschy but fun wax museum directly to its south, **Camden Town's** huge and lively weekend markets off the park's northeast corner, and the lovely canals of **Little Venice** and St. John's Wood with **Abbey Road** (of Beatles fame) to the west. A longer excursion 15 miles (24 km) west brings you to Henry VIII's

Discount Passes

London is a very expensive city—there's no shame in taking advantage of as many discounts as possible. For public transportation, the convenient Oyster card and a variety of Travelcards allow you reduced fares on the Tube, buses, overground rail, Docklands Light Railway, trams, and many mainline railway services. Check *tfl.gov.uk/tickets* for complete information.

The London Pass (*londonpass.com*) provides entry to more than 55 major attractions for one price and offers the option to add on a London Transport Travelcard. The pass also allows you to skip the line at some locations.

Combination tickets are available for many of the city's popular (and high-priced) attractions, such as the London Eye and Madame Tussauds. These can offer big savings in the long run. The London Eye website (*londoneye.com*) lists a variety of options.

London's welcoming pubs—such as the Sherlock Holmes in Westminster—offer respite for visitors.

stunning **Hampton Court Palace,** best reached by cruising up the Thames or via the frequent train service from Waterloo Station.

London is also full of intriguing small museums and houses that often fly under the mainstream radar. Very much worth a visit are the **V&A Museum of Childhood** and the **Geffrye Museum of the Home,** dedicated to the history of domestic life, both in east London; the 19th-century **Old Operating Theatre** in Southwark; and elaborately decorated **Leighton House** near Holland Park in west London.

Sports fans may want to take in a **football (soccer) match**—the Barclays Premier League is often touted as the most exciting league in the world. Chelsea *(chelseafc.com),* Arsenal *(arsenal.com),* Tottenham *(tottenhamhotspur.com),* and West Ham *(whufc.com)* are the top London clubs. If you cannot get a ticket, join Londoners watching the games in the pubs, or book a stadium tour. If cricket is more your style, Middlesex *(middlesexccc.com)* plays its home matches at Lord's, near Regent's Park, and Surrey's home ground is at the Kia Oval *(kiaoval.com),* south of the Thames.

If you need a break from the bustle, London is an excellent base for excursions. **Windsor Castle,** Shakespeare's **Stratford-upon-Avon,** seaside **Brighton,** idyllic **Cambridge,** the Georgian spa town of **Bath,** and the other destinations listed on pp. 219–234 are all within reach on Britain's excellent National Rail *(ojp.nationalrail.co.uk)* lines or by rental car. All major U.S. car rental companies operate in the U.K., or try Europcar *(europcar.co.uk).*

Tipping

In restaurants, check if the service charge has already been added; if not, the usual tip is 10 percent. In pubs and bars there is no tipping except for table service. Taxi drivers expect a 10 percent tip, more if they help with luggage or have to wait. There is no tipping in theaters, cinemas, or concert halls.

HISTORY & CULTURE

▪ Above: Detail of the Buckingham
Palace gate
Opposite: A Yeoman stands tall at
Hampton Court Palace.

LONDON TODAY

London is a living and constantly changing city. Some cities depend on impressive historic buildings for their greatness, others on being the center of government or culture or finance; still others are exciting because they are modern. What makes London unique is that it is all of these in one. It is simply the most culturally rich, stimulating, and dynamic city in the world.

There is, delightfully, too much to do, to see, to visit, and to explore. First-time visitors almost always return to revisit favorite haunts or to explore a little bit more. In fact, about 20 million people visit each year.

London's more than 8 million residents find their great city every bit as exciting.

Come Together: Abbey Road's zebra crossing has become a London landmark.

More than 30 percent were born elsewhere. Of the remainder, many are second- or third-generation immigrants. Some have fulfilled a childhood dream of moving from another part of Britain to the capital. Some have come from farther afield, choosing to leave homelands such as India, Pakistan, and the Caribbean when the British Empire ended after World War II. Others have arrived fleeing political unrest in China, Cyprus, Italy, Kenya, Uganda, and elsewhere. London is truly cosmopolitan. More than 200 languages are spoken. English may be predominant, but you might hear Polish, Chinese dialects, Gujarati, Urdu, Punjabi, Bengali, Turkish, Arabic, Italian, and Spanish on any street corner.

66 **The core of London is spread along the north bank of the twisting Thames River, the capital's backbone.** 99

Entering this pulsating mass for the first time takes one's breath away. Nowhere else offers such quality in such quantity. For instance, most people know that they want to visit the British Museum or the Victoria and Albert Museum, but

few are aware that there are some 300 other museums to choose from—plus myriad commercial art galleries that make London the world center of the art trade. London's theater is legendary, and visitors naturally flock to its many venues. But they are often surprised that they have to choose among more than 100 theaters staging plays or musicals at any one time; some of the best shows may be in theaters well away from the main theater district, the West End.

The museums and theaters are often superb buildings themselves, each telling a tiny part of London's history. Indeed, the quality of London's historic buildings may not surprise the visitor, but the quantity—almost 19,000 protected buildings tucked into every corner of this sprawling city—most certainly does. For instance, Buckingham Palace is not the only royal palace; you can visit six others including the palaces of Westminster, Hampton Court, and Kensington. These palaces are spread out across the expanse of London, so that Hampton Court Palace in the west is about 18 miles (29 km) from Greenwich Palace in the east.

Grasping the general layout of this vast city is the first goal for any visitor. The core of London is spread along the north bank of the twisting Thames River, the capital's backbone. The oldest part, confusingly known as the City, is the tightly packed financial hub. The City's sleek buildings, soaring around the dome of St. Paul's Cathedral and 100 other City churches, are the destination for many of the million or so sharp-suited commuters who, from Monday to Friday, flood into London by train or car. Other City workers cross the capital on the Tube (as the Underground train system is now officially called) or squeeze into red buses.

Outside the City's east wall stand the riverside Tower of London and Tower Bridge. Behind stretches the East End, where the story of London's immigrants and dockworkers unfolds in

■ **The London Eye provides visitors with uplifting vistas up and down the Thames both day and night.**

the streets of Whitechapel and Spitalfields—French Huguenot silk-weavers' fine houses, Jewish synagogues, the Cockney traders of Petticoat Lane market, and the spice-scented streets where many Bengalis now live. Here, too, lives Europe's greatest concentration of artists, designers, and musicians, many using old warehouses as studios. East of the tower, 11 miles (18 km) of docks—left silent when the port moved to Tilbury—have been revived. Known as the Docklands, the area has its own elevated Docklands Light Railway, some daring new buildings, and, farther north, extensive sports facilities—it is here that the 2012 Summer Olympics were held. Opposite the Docklands, on the south bank lie ancient Greenwich Palace and Greenwich Peninsula with its landmark O_2 Arena (formerly called the Millennium Dome).

Hard by the City's north wall, Clerkenwell with its monastic remains leads north to Islington with its elegant houses, thriving fringe theaters, and a plethora of restaurants.

West of the City lies Westminster, London's political and royal center. Here, north of Westminster Bridge, stand the Houses of Parliament, Westminster Abbey, and the government's sprawling Whitehall offices. Buckingham Palace and St. James's Palace are nearby, surrounded by St. James's and Green Parks. This is where smart residential London first grew up, and the area has retained its status—St. James's and Mayfair contain some of London's most stylish shops, art galleries, and restaurants, as well as gentlemen's clubs, both Christie's and Sotheby's auction houses, and deluxe hotels such as the Ritz. London continues westward into the elegant residential and shopping districts of Belgravia, Knightsbridge, and Chelsea. Still farther west lie Kensington, Holland Park, and South Kensington, home to the Science, Natural History, and Victoria and Albert museums. In these areas look for building facades that often have decorated doorways, terra-cotta friezes, or blue plaques noting that a person of historical importance lived at that address. Farther west are former aristocrats' country mansions, now swallowed up by the suburbs: Osterley, Syon House, Kew Palace and Gardens, and finally Hampton Court Palace.

London between the City and Westminster has a distinct character. On the north bank of the Thames, the old lanes and squares of Holborn, Bloomsbury, Covent Garden, and Soho contain the West End theaters and a rich concentration of museums and restaurants. Meanwhile, along the south bank of the Thames, a strip of entertainment centers running from Tower Bridge to Westminster Bridge includes the National Theatre, Shakespeare's Globe theater, and the Tate Modern museum.

London's legal Inns of Court extend through Holborn from Gray's Inn to the riverside Inner and Middle Temples. Leafy Bloomsbury squares are the setting for the British Museum, much of the University of London, and a string of specialist museums stretching down to Covent Garden, a center for theaters, restaurants, shops, and street entertainment. To the west of Covent Garden is Trafalgar Square, where the National Gallery looks down over the fountains to Whitehall and St. James's. A few minutes' walk north from Trafalgar Square, Leicester Square—a focal point of the London night scene—marks the start of Soho. Its southern part is London's Chinatown; its northern part is a mixture of bars, restaurants, and food shops. Theater-lined Shaftesbury Avenue slashes through Soho to Piccadilly Circus. Regent Street, lined with upmarket shops, sweeps elegantly north from here, along Mayfair's eastern edge and up toward Regent's Park. Beyond lie the residential areas of St. John's Wood, hilltop Hampstead, and Highgate.

Despite this variety, Londoners and visitors need to find peace. While the financial markets buzz, there are many ways to relax. London offers countless opportunities for recreation and relaxation, from food to shopping, from theaters to parks. It has more than 6,000 restaurants to choose from; 5,000 or so pubs and bars, many in old buildings or in pretty locations along the river, also serve food; some have music and even theaters.

If relaxation means shopping, try Oxford Street, the longest retail street in Europe. London's two greatest department stores are Selfridges, on Oxford Street, and Harrods in Knightsbridge. Some 350 street markets include Portobello Road's antiques shops

EXPERIENCE:
London Walking Tours

With 2,000 years of history hidden in every nook and cranny of its labyrinth of streets, London is a perfect city for guided walking tours.

The best known and best organized tours are led by **London Walks** (tel 020 7624 3978, walks.com), which offers daily two-hour walks covering topics such as Jack the Ripper, the Beatles Magical Mystery Tour, and the Hidden Pubs of Old London Town. **And Did Those Feet** (chr.org.uk) prides itself on high academic standards, while **Blue Badge** tour guides (guidelondon. org.uk, britainsbestguides.org) offer higher priced (and high-quality) personalized half- and full-day tours. **Londontown. com** provides a variety of guided walks at londontown.com.

and stalls. If relaxation means a walk in a park, make the most of London's parkland. If it means music, you can enjoy the sweet notes of more than 1,000 concerts a week taking place in concert halls, music colleges, churches, and museums.

Despite this banquet of choice, visitors to London can sometimes find themselves choked by crowds of other visitors, unable to taste the essence of the city they have come to visit. If this happens, it is best to leave the lines at Madame Tussauds or the Tower of London behind and hop on a bus or take the Underground to one of the city's more colorful areas. Try Soho or Islington, or take a walk along the south bank of the Thames from Westminster to Tower Bridge.

The Making of London

The twisting, slow-flowing Thames, Britain's longest river, was for many centuries London's nerve center. Roman London stood on its north bank, alongside its vital port. A thousand years after the Romans arrived, Edward the Confessor established his new riverside palace and monastery upstream to the west, on the marshes of Westminster, and so London's second city was born. William the Conqueror consolidated Westminster's position as the royal, political, and religious capital of his new land, while later sovereigns enjoyed a string of palaces built on the banks of the Thames from Hampton Court to Greenwich.

London grew fast. By 1700 its population was around 600,000, making it the largest and fastest growing city in Western Europe. Soon the capital was 20 times the size of the next biggest English city and contained one-tenth of the country's population. The city expanded westward, northward, and, in the 19th century, southward over new river bridges, as well as eastward around the docks. By the 1930s, its population peaked at 10 million.

The river is still a key factor in London's development. In the new century, Docklands has been the largest urban renewal site in Europe, and historic riverside buildings such as the Tower of London and the Houses of Parliament are joined by new ones, including Embankment Place, and the world's largest dome at Greenwich Peninsula.

Parks

Londoners seeking escape on weekends do not need to leave their city. Parks of all kinds enrich the capital, about 1,700 in all. They range from the walled Chelsea Physic Garden

■ Hyde Park is one of many London parks offering a green refuge within the city.

and handkerchief-size City churchyards to the great expanses of Richmond Park and the formal Royal Botanic Gardens. Indeed, nearly 11 percent of Greater London is parkland, a total of 70 square miles (180 sq km).

It was the monarchs who first protected large open spaces for their hunting. Today, these hunting grounds survive as the magnificent royal parks. Hyde Park, formerly considered the fashionable center of London, has fine landscaping and offers activity aplenty. The childlike serenity of neighboring Kensington Park, with its palace backdrop, is quite different. Regent's Park retains the grandeur of its original aristocratic country estate plan. St. James's Park, close to Buckingham Palace, is the place for pageantry, and nearby Green Park offers tranquility and shady trees. In the far west of London, Richmond, the largest royal park, has wonderful views from its hills, while Bushy Park, with its grand chestnut avenue and deer, is tied to Hampton Court Palace. In the east, Greenwich Park sweeps up from gleaming Queen's House to provide the finest panoramic viewpoint of London.

London's other green spaces have evolved in different ways. Hampstead Heath was once common grazing ground. Victoria Park and Battersea Park, opened in 1846 and 1858 respectively, were created to improve local conditions. Peace and quiet can be found in cemeteries and churchyards—St. Dunstan-in-the-East, a secret garden within a ruined church, is especially magical.

Wildlife & Nature

London not only supports a population of over 8 million people, it is a nature sanctuary whose diversity and importance are unrivaled by those of any other capital. London bees produce a good honey, and Richmond Park's 1,000 species of beetle have helped make it a Site of Special Scientific Interest.

Great, thick forests once encircled London, before they were pushed back for agriculture. Vestiges include the spinneys of Highgate Woods and Holland Park and some of the ancient oaks of Richmond Park. The 18th-century Enlightenment and Picturesque movements awakened Londoners to nature's beauties, both tamed and untamed. It was at this time that Kew's Royal Botanic Gardens were planted.

In the 19th century, the Victorians replaced many traditional limes, elms, and chestnuts with plane trees (see sidebar above). They also controlled their parkland vistas by introducing evergreen oaks, copper beeches, false acacias, arbutus, and trees of heaven.

Other parts of London are truly wild, notably the neglected cemeteries where hedgehogs, weasels, frogs, and foxes have resettled. And birds—redstarts, kestrels, and herons—have returned to London, to join the pigeons, sparrows, and seagulls. ∎

London Plane Trees

London is lucky to have benefited from the plane tree. This hearty, quick-growing shade tree has claimed the city as its own, standing sentry along its streets, filling the peaceful parks, and providing a green ornament for its squares.

The London plane can grow to heights of about 98 to 130 feet (30–40 m) and is especially adept at urban living. Air pollution gets absorbed in the tree's thick outer bark, which is then shed as needed, revealing a healthy layer. The plane can be easily transplanted and does well in the typical hard-packed London soil. Plus, its strong limbs can survive wind and heavy rain better than most, helping it stand tall when other trees might cry uncle. Its ability to thrive, even during London's most polluted days, is a fine example of evolutionary adaptation.

HISTORY OF LONDON

It is people who have, over the centuries, shaped the London we know today. Some have left a tangible legacy: The Romans left their Temple of Mithras, Samuel Pepys his vivid diary, and William Hogarth his caricatures of 18th-century life. London today is the city created by all those who have taken part in its 2,000-year history.

Roman London

London might have been born in 54 B.C. when Julius Caesar and his Roman army attacked the Catuvellauni forces who held two hills beside the Thames, at the point where it stopped being tidal and could easily be forded. But Caesar instead returned to Gaul (France). It was under Emperor Claudius, in A.D. 43, that the Romans came back and founded Londinium port on the same spot. They built the first London Bridge, linking their ports on the southeast coast (now Kent) to Camulodunum (Colchester), capital of their British province.

After a revolt of the British tribes, led by Queen Boudicca of the Iceni, who burned the city down in A.D. 61, the Romans made Londinium their capital. A tall, thick wall protected its 30,000 to 60,000 inhabitants. Public buildings included baths, temples, gardens, a basilica, and a forum. But in 410, mirroring Rome's decline, Roman troops left London.

> " The young Viking Dane Cnut (r.1016–1035) chose London, not Winchester, as his capital—a position it would never again lose. "

Saxons & Vikings

After the Romans left, London dwindled. However, its location ensured that trade continued—and its wealth attracted invaders. Over the next three centuries, Angles and Saxons from northwest Germany gradually established small kingdoms in England—Kent, Mercia, Wessex, and others. Saxon London, called Lundenwic, was sited along the Strand. Through the sixth and seventh centuries it prospered with international trade.

But there were other eyes on London. Viking longships left Norway, Sweden, and Denmark to raid England. In 842 and 851, Danish Vikings stormed London, and in 872 they made it their headquarters. It was Alfred (r.871–899), the Christian king of an enlarged Wessex, who recaptured the city in 886 and made peace with the Danes. Although Winchester was the royal capital, Alfred made Lundenwic the power base. He moved the earlier Saxon settlement from the Strand, where enemy longships could easily beach, back inside the walls and renamed it Lundenburh. He repaired the defenses and invigorated international trade, devising a countrywide code of law and a system of taxation and instituting military service. When the Danes returned in 980, the state was strong enough to hold firm, even if hefty "Danegeld" tribute was needed to buy off war.

But these payoffs didn't protect England from the eventual arrival of the Danes as rulers of England. The young Viking Dane Cnut (r.1016–1035) chose London, not Winchester, as his capital—a position it would never again lose. Cnut brought prosperity to the country and patronized the church.

Medieval London

In the years 1042 to 1485, Westminster was established as the seat of the monarchy, while the City's merchants exercised more and more control over their city and their kings.

When Edward the Confessor (r.1042–1066) dared not make his pilgrimage to Rome (he feared a coup if he left the country), Pope Leo permitted him to restore the modest Westminster Abbey instead. Thus began one of London's greatest building projects: the

■ The Battle of Hastings in 1066 brought Normans into England and into London.

Street Names That Tell a Story

Doesn't Pudding Lane sound like a charming cobblestoned alley, evoking images of good-natured vendors selling sweets to happy children? Think again. "Pudding" was actually the medieval term for animal guts, and Pudding Lane was a street by the riverside that housed many a butcher shop. Animal innards were tossed out the overhanging windows, and gravity, time, and the occasional broom would funnel the pudding down the sharply pitched street into a waste removal system of barges on the Thames.

London is full of evocative street names. Many derive their names from the ancient businesses plied there: It's clear what was sold on Poultry Street, Wood Street, Milk Street, Honey Lane, and Bread Street, all located near or on the old market at Cheapside. Less obvious is the origin of Friday Street's name, until we learn it led directly to Cheapside's fishmongers.

Other London street names tell a variety of different stories: Houndsditch, at the east end of the City, was a ditch just outside city walls where, in the Middle Ages, the bodies of dead dogs were unceremoniously tossed; Cockpit Steps, in Westminster, was the site of royal cockfights; Old Jewry, a street near the present-day Guildhall, was a Jewish settlement in Anglo-Saxon times; and Clink Street in Southwark marks the location of the old Clink prison (long since gone), which endowed the language with a short and sweet English nickname for a jail.

monastery, abbey church, and royal palace of Westminster. But it was Edward's cousin, William (r.1066–1087), Duke of Normandy, who established Westminster as the seat of royal and state power. Invading England in 1066, he crushed Edward's successor, Harold, at the Battle of Hastings. Norman rule, with imported administrators and soldiers, replaced Anglo-Saxon; and, to keep watch over the City merchants, William (later known as The Conqueror) built the Tower of London.

William's great tax survey of England, the Domesday Book, reveals an ordered society that would thrive under Norman and Plantagenet rule. This was a period of Crusades abroad and extensive monastic building at home. Between 1077 and 1136, 13 monasteries and 126 churches were built in and around London's wall, including St. Bartholomew's Church and Hospital. At Westminster, Henry III (r.1216–1272) began the Gothic rebuilding of the Abbey in 1245.

In the City, the merchants won the right to be self-governing in 1191. In 1215 King John (r.1199–1216) put his seal to the Magna Carta, which curbed his powers. By 1295, the Model Parliament of Edward I (r.1272–1307), government was by consent, not rule.

The next century witnessed the Black Death (1348–1350) epidemic, when half of London's population died; the Peasants' Revolt of 1381, which Richard II (r.1377–1399) quelled at Smithfield; and the Wars of the Roses (1455–1485) inheritance dispute. On a happier note, in 1477 William Caxton produced the first book printed in England on his Westminster press.

Tudor London

When Henry VII (r.1485–1509) came to the throne, ushering in Tudor rule (1485–1603), London's prosperity and status surged forward, out of the medieval world into the Renaissance and onto the international stage.

War-torn England recovered under strong rulers, and the benefit was felt most in London. Commerce expanded. Wharves lined the riverfront. In 1566, Thomas Gresham built the Royal Exchange to enable London financiers and merchants to compete with Antwerp. London's population leaped from 75,000 to 200,000, making it the fastest-growing European city, and equal in size to Paris and Milan.

Trade boomed as merchant-adventurers opened up new trading routes, to Asia for silks and spices and to America for tobacco and sugar. At Deptford and Woolwich, a navy was built up that would quash Philip II's Spanish Armada in 1588 and enable Francis Drake, Walter Raleigh, John Hawkins, and others to explore new trade routes, laying the foundation for the colonies of the British Empire.

The church, however, was turbulent. Henry VIII (r. 1509–1547), lacking a male heir, instructed his lord chancellor, Cardinal Wolsey, to win permission from the pope to divorce Catherine of Aragon. When he failed, the king dismissed him, took over his palatial homes at Hampton Court and Whitehall, and from 1532 to 1534 broke with Rome to become Supreme Head of the English Church. The Reformation began. It promoted Protestant ideas, English-language Bibles, and the Dissolution of the Monasteries (1536–1540). About 800 religious houses were closed, 20 of them in and around London. The capital's atmosphere and character were profoundly altered as secular power replaced the religious influence.

Henry was succeeded by his son, the boy-king Edward VI (r. 1547–1553), his daughter Mary I (r. 1553–1558), and then his younger daughter, Elizabeth I (r. 1558–1603).

■ The Palace of Westminster was the principal London royal residence until the reign of Henry VIII.

With her heady mix of intelligence, charm, and arrogance, she gave her name to an age: the Elizabethan Renaissance. This was the age of the first custom-built theaters (where Shakespeare's plays were performed), of art patrons, and of pageantry.

Stuarts & Revolution

After Elizabeth's death, Londoners celebrated King James VI of Scotland as their James I (r. 1603–1625), the first Stuart sovereign of England. The Stuarts (1603–1714, except for 1649–1660, the period of the Republic) failed to unite Catholics and Protestants.

Parliament turned against the extravagant, well-meaning monarchs. Protestants left for the New World—the Pilgrim Fathers sailed on the *Mayflower* from Southampton in 1620. Papists threatened the king's life—Catholic conspirators tried to blow up the royal family and Parliament in 1605. Finally, after Charles I (r. 1625–1649) was executed for treason (see sidebar this page), Oliver Cromwell and his Puritan followers formed the Commonwealth (1649–1653), and then the Protectorate (1653–1659).

Their Puritan London did not last. Soon after Cromwell's death, the monarchy was restored and Charles II (r. 1660–1685) took the throne. This marked the start of the Restoration, where dramatist John Dryden, composer Henry Purcell, scientist Isaac Newton, painter William Hogarth, and architect Christopher Wren were key figures in a creative outburst. But Parliament's attempts to restrict royal power soon broke down.

When Charles's Catholic successor James II (r. 1685–1688) fled to France, the bloodless Glorious Revolution witnessed Parliament inviting the Dutch Prince William of Orange (r. 1689–1702) and his wife, Mary (r. 1689–1694), both Protestants, to take the throne. They signed the Bill of Rights (1689), limiting the monarch's power and excluding Catholics from the throne. In Parliament, modern elements of government evolved, such as political parties, cabinet government, and the limited parliamentary term. Later, under Queen Anne (r. 1702–1714), Scotland and England signed the Act of Union (1707).

Meanwhile, Londoners had suffered the Great Plague, which killed some 110,000 in 1665, then the Great Fire of London, which raged for four days in 1666 and destroyed

The Execution of Charles I

In 1648, with the English Civil War finally over, a tribunal assembled by Oliver Cromwell and his Parliamentarians sentenced defeated king Charles I to death, citing his "wicked design to erect and uphold in himself an unlimited and tyrannical power to rule according to his will, and to overthrow the rights and liberties of the people of England."

The sentence of beheading was carried out on January 30, 1649. Charles was led through Banqueting House, then part of Whitehall Palace, to the makeshift scaffolding erected outside. He wore extra-heavy clothing, as the day was very cold and he was concerned that visible shivering would be construed as cowardice by the thousands of spectators in the crowd.

The king acted with poise and dignity on the scaffold. Charles asked the executioner that the fatal blow not be struck until he had stretched his hands out wide by his side, signaling his readiness. After adjusting the executioner's block, the king lay in position, spoke softly to himself, and gave the agreed-upon signal. Charles was beheaded in one stroke. By all accounts, the act was greeted with a woeful combination of groans, cries, and stunned silence.

GEORGE II.
1727 – 1760

GEORGE III.
1760 – 1820

GEORGE IV.
1820 – 1830

St.Vincent

1977

A 1977 St. Vincent stamp shows English kings George II, George III, and George IV.

four-fifths of the wood-built City. Afterward, the wealthy moved westward and architect Wren's St. Paul's Cathedral and churches gave new character to the City. A financial explosion stimulated by William Paterson's new Bank of England (1694) generated ideas that would produce the Stock Exchange, the Baltic Exchange, and Lloyd's.

Georgian London

When Queen Anne died without a direct heir, the crown went to the great-grandson of James I, the German-speaking Elector of Hanover named George. Thus began the Hanoverian line that continues today, called Windsor since 1917.

Under the Georges—George I (r. 1714– 1727), George II (r. 1727–1760), George III (r. 1760–1820), and George IV (Prince Regent 1811–1820, king 1820–1830)—London prospered as never before. Trade and the arts flourished, and the population doubled to one million. London became Europe's largest city.

This huge metropolis needed houses. The wealthy moved westward again, first toward the Court at St. James's and then over the Bloomsbury fields, and northward up to Islington, Hampstead, and Highgate. Inspired by Inigo Jones's Covent Garden Piazza of 1631 and Henry Jermyn's lucrative development of St. James's Square in the 1660s, developers coated aristocrats' London estates with terraces and squares to create Mayfair, Marylebone, and later Belgravia. London also expanded southward: Westminster Bridge opened in 1750, and others followed. Northward, the flamboyant Prince Regent and his architect, John Nash, laid out Regent Street and Regent's Park and Canal in 1811–1828.

Grand private mansions were also built, such as Apsley House, Kenwood, Syon, and Osterley, where Scottish architect Robert Adam introduced his delicate neoclassicism. Indeed, classicism and intellectual inquiry were fundamental to the 18th-century Enlightenment movement. In London it found expression in David Garrick's classical theater, Lord Burlington's Palladian villa at Chiswick, and in the establishment of learned and artistic societies such as the Royal Society of Arts (1754) and the Royal Academy (1768).

London's wealth rested on trade. The industrial revolution and the expansion of the empire made London the world's largest port in 1800—up to 8,000 ships might be on the Thames at any given time. To thwart pilferers and speed up the unloading of cargo, the merchants built walled, enclosed docks, an 11-mile-long (17.7 km) system completed in 1921.

Victorian London

In 1837 the young Victoria ascended the throne to reign for 63 years. She gave her name to an age of change, invention, growth, and contrast, particularly in her vast capital—now the center of an empire that stretched across the world. Colonialism became imperialism; in 1877, Victoria became queen-empress of India.

During the 19th century, London's population exploded from one million to more than six million people. Despite Victorian London's wealth, the issues of transportation, water supply, sewage, and slums posed huge challenges. Nevertheless, entrepreneurs, philanthropists, and entertainers prevented the city from grinding to a standstill.

London was now too big to walk across, too widespread to be served by the Thames ferries. In 1829, London's first regular public horse-dawn bus service started. Electric trams followed in 1901, motor buses in 1905.

London's first railway opened in 1836. Two years later, Euston terminus was built; there were a dozen more by 1899, making the capital easy to visit. From 1851, the North London Link brought workers from outlying London villages to the docks. The railway companies' need to issue precise timetables resulted in the establishment of British Standard Time in 1884, and it was soon adopted around the world. The world's first underground railway had opened in 1863; the first deep-dug lines for electric trains, soon known as the Tube, followed in 1890.

> **Despite Victorian London's wealth, the issues of transportation, water supply, sewage, and slums posed huge challenges.**

People migrated from the countryside in droves. There were also waves of immigrants. Following the Irish potato famine of 1845–1848, 100,000 Irish arrived, cramming into speculators' tenement housing, which, lacking drainage and running water, quickly became slums. Later, in the 1880s, more than 100,000 Jews arrived, fleeing anti-Semitic pogroms in Russia and Eastern Europe. Many settled in Whitechapel in the East End.

London had been seriously overpopulated since the 1830s, and its hygiene infrastructure collapsed. More than 400 sewers emptied into the Thames. Typhus, smallpox, and cholera were rampant. After the 1848–1849 cholera epidemic and the Great Stink of 1858 (when the stench of a hot summer and the overflow of human waste finally jolted

■ **Firemen hose down wreckage after a bombing raid during World War II.**

the city into action), engineer Joseph Bazalgette designed London's first sewage system. He then created the Embankments, built between 1864 and 1874, reclaiming land from the Thames to house a trunk sewer, an underground railway, gas mains, and a water conduit, with a road and public gardens above.

Prince Albert, Queen Victoria's Consort, realized his grand plan for promoting learning and trade. On May 1, 1851, his Great Exhibition opened, displaying "the Works of Industry of all Nations" in a great glass hall in Hyde Park, designed by a gardener, Joseph Paxton. Six million people visited it, a third of the British population. Afterward, Albert was the vision behind a permanent showcase of science and the arts in South Kensington. Beginning with the Victoria and Albert Museum in 1855, museums, colleges, and institutions soon covered an area fondly known as Albertopolis.

Londoners needed lighter entertainment, too. By the 1890s, London had 38 West End theaters and was the theater capital of the world. In the East End, Marie Lloyd was one of the stars who sang in more than 30 music halls, each seating up to 1,400 spectators. Meanwhile, countless heroes of empire, science, and the arts were honored with public statues, most notably Admiral Lord Nelson in Trafalgar Square, named for the battle in which he died defeating the French.

St. Pancras International

While London may best be known as a city of ancient tradition, St. Pancras train station is a symbol of its future. The station was dramatically refurbished from 2001 to 2007, and in 2007 it became the London terminus of the Eurostar trains to Europe.

A shiny new train terminal, built below the original 250-foot (75 m) arching roof of the Gothic Victorian structure, greets visitors stepping off from Belgium and France with a range of shops, restaurants, cafés, pubs, and wine bars, including an impressive 315-foot-long (96 m) champagne bar.

But all is not metal and glass. Keep an eye out for statues of wyverns—mythical winged reptiles with the heads of dragons—that were the emblem of the Midland Railway Company, which built this fine terminus for their railway in the 1860s.

Twentieth-Century London

Under Edward VII (r. 1901–1910), Victorian grandeur acquired a certain extravagance and decadence that was halted by World War I. George V (r. 1910–1936) saw his capital suffer Zeppelin raids, unemployment, overcrowding, and an influx of refugees. George VI (r. 1936–1952) witnessed the World War II bombs, the arrival of Polish refugees, the dissolution of the empire, and, in 1948, the creation of the Commonwealth. Since 1952, his daughter Elizabeth II has reigned over a truly multicultural London, whose cosmopolitan outlook continues to enable waves of innovation to influence the rest of the world.

The 20th century saw great physical change in London. It began when Aston Webb laid out a royal processional route from Buckingham Palace, along The Mall to Admiralty Arch. After World War II, bomb sites such as the Barbican were rebuilt as high-rise housing, and developers took advantage of the property slump—most of Mayfair's mansions were destroyed at this time. This gave energy to the burgeoning conservation movement, whose advocates fought to save Covent Garden, Islington, and other areas.

After London Port was moved to Tilbury, the docklands slowly closed down. Then, in 1981, the world's largest urban renewal program began, heavily backed by the government. The profitable deregulations of the financial markets in 1986—"the Big Bang"—led the City to rebuild half of its office space; the following year saw Rupert Murdoch's revolution in newspaper production silence London's home of printing, Fleet Street.

London's people changed, too. When the population of Greater London peaked at ten million in the 1930s, housing was short, the smog was unhygienic, and one million people worked on the docks. Political refugees were also arriving by the thousands: Jews went to the East End, then to northern areas such as Golders Green, Edgware, and Stamford Hill; Turkish Cypriots settled in Haringey and Stoke Newington, and Italians in Clerkenwell. After World War II, more than one million Londoners left for the verdant suburbs. Their houses were often divided up for the thousands of immigrants coming from the Commonwealth—Jamaicans went to Brixton and Stockwell, Trinidadians and Barbadians to Notting Hill, Asians to Southall, and Hong Kong Chinese to Soho.

Amid these crises and upheavals, London witnessed many landmark events—the first BBC broadcasts (radio in 1922, TV in 1936), all women over 21 winning the vote in 1928, and in 1951, the Festival of Britain. Held on the south bank of the Thames to raise Londoners' morale after postwar austerity, the festival marked a release of new creative energy. South Bank now has one of Europe's largest arts complexes.

The Swinging Sixties followed, and then an outpouring of innovative music, art, architecture, and fashion. Terence Conran, Andrew Lloyd Webber, Norman Foster, Vivienne Westwood, and many more lifted London's status. The city was once again a fashionable and exciting place in which to live and work.

The Twenty-First Century

The new millennium witnessed Eurostar trains running from London to Paris via the Channel Tunnel and a revitalization of the London riverscape for public buildings, such as Tate Modern at Bankside, and residential warehouse conversions.

The city and nation suffered a painful blow on July 7, 2005, when 52 people were killed in four coordinated terrorist bombings on the London public transportation system. A memorial to the victims stands quietly at the eastern edge of Hyde Park.

More recently, and more happily, the wedding of William, Duke of Cambridge (second in line to the throne), to Kate Middleton in 2011 and that of his brother, Harry, to Meghan Markle in 2018 were much celebrated and watched by billions around the globe. The renewed popularity of the royal family grew with the birth of William and Kate's children—George Alexander Louis (2013), Charlotte Elizabeth Diana (2015), and Louis Arthur Charles (2018) but was shaken once again when Harry and Meghan announced that they were giving up their royal titles only a few months after their son, Archie, was born (2019). The British dubbed the choice made by the Duke and Duchess of Sussex "Megxit" in a play on words that imitated "Brexit," which had become official the same month, on January 31, 2020, more than three years after a referendum had ratified the withdrawal of the United Kingdom from the European Union.

Looking to the future, the legacy of the 2012 Olympics continues the revitalization of the East End. Meanwhile, work continues on the Crossrail, the new railway line whose main section will be inaugurated in 2020, connecting dozens of existing railway and tube stations, thus solving some of the traffic problems in the city. ■

Prince Harry and Meghan Markle on their wedding day (May 19, 2018)

THE ARTS

London is remarkable not for its cultural cohesion but for its cultural diversity. Almost everything you might ever want is here—it is merely a question of finding it: a thousand years of architecture, painting stretching back to early Gothic delights, statues from the Romans onward, and music and theater of every description. London's museums, galleries, churches, and open houses can be overpoweringly rich. If the Victoria and Albert Museum is too exhausting to contemplate, you can always visit smaller galleries.

In London, art is unavoidable. Commercial galleries and auction houses show art on the move. Sculptures spangle London's streets and parks. Both private houses and impressive public buildings may be decorated with fine ironwork or terra-cotta friezes—you have only to lift your eyes above street level to see them.

Architecture

London has superb examples of virtually every British architectural style. Westminster's story leads through grand public buildings, such as Westminster Abbey, and the royal palaces and parks. It also includes the aristocrats' mansions and amusements. In the City the remains are a rich mix of livery halls, offices, dealing rooms, and markets that culminate in Broadgate and the Dockland's Canary Wharf developments.

> **Westminster's story leads through grand public buildings, such as Westminster Abbey, and the royal palaces and parks.**

Pre-Norman Remains: Evidence of occupation in the London area goes back to about 500,000 B.C., but the most substantial pre-Norman remains are Roman. Archaeologists have located the forum, basilica, amphitheater, governor's palace, and public bath sites. The Museum of London possesses some fine mosaic floors and a wall painting from Southwark. In the City, there are thick chunks of Roman wall at Trinity Square and on Tower Hill and a section of amphitheater beneath Guildhall Art Gallery.

Norman Castles & Churches: The houses of London's Saxon, Norman, and medieval merchants and craftsmen were built of wood and plaster, so they did not last. Just before the Norman Conquest, the Saxon King Edward the Confessor built Westminster Abbey (consecrated 1065), inspired by buildings at Jumièges and Caen in France. The Romanesque style he adopted, with its chunky piers, rounded arches, galleries, and open timber roof, was so widely used by the Normans that in Britain it is known as Norman style.

William I built a ring of castles, including Windsor, around his capital, and his White

(continued on p. 34)

■ St. Paul's, built in the 17th century, is England's only domed cathedral.

TRADITIONAL ENGLISH FOOD

Like airplane food, English cuisine suffers from a serious lack of respect. Never mind that London is one of the hottest cities on the planet for fine dining—it's the traditional fare that usually takes the brunt of the jokes. But what's not to love?

Fish and chips shops are a traditional, but increasingly rare, London sight.

The English custom of boiling vegetables beyond recognition is largely a thing of the past. If it's comfort food you're looking for, London delivers.

The Traditional English Breakfast

Start your day with a traditional English breakfast, which is usually made up of eggs (most often fried, though sometimes scrambled or poached), back bacon, grilled tomatoes, baked beans, fried mushrooms, black pudding, English sausages, and toast. Sometimes kippers (very salty, smoked herring) is on the menu as well. Nearly all hotels and cafés offer some variation of the English breakfast, though many pubs also offer the meal throughout the day. Standout breakfasts can be had at **Simpson's-in-the-Strand** (100 Strand, WC2, tel 020 7420 2111, Underground Temple, simpsonsinthestrand.co.uk,

$$), the **Wolseley** restaurant (160 Piccadilly, W1, tel 020 7499 6996, Underground Green Park, thewolseley.com, $$$$), or at any of the four **Richoux** (172, Piccadilly, W1, tel 020 7493 2204, Underground Green Park, richoux.co.uk, $$–$$$) restaurants around the city.

Pub Grub

If, by chance, you find yourself in a pub during lunch, there will most likely be several reliable dishes on the menu, all falling under the rubric of "pub grub." Try the Ploughman's Lunch, a hearty meal that usually consists of a thick slab of farmhouse cheddar cheese, tangy relish (called "pickle" in England), salad greens, pickled onions, and fresh, crusty bread. Other tasty fare includes meat- and/or vegetable-filled savory pastries (called pasties) and pies (steak & kidney being the most famous, but many others are available); English sausages with mashed potato, gravy, and peas (aka bangers and mash); shepherd's pie; and traditional roasts of beef, pork, or lamb.

Meanwhile, gastropubs are taking pub food firmly into the 21st century. What began as an isolated effort to upgrade the offerings of pub kitchens with refined, creative menus is now a major foodie movement. Gastropubs are sweeping across London and can be found in nearly every neighborhood; check with your hotel concierge or local friends for recommendations. Some of the tried and true include the **Eagle** (159 Farringdon Rd., EC1, tel 020 7837 1353, Overground Farringdon, theeaglefarringdon. co.uk, $$–$$$) in Clerkenwell, the **Charles Lamb** (16 Elia St., N1, tel 020 7837 5040, Underground Angel, thecharleslamb.co.uk, $$–$$$) in Islington, and the **Gun** (27 Coldharbour, E14, tel 020 7515 5222, thegundocklands.com) in Docklands.

Dinner Fare

In addition to the traditional dinnertime roasts, several restaurants specialize in British meats and game. Established in 1798, **Rules** (35 Maiden Lane, WC2, tel 020 7836 5314, Underground Leicester Square or Covent Garden, rules.co.uk, $$$$) in Covent Garden is the oldest restaurant in London and the place to go for seasonal game,

including grouse, pheasant, and deer.

St. John (26 St. John St., EC1, tel 020 7251 0848, Uderground Barbican, Overground Farringdon, stjohnrestaurant.com, $$–$$$), appropriately located near the Smithfield Meat Market, is a highly celebrated restaurant that specializes in "nose-to-tail" dishes that waste no part of the animal—but its menu is extensive enough to also please those less enamored with offal.

Pie & Mash

An East End staple for centuries, traditional pie and mash shops are sadly on the endangered species list. The bill of fare consists of a hearty minced-meat pie accompanied by a healthy spoonful of mashed potatoes, all buried in green "liquor"—a seasoned parsley-based broth that has nothing to do with alcohol. Jellied or stewed eels are usually the only other offerings.

A few authentic pie and mash shops remain around London. Two old-timers worth a visit: **F. Cooke** (150 Hoxton St., N1, tel 020 7729 7718, Overground Hoxton, $) in East London's hipster Hoxton neighborhood, and **M. Manze's** (87 Tower Bridge Rd., SE1, ttel 020 7837 5270, Underground Borough, manze.co.uk, $) south of the Thames (and at two other locations).

EXPERIENCE: Sampling Fish & Chips

Another dying tradition to bemoan: the decline of corner fish and chips shops, which used to be found in every neighborhood but now are few and far between. Even so, the renowned hot battered-and-fried fish (usually cod, plaice, or haddock) and the thick wedge potato fries (served with salt and vinegar) are worth seeking out.

A high-end option is the **Sea Shell of Lisson Grove** (49–51 Lisson Grove, NW1, tel 020 7224 9000, seashellrestaurant.co.uk, $$–$$$), near the Marylebone Tube station, which has been serving fresh fish and chips to London's jet set for 40 years.

Other recommendations include

Rock & Sole Plaice (47 Endell St., WC2, tel 020 7836 3785, rockandsoleplaice.com, $$–$$$), in Covent Garden, a popular haunt of Londoners and tourists alike for more than 100 years; **J Sheekey** (28–32 St Martin Ct., WC2, tel 020 7240 2565, Underground Leicester Square, j-sheekey. co.uk, $$$$), another popular, century-old Covent Garden purveyor of the tried and true (with modern choices as well); and the **Golden Hind** (71a–73 Marylebone Ln., W1, tel 020 7486 3644, Underground Bond Street, goldenhindrestaurant.com, $), a local favorite since 1914, tucked away in the quiet Marylebone neighborhood north of Oxford Street.

■ **Henry VIII added on to Cardinal Wolsey's Hampton Court Palace.**

Tower (1078–1097), kernel of the Tower of London, is an important example of Norman military architecture. Built of Caen stone, the walls are 12 feet (3.6 m) thick, and the square plan contains three rooms on each floor; the cupolas on the corner towers are 14th-century additions. A masterpiece of Norman ecclesiastical architecture is the White Tower's St. John's Chapel: tiny, simple, and with two massive arches.

In London the best surviving Norman church is St. Bartholomew the Great, built in 1123 as part of the priory and hospital, and now the City's only surviving 12th-century monastic church.

Medieval Architecture: Medieval London's walls, with towers and seven double gateways, are still identifiable by street names such as Aldersgate, Aldgate, and Bishopsgate. They surrounded a city made up of flimsy wooden houses, livery company halls, and about 140 churches. The circular Temple Church in Inner Temple, begun in 1160 and enlarged in 1220, is one of London's earliest buildings constructed in the Gothic style, seen in the pointed arcade arches.

Surviving medieval buildings include the labyrinth of Inner and Middle Temples dating from 1350 and Lincoln's Inn from 1400. Richard II's Westminster Hall, with its spectacular hammerbeam roof, was started in 1394, while City merchants built their Guildhall between 1411 and 1440. Archbishop Morton built the redbrick gatehouse of his Lambeth Palace around 1495.

The most impressive of the 20 medieval religious houses in London was Westminster Abbey, the royal abbey Church of St. Peter, together with its monks' cloisters. In 1245, Henry III demolished it and began building a lavish Gothic church. Four monastic houses stood just north of the City: St. Bartholomew's Priory, Charterhouse Monastery, St. John of Jerusalem's Priory, and Clerkenwell Nunnery. St. John's great gateway evokes their grandeur.

Tudor Buildings: Some of the most glorious buildings seen in London today were built as expressions of the capital's growing world status under the Tudor sovereigns, who ruled from 1485 to 1603. Henry VII added his soaring, lacelike chapel to Westminster Abbey in the early 1500s. The fine fan vaulting and large windows typical of this period give it a spiritually uplifting airiness. A rare, surviving domestic building, Charterhouse Priory's heavy Washhouse court, built between 1500 and 1535, contrasts sharply.

A major catalyst for this growth was Henry VIII's Dissolution of the Monasteries (1536–1540), which released large swaths of land for building by royals, aristocrats, and developers. While the monarchs concentrated on their palaces and parks, aristocrats and bishops built along the Strand. This was the riverfront that stretched between the City and Westminster. These buildings survive only in street names—Bridewell, Savoy, Northumberland.

> " While the monarchs concentrated on their palaces and parks, aristocrats and bishops built along the Strand. "

The Old Hall of Lincoln's Inn, built in 1492 as housing for the lawyers who resided there, gives an idea of how most of Tudor London must have looked. There is also Camden's Staple Inn, a group of 16th-century domestic houses built in 1586: The half-timbering, horizontal strips of windows, high gables, and overhanging upper floors are typical of the period, although brick houses with chimneys and glass windows were growing in number.

The Tudor monarchs realized the importance of an outward show of power. Henry VII started the royal wave of secular building with Richmond Palace and Baynard's Castle at Blackfriars, both completed in 1501. When Henry VIII came to the throne in 1509, he inherited these, along with the Tower of London, Eltham Palace, and others—some 16 residences within a day's ride of the capital.

At Greenwich, Henry built tennis courts, a tiltyard (medieval knights' competition area), and a large royal armory that could compete with continental products. With the fall of Cardinal Wolsey, he seized Whitehall Palace and added entertainment areas and riverside State apartments, painting the brickwork red, white, and black. At Wolsey's already vast Hampton Court Palace, he built a great hall, chapel, kitchens, and service courts. Henry also seized the former leper hospital of St. James's. It is in these last two that Tudor palace-building can best be seen today.

While advances were made in domestic housing, overpopulation in the City led to multiple occupancy of houses, poor hygiene, more fires, poverty, and an increase in fatal illnesses—smallpox, tuberculosis, and bubonic plague. A royal proclamation in 1580 forbade the building of any new houses or the subdivision of any existing ones.

Stuart & Georgian London: Inigo Jones gave Stuart London its first Palladian buildings—Queen's House at Greenwich, built in 1616, Banqueting House at Whitehall in 1619, Queen's Chapel by St. James's Palace in 1623–1627, St. Paul's Covent Garden in 1631–1638, and London's first square, Covent Garden Piazza, in 1631.

The Great Fire of 1666 provided the impetus for further change. In 1667 the first Building Act was passed: All structural walls were to be of brick or stone, and the only projections allowed were balconies. There were also rules governing foundations, timbers being near chimneys, house heights, street widths, and other requirements. The aim was to raise building and safety standards and to control town planning. The result was that plain, flat-fronted terraces and squares would be built over the fields as London expanded, creating the classic character of residential Georgian London.

> " The capital's post-fire architectural hero was Sir Christopher Wren, who rebuilt St. Paul's Cathedral, beginning in 1675. "

The capital's post-fire architectural hero was Sir Christopher Wren, who rebuilt St. Paul's Cathedral, beginning in 1675. Wren also designed 51 churches to surround St. Paul's and worked extensively for the royals at Kensington and Hampton Court Palaces, and at Chelsea and Greenwich Hospitals.

The 18th-century Enlightenment attracted a plethora of fine classical architects to London. Nicholas Hawksmoor's Christ Church in Spitalfields, completed in 1714, and James Gibbs's St. Martin-in-the-Fields, of 1721, were two of many new churches. Impressive public buildings included William Kent's Treasury of 1733, William Chambers's Somerset House of 1776, and Robert Smirke's British Museum of 1823. Meanwhile, Lord Burlington's Chiswick House of 1725, and Robert Adam's remodeling of Syon, Osterley, and Kenwood mansions in the 1760s, introduced new lightness and elegance to classical buildings. Finally, the Prince Regent employed John Nash from 1816 to 1828 to create the great sweep of Regent Street and Regent's Park, all coated in gleaming, white stucco.

Victorian & Edwardian Architecture: As the London of Queen Victoria transformed itself into the huge capital of an empire, sweeping changes took place in many spheres. In architecture, classicism was challenged by a Gothic revival and by a return to a redbrick, vernacular style inspired by Christopher Wren.

Nineteenth-century developers followed the lead of Georgian builders, whose planning centered on garden squares. Thomas Cubitt's Belgravia by Buckingham Palace was the grandest. Other developments included west London's Cadogan and Ladbroke estates, and the Islington squares. Bedford Park, begun in 1875, and Hampstead Garden Suburb, begun in 1906, broke new ground in suburbia.

There was a proliferation of public buildings aimed at bringing education to the general public, among them William Wilkins's National Gallery of 1832 and the glasshouses (greenhouses) of Kew. The South Kensington buildings stimulated by the Great Exhibition of 1851 included Alfred Waterhouse's Natural History Museum and Richard

Norman Shaw's Royal Geographical Society, both of 1873, and Sir Aston Webb's Victoria and Albert Museum of 1899. Westminster changed radically: The Houses of Parliament suffered a disastrous fire in 1834 and A. W. N. Pugin and Charles Barry designed the new Houses of Parliament in elaborate Victorian neo-Gothic.

London's vastly increased size necessitated improvements in its infrastructure. New communications demanded new types of building: Sir George Gilbert Scott designed the Gothic St. Pancras railway station and adjacent hotel of 1868–1874. Wide Shaftesbury Avenue was one of several new roads that sliced through slums.

London's Buildings, 1900–Present: London's population today is only slightly higher than what it was in 1900 when, at around 7 million, it was the world's most populated city—New York had 4 million people, Paris 2.7 million.

▪ **The graceful curves of the Nelson Stair at Somerset House**

Trafalgar Square's Fourth Plinth

While Trafalgar Square has always been synonymous with the towering statue of Horatio, Lord Nelson, more contemporary art has also been on show in recent years.

Behold the Fourth Plinth. Although the rest of Trafalgar Square was completed in the 1840s, the plinth (a statue base) in the northwest corner of the square remained vacant after funding ran out.

That changed in the 1990s when three artists were commissioned to create works that, one after the other, would temporarily call the plinth their home. The program proved so popular that the Fourth Plinth is now formally being used to display innovative contemporary art.

Works in recent years have included a 20-foot-long (6 m) ship in a bottle (appropriately featuring Admiral Nelson's ship, H.M.S. *Victory*) by Yinka Shonibare, and Anthony Gormley's "One and Other," where everyday Brits occupied the plinth for one hour. This went on every hour, 24 hours a day, for 100 days.

A display in the basement of nearby St. Martin-in-the-Fields church shows all the short-listed entries for the artwork to be featured next. The Fourth Plinth even has its own website *(london.gov.uk/fourth plinth)*, where you can keep abreast of the latest proposed new displays (and vote for your favorite).

In the 1920s and '30s, crowding, smog, and dirt generated a middle-class exodus to the suburbs, hastened after World War II. Garden suburbs were seen as the idyllic solution to the ills of city life. Nevertheless, the city's population and boundaries continued to grow, and in the 1930s peaked at about 9 million.

After World War II damage, postwar construction focused on much needed housing, including the City's large Barbican Estate, begun in 1959. In the public sector, Robert Matthew's Royal Festival Hall was built for the 1951 Festival of Britain and marked the start of the Southbank Centre arts complex.

The 20th century saw several interesting theaters added to London's many. They include the Savoy of 1929, Sir Denys Lasdun's Royal National Theatre of 1967–1977, and the re-created Shakespeare's Globe, opened in 1997 (the last two offer tours).

In the 1960s, undistinguished development, coupled with plans to destroy Covent Garden Market, St. John's Wood, and other areas, stimulated the conservation movement and the call for a change of style. Buildings by Frederick Gibberd, James Stirling, Richard Rogers, Terry Farrell, and Nicholas Grimshaw have introduced new ideas. In the 1980s, the Docklands revival began, the commercial "Big Bang" led to City rebuilding, and new life was injected into the riverside. More than 30 major London millennium building projects kick-started the 21st century. The new City Hall, Portcullis House, the "Walkie-Talkie" building at 20 Fenchurch Street, and 30 St. Mary Axe (aka the "Gherkin") keep London ever changing. Meanwhile, in the far eastern reaches of the East End, among the latest transformations in London are the areas built for the 2012 Olympic and Paralympic Games, and the redevelopment of King's Cross district.

Plaques & Statues

Thousands of Britain's heroes and villains people the streets, squares, and churches of London with their memorials.

Some are grand: Nelson's statue stands on a tall column and is set in a square named after his great battle, Trafalgar. Others are remarkably modest: The architect of a great sweep of central London, John Nash, has merely a bust in the colonnade of All Souls Church, Langham Place, which he designed. A few have several memorials: The achievements of Prince Albert were recognized in the splendid Albert Memorial in Kensington Gardens, in Charles Bacon's equestrian statue at Holborn Circus, on the facade of the Victoria and Albert Museum, and elsewhere too. But it is the Duke of Wellington— neither king nor prince but one of Britain's greatest generals—who has three equestrian statues: inside St. Paul's Cathedral, in front of the City's Royal Exchange, and in front of Apsley House at Hyde Park Corner.

■ Twentieth-century paintings hang on transparent dividers at the National Portrait Gallery.

Great Museums

London has more than 300 permanent museums and galleries, large and small, general and specialist. Some are custom-built; others are collectors' homes; all exist thanks to the work of remarkable people.

The British Museum, the capital's first great national public collection, is one example. Sir Hans Sloane died in 1753, leaving his extensive library and collections of fossils, coins, minerals, and more to the nation—subject to a £20,000 ($32,000) payment to his daughters. The museum opened in Montague House on January 15, 1759, and moved into Robert Smirke's new building in 1838.

The National Gallery, founded in 1824, exists thanks to the gift of 38 paintings by financier John Julius Angerstein. Other national collections include the National Portrait Gallery, the National Maritime Museum, the Science Museum, and the Victoria and Albert Museum, which holds the national collection of decorative and fine arts. The Tate Gallery is divided into two sections, British art in Tate Britain on Millbank, and international modern art in Tate Modern in the refitted Bankside Power Station.

More personal collections include the Dulwich Picture Gallery, opened in 1814 as

■ **J. M. W. Turner's "The Fighting Temeraire" (1839) hangs in the National Gallery.**

the country's first public art gallery, and the Iveagh Bequest and Suffolk Collection in Kenwood House in Hampstead. In the house-museums the stamp of the collector's personality is even stronger, lingering on in his or her residence, whether it is the grand Ham House, Osterley Park, Apsley House, the Wallace Collection, or the more intimate Sir John Soane's Museum, Dr. Johnson's House, and Leighton House. Palaces fulfill this role, too, especially Kensington and Hampton Court.

Finally, there are the specialist collections: the Design Museum; the Museum of London and Museum in Docklands, which tell the capital's own story; and Julius Wernher's treasures in Greenwich's lovely Ranger's House.

Artists in London

Painters from the world famous to the quietly anonymous have recorded almost every important event, building, and person of London's history since the 16th century: What the Globe Theatre and Old St. Paul's Cathedral looked like, the extravagance of the Lord Mayor's rich pageant, the formal opening of St. Katharine Dock.

Hans Holbein painted portraits of grandees, while Wenceslaus Hollar, from Prague, worked for the Earl of Arundel drawing the best and most detailed views of 17th-century London that exist, working on the roof of the earl's Strand mansion. Later, patronage reached a peak under Charles I, who employed Sir Anthony Van Dyck for nine prolific years and also commissioned Sir Peter Paul Rubens to paint the ceiling of Banqueting House. Thomas Rowlandson and William Hogarth caricatured the city's seamier side. In contrast, Canaletto, Claude Monet, Joseph Mallord, J. M. W. Turner, James Whistler, and André Derain all eulogized the Thames.

A considerable number of paintings by artists working in London are to be found in Hampton Court and Buckingham Palaces, as well as in some museums and galleries. The Museum of London has 20,000 paintings, prints, drawings, and other exhibits, usually chosen for their image rather than the fame of their author. One is a picture by Abraham Hondius of the Thames frozen over in 1677. In another work, Henry Moore records Londoners taking refuge in Underground stations during World War II.

Holbein the Younger came to London in 1526, and later entered the service of Henry VIII. At Henry's Bridewell Palace on Fleet Street, he painted his remarkable double portrait, "The Ambassadors," now in the National Gallery. Here, too, are pictures by Van Dyck and Thomas Gainsborough, who first came to London in 1740. Next door, the National Portrait Gallery has plenty of personalities painted in their home city, such as John Hayl's portrait of diarist Samuel Pepys and Tom Phillips's of theater director Sir Peter Hall. The Imperial War Museum has a rich collection of 20th-century pictures by artists such as Paul Nash, Stanley Spencer, and David Bomberg. Among the smaller museums, Sir John Soane's stacks up the Hogarth series, and Kenwood House has paintings by Sir Joshua Reynolds, who lived in London from the 1740s.

Occasionally, a London artist's home survives as a house-museum. Lord Leighton's splendid indulgence is in Holland Park, Linley Sambourne's overstuffed home is preserved in Kensington, and Hogarth's country cottage hides between a noisy roundabout and elegant Chiswick House.

Tate Britain has plenty of London artists' work on view. Turner, a Londoner by birth, studied at the Royal Academy and always returned to London after his European tours. Tate Britain's Clore Gallery houses his works, while the main buildings may at any time have on display John Constable's "The Opening of Waterloo Bridge," Charles Ginner's "Piccadilly Circus," and works by R. B. Kitaj, Peter Blake, Howard Hodgkin, Rachel Whiteread, Damien Hirst, and Fiona Rae.

Today London is seething with artists from all over the world; one estimate puts 10,000 working in the East End alone. Howard Hodgkin, Gilbert & George, David Hockney, Bridget Riley, and Maggie Hambling are among the older generation of artists living in the capital city.

The annual Turner Prize is the most prestigious contemporary art award and acts as a yardstick for the way art is moving. Hodgkin was an early winner; Damien Hirst (famous for his pickled and chopped-up animals) and Rachel Whiteread (who represents inside spaces as dense matter) have both won it. Others to look out for include Jenny Saville, who paints the best flesh since Rubens, and Charlotte Prodger, who won in 2018.

> **The annual Turner Prize is the most prestigious contemporary art award and acts as a yardstick for the way art is moving.**

To see new movements in the art world, visit shows at the Whitechapel Art Gallery, recently reopened after doubling its exhibition space. Near here, the new galleries in the Old Truman Brewery building in Brick Lane and others in Hoxton Square show the cutting edge of contemporary art. In the West End, shows at the Photographers' Gallery are always worth seeing—further info can be found in *Time Out* (either online or in its weekly print magazine). Farther west, the Serpentine Gallery in Kensington Gardens is a wild card in conservative Kensington, and the innovative (and free) Saatchi Gallery offers rotating exhibits in the heart of Chelsea.

Literary London

Throughout its 2,000-year history, Londoners and visitors have documented the city in diaries, chronicles, poetry, and fiction. Reading some of these is one way of getting to know the London atmosphere at different historical periods.

The earliest known description of London is by the Roman historian Tacitus. He wrote that during Boudicca's revenge "the enemy massacred, hanged, burned and crucified with an energy that suggested . . . retribution would soon be visited upon them." From a later age, detailed descriptions of the city include the remarkable one of Elizabethan London by retired tailor and self-taught historian John Stow, in *A Survey of London,* published in 1598.

Meanwhile, the first English-language poem about London, *To the City of London* (circa 1501), once attributed to Scottish poet William Dunbar, ends with the accolade "London, thou art the flower of cities all."

Some remarkable diaries survive from the 17th and 18th centuries. The little-known John Manningham described Elizabeth I's calm death in his diary: "At about three o'clock her Majesty departed this life, mildly like a lamb, easily like a ripe apple from a tree." Samuel Pepys's diary of 1660–1669

is better known. In it, the details of his daily life hopping on boats to move from the City to Whitehall Palace, or playing music and going to church, vividly conjure up the Stuart Restoration, and are as interesting as his spectacular account of the Great Fire of 1666. In the same way, John Evelyn, whose diary spans the years from 1640 to 1706, is as keen to describe William and Mary's new Kensington Palace as the beaching of a whale at Greenwich or Cromwell's funeral—"the joyfullest funeral that I ever saw." The Scot James Boswell kept his *London Journal* in 1762–1763, in which he is depressed by the "tumultuous scene" in Parliament, enjoys a friendship with the popular actor-manager David Garrick, and is, like Pepys, indiscreet on the subject of love.

Diaries were kept by many 19th-century Londoners, from schoolboy John Thomas Pocock to Queen Victoria, and by visitors, from the Frenchmen Gustave Doré and Blanchard Jerrold to American Nathaniel Hawthorne.

■ **Oscar Wilde found success as a playwright in Victorian London.**

London comes alive in the great Victorian novels. Thackeray's *Vanity Fair* paints social London during the Regency period, when Knightsbridge was almost in open country. In contrast, Charles Dickens's novels sum up deprivation and squalor. In *Sketches by Boz,* St. Giles slums are described as "wretched houses with broken windows patched with rags and paper . . . filth everywhere—a gutter before the houses and a drain behind them."

London's Antiquarian Bookstores

London is a bibliophile's kind of town. An excellent array of antiquarian booksellers could keep you browsing for days on end.

Charing Cross Road, north of Trafalgar Square, is home to a slew of secondhand, rare, and collectible booksellers, including **Quinto Bookshop** *(72 Charing Cross Rd., WC2, tel 020 7379 7669, quintobookshop .co.uk);* **Francis Edwards Antiquarian Booksellers** *(francisedwards.co.uk),* established in 1855 and sharing the same premises as Quinto; and **Henry Pordes Books** *(58–60 Charing Cross Rd., WC2, tel 020 7836 9031, henrypordesbooks.com).* **Cecil Court,** a charming pedestrianized alley off the east side of Charing Cross Road, contains several more. Check *cecilcourt .co.uk* for a complete list.

Fans of the Helene Hanff book (and movie) *84 Charing Cross Road* might be disappointed to learn that Marks & Co., the bookstore featured in the memoir, is no longer in business. The store was on the east side of Charing Cross Road, just north of Cambridge Circus. A restaurant now occupies the site, but a plaque notes the shop's location.

TheBookGuide *(inprint.co.uk/thebook guide/shops)* lists antiquarian bookshops in London (and elsewhere).

To get a flavor of the variety of London lives in the 20th century would require a dip into, perhaps, Beatrice Webb's diary, Bertrand Russell's autobiography, and Arnold Bennett's journals. George Orwell's journal, Laurie Lee's autobiography, Raymond Chandler's letters, Sir Winston Churchill's copious writings, John Betjeman's poems, and Martin Amis's novels make an equally diverse set.

But it is William Wordsworth's radiant celebration of the city in his sonnet "Upon Westminster," written in 1802 after he crossed Westminster Bridge in the dawn coach, that still encapsulates the romance of London beginning with: "Earth has not anything to show more fair; . . . This City now doth, like a garment, wear/The beauty of the morning; silent, bare,/Ships, towers, domes, theaters, and temples lie/. . . All bright and glittering in the smokeless air."

Few contemporary authors can match the outpouring of quality prose about London written down the centuries. Martin Amis is an exception, seen in his novels *Money* and *London Fields,* as is Michael Moorcock, whose many books set in London include *Mother London.* Peter Ackroyd writes both biography (on Dickens, for instance, and on London itself) and novels. His *Hawksmoor* is set in Spitalfields, *The House of Doctor Dee* concerns an Elizabethan alchemist, and *The Lambs of London* is set in 19th-century Holborn.

Monica Ali's acclaimed 2003 novel, *Brick Lane,* explores the life of a young bride in London's Bengali community. But perhaps it is Iain Sinclair who touches the raw nerve of London today, setting many of his books in the City, the Docklands, and even beyond *(The Last London, 2017).* His novels include *Lud Heat* about the founder of London.

Performing Arts

Up to a thousand concerts are given in London every week. There are also operas, plays, musicals, and ballets performed in theaters, rooms, gardens, churches—almost any kind of space.

London has always offered plentiful and innovative entertainment, bewildering visitors with its sheer quantity of plays and shows available. In 1599, Thomas Platter, a visitor from Basel, remarked that "every day at two o'clock in the afternoon . . . two and sometimes three comedies are performed at separate places, wherewith folk make merry together, and whichever does best gets the greatest audience."

> 66 **From the 1840s onward, London witnessed an explosion in theater, music halls, and entertainment of all kinds.** 99

The Elizabethan stage was, at this period, in its infancy, mixing traditions of secular plays performed in the yards of inns with dancing, singing, and the baiting of bears and bulls. The Puritan City fathers banned theater from the City in 1574. Two years later, James Burbage built London's first permanent playhouse at Shoreditch City. In 1587 the Rose was the first of four theaters to open at Southwark, which soon became London's entertainment center. Here Burbage opened his Globe in 1599. More than 2,000 people would cram into the circular, tiered, wooden theaters to watch plays by Shakespeare, Ben Jonson, and Thomas Dekker, although use of the open-air venues depended upon good weather.

With Charles II's restoration, theater returned to the city center. Plays were an almost daily event at Whitehall Palace. The king granted two men permission to produce public plays: Thomas Killigrew, who opened the Theatre Royal, Drury Lane, in 1663, and William D'Avenant, whose theater at Lincoln's Inn Fields had the first proscenium arch and facilities to set scenery during a play.

Throughout the 18th century, only two theaters and companies were allowed to work inside the city, Drury Lane and the Opera House in Covent Garden; the many others were illegal. London theater later suffered its second perse-cution in 1737, when Henry Fielding's crude satires at the old Theatre Royal in the Haymarket caused the Lord Chamber-lain to exercise his power of censorship, lifted only in 1968.

Despite strict censorship, theater and entertainment flourished. David Garrick was the actor-manager who revived classical theater and treated Shakespeare with a new respect. He demanded that actors learn their parts, improved production, and transformed audience behavior, which had often been raucous—people would walk across the stage to chat with friends during performances. In 1728 the first performance of John Gay's *Beggar's Opera* marked the arrival of English opera. Meanwhile, 18th-century Lon-don was full of musical activity, both amateur and profes-sional. Concert rooms and theaters were opened to cater to the increased demand for concerts, opera, and masquerades: Mozart appeared at the Hanover Square Rooms, J. S. Bach and Haydn conducted their own compositions, and Handel composed operas, concerts, and chamber works.

From the 1840s onward, London witnessed an explosion in theater, music halls, and entertainment of all kinds. The music halls grew out of informal sing-alongs held in taverns. By the end of the century, huge halls were built. The lavishly renovated Hackney Empire flourishes in north London. The Coliseum, opened in 1904, had a stage large enough to hold a chariot race, with an audience capacity of 2,558, still London's largest. These variety theaters attracted a new audience, the middle-class visitor to London. Gradually, the vulgarity was tempered, so that Sarah Bernhardt played at the Coliseum, Sir Thomas Beecham conducted excerpts from *Tannhäuser* at the Palladium, and one music hall even put a cricket match on stage.

In theater, the great actor-managers dominated. Herbert Beerbohm Tree built Her Majesty's Theatre and staged *A Midsummer Night's Dream,* with real rabbits hopping about the Athenian woods set, and, in 1895, Oscar Wilde's *An Ideal Husband.* Sir Henry Irving made Ellen Terry his leading lady at the Lyceum, which he managed for 24 years from 1879. Richard D'Oyly Carte staged Gilbert and Sullivan operettas, including *The Mikado,* at his Savoy Theatre with such success that the profits financed the building of his deluxe Savoy Hotel next door.

The cast of the West End musical *Let It Be* re-creates London's Swinging Sixties.

Landmark events in London theaterland included Richard Wagner conducting *The Ring* at the Royal Opera House in 1867 and Anna Pavlova making her London ballet debut at the Palace Theatre in 1910. This theater, restored by Andrew Lloyd Webber, is where his *Jesus Christ Superstar,* written with Tim Rice, became London's longest-running musical until it was eclipsed by another of his productions, *Cats* (now closed), and later by *Les Misérables* (still going strong).

Meanwhile, Harley Granville-Barker dazzled Londoners at the Royal Court in Chelsea, where he staged 32 plays from 1904 to 1907, including the first performances of George Bernard Shaw's *Candida.* More recently, Sir Peter Hall was the first director of the National Theatre when it finally opened in 1976, the realization of an idea put forward by Garrick.

Today, some of London's most interesting theater is found in the "Off–West End" and "fringe" venues. The Royal Court, Almeida, Hampstead, Old Vic, Young Vic, and Donmar Warehouse theaters stage many of London's most innovative productions. Avant-garde fringe theaters, often housed in pubs, warehouses, and small upstairs rooms, are dotted across the capital. Ones at the forefront include the King's Head, Riverside Studios, The Bush, BAC, and Tricycle; others, often more offbeat, include the Etcetera Theatre, Old Red Lion, and The Finborough (for more information see Travelwise pp. 263–264).

Back in the mainstream, the auditoriums of the state-funded National Theatre and Shakespeare's Globe show traditional and contemporary plays, and some musicals, in repertory. This enables visitors to see a number of productions in any week. The traditional Victorian and Edwardian theaters of the West End stage more conventional productions and long-running musicals, including *Les Misérables* and Andrew Lloyd Webber's *Phantom of the Opera.* The rebuilt Sadler's Wells Theatre focuses on ballet and some opera and stage productions. Currently, opera is staged in several renovated or restored theaters: Royal Opera House, Coliseum, Savoy Theatre, Sadler's Wells, and Hackney Empire. ■

EXPERIENCE: Explore the London of Film

London is a living movie set—only Hollywood and New York can claim to have had more films set within their borders.

Notable movies filmed in the city include *Bridget Jones's Diary, The Da Vinci Code,* and many scenes in the popular *Harry Potter* series. London also features heavily, of course, in the series of movies featuring that most British of heroes, James Bond, including *Die Another Day, For Your Eyes Only,* and *Skyfall.*

A host of companies offer regular walking and bus tours of famous London film sites. Try **Celebrity Planet** *(tel 020 7193 8770, londoncelebritytours.wordpress.com,*

$$$$), which offers exciting tours to the homes of celebrities and the most famous film sites; and **Brit Movie Tours** *(tel 0844 2471 007, britmovie tours.com, $$$$),* which offers an extensive tour of James Bond's London.

True film buffs should plan a visit to the **BFI,** the British Film Institute *(bfi.org.uk; see* Travelwise p. 263). This repository of all things related to British film holds special events and exhibitions and includes the Mediatheque, a screening room where you can request a free private viewing of any of nearly 2,000 film and television titles from the BFI archive.

Twisting and turning past London's history—customhouses, quays, palaces, parliamentary buildings, and the Tower of London

THE THAMES

Looking toward the South Bank district along the Thames at twilight

THE THAMES

The Thames is narrow as it runs northward from Hampton Court Palace, passing in great curves through the once rural villages of Twickenham, Richmond, Kew, Chiswick, and Barnes—now swallowed up by the mass of Greater London. Then it swings eastward into the city center. The last eight of London's 34 Thames bridges cluster close together and beyond the final one, Tower Bridge, the waters of the widening river slip slowly around the Isle of Dogs peninsula and through the great metal fins of the Thames Barrier.

Along the Thames stand buildings that testify to the river's role in history. For centuries, the river was the main highway for Londoners, and a facade within view of it was prestigious, as it still is. St. Paul's Cathedral, the Tower of London, and Westminster's Houses of Parliament are all close to the Thames.

Kings and queens, accompanied by boatloads of courtiers and musicians, would be rowed up and down the Thames between their riverside palaces at Greenwich,

the Tower of London, Whitehall, Westminster, Richmond, and Hampton Court. Aristocrats often chose rural locations upstream from the city, for their homes—Ham House, Syon House, and Marble Hill House are the most impressive survivors. And there are several riverside parks: Greenwich downstream, and Battersea, Kew, Richmond, and Hampton Court's Home and Bushy Parks upstream.

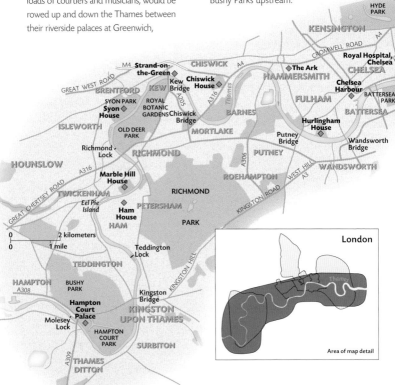

■ Vauxhall Bridge is among 34 that span the Thames.

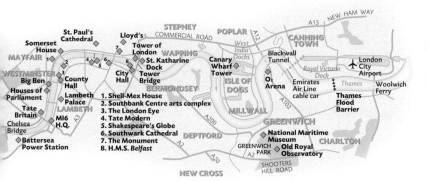

1. Shell-Mex House
2. Southbank Centre arts complex
3. The London Eye
4. Tate Modern
5. Shakespeare's Globe
6. Southwark Cathedral
7. The Monument
8. H.M.S. Belfast

Today, energetic riverfront building marks the rediscovery of the Thames. The redevelopment of the Docklands, in particular the Isle of Dogs, has been infectious. Riverside buildings that have lost their original purpose, such as Bankside Power Station and County Hall, now breathe again as they are put to new uses. Dramatic modern buildings are being added, including City Hall at Southwark.

Forgotten harbors, such as St. Katharine and Chelsea, have been redeveloped. River taxis beat rush-hour roadblocks, and the Millennium Bridge spans the Thames from St. Paul's to Bankside. As for strolling, the Thames Path (a walk along both the north and south banks) has brought Londoners close to their river again. ■

THE HISTORICAL PORT

Once the biggest port in the world, London no longer sees laden ships coming and going up the Thames. And the boats traversing it now, for pleasure or transportation, are few compared to those of the past, when much of Britain's wealth flowed in and out of the river.

■ Canaletto's "The Thames on Lord Mayor's Day," circa 1747

The Roman port flourished on what is now Cornhill, with a wooden bridge, warehouses, and quays. The Anglo-Saxons traded with France and the Rhineland, then ventured farther to the Baltic and Middle East. In Tudor times, merchants built up the port to the point where about 40,000 people lived off the river, from bargemen and boatbuilders to stevedores and porters—and 2,000 boats ferried people up and down the river highway. Trade soared in the 17th and 18th centuries, and London became the world's largest port. In 1802 the new enclosed docks relieved the Thames of its shipping jam. By 1900, a million people worked in the port, but when the port moved to Tilbury in 1965, London's river fell silent.

Amid the bustle of trading, London's river pageantry was always impressive. King Henry VIII's ostentatious minister, Cardinal Wolsey, would dress in crimson satin to be rowed in his barge from Westminster to Greenwich to visit the king. The best shows on the Thames were those staged by the Lord Mayor. From 1422 to 1846, each year Livery Company barges escorted the Lord Mayor elect to Westminster, to seek the sovereign's approval.

By the mid-19th century, the river was little more than an open sewer, slowly carrying the industrial and domestic effluent of London out to sea. But after Queen Victoria's lawyers won back the crown's river rights from the City Fathers in 1857, engineer Joseph Bazalgette designed London's first city-wide sewage system. He also found a solution to the Thames's poor state of hygiene and the frequent winter freeze-ups that threw London into chaos. Inspired by Wren's suggestion of a river wall, he devised a land-reclamation scheme that narrowed the Thames and made the water flow faster. This embankment included a road on top to relieve the congested city, public gardens, and a tall river wall to combat floods.

Thames Revival

When the docks moved and industry was no longer allowed to dispose of its waste straight into the river, the quality of London's river water improved dramatically. Today, more than 100 species of fish live in the city stretch, including perch, sea stars, mussels, and eco-fragile salmon. With cleaner water, overhauled bridges, and new riverside buildings, Londoners have rediscovered their riverscape.

The revival began in the 1980s. The government's Docklands project was born in 1981. The aim was to reshape the 8.5 square miles (22 sq km) of disused docklands with houses and offices. Soon individual developments were under way the length of London's riverbank. Old warehouses were converted to apartments. New office blocks arose, reflected in the waters of the old docks, which have been kept for their recreational potential.

Up at Hammersmith, architect Richard Rogers converted an oil depot into offices and apartments in 1987, creating a new working community. Nearby, Ralph Erskine's fun-shaped The Ark, of 1991, is a brave attempt at an ecologically sound office building.

Chelsea Harbour, where coal barges unloaded their cargo until 1960, was developed in 1986–1987 into a luxurious riverside community. On the opposite bank, a simple concrete-and-glass building by Norman Foster houses his own architectural practice.

In central London, Farrell's Embankment Place, built in 1987–1990 as an office block dramatically suspended over Charing Cross railway station, was the first of several major riverside projects. Michael Hopkins's severe Portcullis House at Westminster and Lifschutz Davidson's remodeling of Hungerford Bridge followed upstream; and a string of South Bank transformations and creations appeared, from County Hall to the Oxo Tower.

Downstream from here is the dynamic revival of Somerset House, the pedestrian-only Millennium Bridge (2002), the Shard (2012), and the remodeling of Bankside Power Station into Tate Modern. Beyond lie Foster's elliptical City Hall and the converted warehouses of Shad Thames and Docklands.

Frost Fairs

Climate change is not a topic unique to our times. From the 14th to the 19th century, a "little ice age" held northern Europe in its grip. During these centuries, the Thames froze over more than a dozen times, allowing the citizens of London to set up Frost Fairs—winter festivals on the iced-over river that featured sports, entertainment, and plenty of food and drink.

Another reason for the freeze-overs was the Thames's slow-moving waters—the banks were wider then, and old London Bridge's many arches further slowed the river. A 19th-century government project to build embankments and remove some of the arches sped up the river's flow, ending freeze-ups.

The first organized Frost Fair took place in the 17th century. Vendors roasted and sold mutton and oxen; booths were set up for souvenirs and snacks; swings, sideshows, puppet shows, and merry-go-rounds were built; and people played hockey and (English) football.

Never a people to forgo a chance to set up shop, entrepreneurial Londoners were adept at cashing in on the festive atmosphere of the fairs. Admission fees were charged for most events, and a popular contemporary rhyme alerts us to the pricing patterns: "What you can buy for threepence on the shore, will cost you fourpence on the Thames, or more." Frost Fairs continued until 1813, the last time the Thames froze over.

TWO THAMES BOAT TRIPS

Taking a pleasure boat trip on the Thames is a delightful way to appreciate how this great river was the backbone of the capital's development. From Westminster pier, you can take a short, urban journey downstream past the City of Westminster and the City of London, or a longer rural journey upstream, gliding through increasingly green areas of outer London.

■ A tour boat approaches Tower Bridge.

Down the Thames: Westminster to Greenwich

Starting from Westminster pier, some boats swing around beneath Westminster Bridge for a panoramic view of the Houses of Parliament before moving downstream, with County Hall on the right. Bazalgette's Victoria Embankment, left, has the Portcullis House, Whitehall Court, and the National Liberal Club, built in the 1880s. Behind Whitehall Stairs—there were once hundreds of river stairways like this giving access to the river—stood Whitehall Palace.

Under Hungerford Railway Bridge, Farrell's new offices are suspended above older Charing Cross station, to the left. The Southbank Centre arts complex is right, Charing Cross Pier and Embankment Gardens left, where the Duke of Buckingham's water gate survives to evoke the Strand's past glories. From here, Victorians took steamboats on day trips down to seaside towns on the Thames estuary. On the skyline you see the Shell-Mex House of 1932, with clock, and the newly refurbished Savoy Hotel (Mackmurdo, 1903–1904). Monet painted his views of Waterloo Bridge from one of its rooms. At Victoria Embankment the misnamed Cleopatra's

Needle—London's oldest monument, dating from 1450 B.C.—is an obelisk of pink granite from Heliopolis in Egypt.

Under Waterloo Bridge, the National Theatre is to the right. Somerset House is to your left, then Inner Temple Gardens and the riverside, cast-iron griffins marking the boundary of the City. After Blackfriars Bridge, you can see Millennium Bridge and, on your left, St. Paul's, a peculiar building nicknamed "Walkie-Talkie," and the vast, oddly-shaped 30 St. Mary Axe, widely known as the "Gherkin." Bankside Power Station, now Tate Modern, is on the right, with the new Shakespeare's Globe beyond.

Southwark Bridge and Cannon Street Railway Bridge come next, then the Doric column of the Monument, to the left,

commemorating the Great Fire, the modern London Bridge marking Roman London's beginnings, Hays Galleria, H.M.S. *Belfast*, and the curved glass of City Hall.

The medieval Tower of London is on the left, and Tower Bridge spans the river beside it. The revived Docklands line the widening river as it sweeps through the Pool of London, until recently filled with ships. To the right are the areas of Shad Thames, Bermondsey, Rotherhithe, and Deptford. To the left are Wapping, Shadwell, and Limehouse. The soaring towers of Canary Wharf, on the Isle of Dogs peninsula, face across the Thames to Greenwich. Beyond lies the O_2 Arena, the massive sports and concert venue on Greenwich Peninsula. Farther downstream, past the Emirates Air Line cable cars

EXPERIENCE: Taking to the Thames

No trip to London would be complete without taking to the water in some fashion. Tourist and commuter services launch from both banks of the Thames.

River Bus services, generally catering to commuters, are a fun way to move about the city: **MBNA Thames Clippers** (tel 020 7001 2200, thamesclippers.com, $$) runs frequent commuter boats from Royal Arsenal Woolwich Pier in the east to London Eye pier in the west, with convenient stops. Check out **London Transport** (tel 0343 222 1234, tfl.gov.uk) for additional information.

Many operators offer leisure tours along the Thames. Most run sightseeing cruises, while others specialize in brunch, dinner, jazz, and other themed tours. Options include **The London Eye River Cruise** (tel 0871 781 3000, londoneye .com, $$$$); the **Westminster Passenger Service Association** (tel 020 7930 2062, thamesriverboats.co.uk, $$$$), which runs the only scheduled service upriver to Kew and Hampton Court; **Crown River Cruises** (tel 020 7936 2033, crownriver .com, $$$$); **City Cruises** (tel 020 7936 2033/3383, citycruises.com, $$$$); and **Thames River Services** (tel 020 7930 4097, thamesriverservices.co.uk).

Thrill seekers might like dashing along the river on **London RIB** (tel 020 7928 8933, londonribvoyages.com, $$–$$$), a speedboat; while the **London Duck** (Chicheley St., tel 020 7928 3132, london ducktours.co.uk, $$$$) is ideal for families and offers a land and river tour in an amphibious WWII landing craft.

soaring across the water (the only cable car in London), the shining fins of the Thames Flood Barrier, a series of gates, straddle the river at Woolwich.

Up the Thames: Westminster to Hampton Court

From Westminster pier, the boats pass under Westminster Bridge. The Houses of Parliament and Victoria Tower Gardens are on the right, with Lambeth Palace and the floating fire station on the left. After Lambeth Bridge, Bazalgette's embankments support Pimlico's Tate Britain on the right.

INSIDER TIP:

Held in September each year, the Totally Thames Festival [totallythames. org] features art, food, music, and tall ships.

—LARRY PORGES
National Geographic
Travel Books editor

Beyond Vauxhall Bridge and Farrell's MI6 headquarters, energy from Battersea Power Station, on the left, is used to heat Dolphin Square's apartments, on the right. After Chelsea Bridge the banks look more rural: Battersea Park, with its Peace Pagoda, on the left, and, on the right, the gardens of the Royal Hospital Chelsea, the site of the annual Chelsea Flower Show. Albert Bridge springs from the core of old Chelsea village, to the right. After Battersea Bridge,

familiar from Whistler's paintings, is Chelsea Harbour. Turner painted sunsets from the tower of riverside St. Mary's Church, Battersea.

Around a great bend in the river, Hurlingham House, right, built in 1760, and its gardens are now a private sports club. Bazalgette's Putney Bridge replaced the 1729 wooden one, which was the Thames's second longest span when it was built. Bishops Park is on the right, boathouses on the left—the Oxford v. Cambridge Boat Race starts here. Ralph Erskine's The Ark is visible on the right before you reach castellated Hammersmith Bridge.

Chiswick's Malls, on the right, are lined with handsome houses; pretty Barnes village is to the left. After Duke's Meadows, right, comes Chiswick and its elegant bridge, then Kew railway and road bridges, with Strand-on-the-Green's charming cottages on the right. The Royal Botanic Gardens (see pp. 192–193) at Kew follow, left, with their riverside palace, and on the opposite side gleaming Syon House (see p. 195). After Richmond Half-Tide Weir and Footbridge come Twickenham and Richmond Bridges. Here stand the remains of Richmond Palace, behind the riverside Asgill House, built in 1758. Richmond Park and Ham House follow, left, with Marble Hill House on the right.

Teddington Lock and Weir mark the end of the tidal stretch of the Thames. After Kingston Bridge and the great sweep past Home Park, Tijou's grand river gates announce Hampton Court Palace (see pp. 197–200). ■

Churches by Christopher Wren and skyscrapers in a maze of narrow lanes that date from the capital's origins

THE CITY

The Lord Mayor's coach, Museum of London

THE CITY

Much of the City's 2,000 years of busy history has left traces in this district. The two defendable hills that attracted the Romans to this spot are still clear to see: Ludgate, on which St. Paul's Cathedral now stands, and Cornhill. Here, 40 miles (64 km) up the Thames from the sea, the river could be forded and the gravel riverbed bridged. The north bank was firm, and streams from Highgate and Hampstead provided fresh water— the Walbrook ran through the new settlement, the Fleet formed the western boundary.

The Romans' basilica and forum stood on Cornhill, where Lombard Street now runs; the remains of one of their temples, dedicated in the third century A.D. to Mithras, the god of a mystery cult, are visible in Queen Victoria Street (see sidebar p. 69). Around A.D. 200, the Romans encased their 330-acre (133 ha) city with a tall, thick wall of Kentish ragstone, 3 miles (5 km) long and pierced by seven gates. Today, chunks of wall, with medieval repairs, survive in the Barbican Centre, in and near the Tower of London, Noble Street, and elsewhere. The gateways survive in place-names only and include Aldgate, the poet Geoffrey Chaucer's home (1342–1400); Bishopsgate, whose road led all the way to Hadrian's Wall in the north

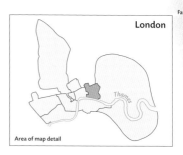

Area of map detail

London

CLERK
CLERKEN-
WELL
GREEN

Farringdon

of England; Moorgate, beyond which lay marshy land; Cripplegate, which led to a medieval suburb and to Islington village; and Aldersgate, which led to the monasteries of Clerkenwell and to Smithfield market.

When medieval London burst out of the walls, it crept westward toward its rival, Westminster. The City boundaries barely changed. Even today, the City's nickname, "the Square Mile," is a roughly accurate description of the Roman settlement.

Then two dramatic events occurred. Plague was endemic to London, but in April 1665, what was to be the worst outbreak since the Black Death of 1348–1350 began, killing an estimated 110,000 people before the cold weather brought it to a halt. The next year, on September 2, fire broke out at about 1 a.m. at Thomas Farrinor's bakery on Pudding Lane. By morning, 300 houses and part of London Bridge were alight. The strong east wind fanned the fire as it gobbled up the pitch-coated wooden buildings. Over the next two days, the flames ate up Lombard Street, Cheapside, St. Paul's Cathedral, and

NOT TO BE MISSED:

Touring glorious St. Paul's Cathedral, including climbing up to the dome for spectacular views of London 58–61

A lunchtime concert in one of Wren's City churches 59

Visiting the City's art collection in the Guildhall Art Gallery 65

Taking a wander through the tiny lanes and atmospheric back alleys of the historic Cloth Fair area 67

Viewing London's history at the Museum of London's extensive collections and exhibits 68–69

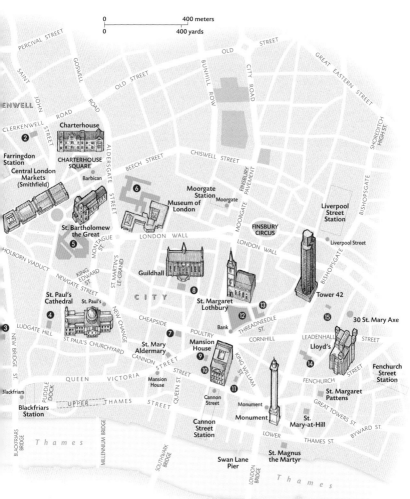

Inner Temple. On September 5, the fire checked, but not before four-fifths of the City—including 13,000 houses, 87 churches, and 44 livery halls—had been burned.

While embers were still glowing, Charles II pledged that the city would be rebuilt. Sir Christopher Wren's dream of a city of avenues radiating from a new St. Paul's was impractical, partly because the guilds would not give up their land. Instead, fireproof brick houses were built following the medieval street plan. ■

① St. James Clerkenwell ② St. John's Gate ③ St. Bride's ④ St. Martin-within-Ludgate ⑤ St. Bartholomew's Hospital ⑥ The Barbican ⑦ St. Mary-le-Bow ⑧ St. Lawrence Jewry ⑨ Temple of Mithras ⑩ St. Stephen Walbrook ⑪ St. Mary Abchurch ⑫ Bank of England & Museum ⑬ Stock Exchange ⑭ Leadenhall Market ⑮ St. Helen Bishopsgate

ST. PAUL'S CATHEDRAL

This is the cathedral church of the London diocese—a church for Londoners, while Westminster Abbey serves the nation. St. Paul's was founded by King Aethelbert of Kent for the missionary monk Mellitus. This, the fifth church on the site, is England's only baroque cathedral, the only one with a dome, and the only one built between the Reformation and the 19th century. It was also the first to be constructed entirely by a single architect, Sir Christopher Wren.

Sir Christopher Wren's vision of St. Paul's Cathedral included a massive dome.

St. Paul's Cathedral

- Map p. 57
- Ludgate Hill, EC4
- 0207 246 8348
  Reception
  Mon.–Fri., 9
  a.m.–5 p.m.:
  0207 246 8350.
  Visit inquiries:
  020 7246 8357
- Closed Sun.
  except for
  services & for
  special events
- $$
- Tube: St. Paul's,
  Mansion House,
  Blackfriars
  Rail: City
  Thameslink

stpauls.co.uk

The foundation stone was laid on June 21, 1675. Boatloads of Portland stone from Dorset were delivered to the nearest wharves, and the bulk of the cathedral was built by 1679. Wren's son put the last stone on the lantern supporting the triple-layered dome in 1708, and the cathedral was completed in January 1711. The entire building recently underwent a 15-year, £40 million ($64 million) restoration and cleaning of both interior and exterior stonework, statues, and mosaics to commemorate the 300th anniversary of the cathedral's consecration in 2011.

Exterior

Before going into the cathedral, stand well back on Ludgate Hill and look at St. Paul's in its entirety. The building is arranged in four volumes: the dome and crossing, the nave and choir, the transepts, and the west end. The dome rests on a wide drum—which provides an open terrace—and is made of an inner curved brick structure, an intermediate brick cone that supports the lantern, and an outer wooden casing covered in lead. The grand facade has a pediment relief of the Conversion of St. Paul. Pilasters and pediments give the building baroque movement.

Interior

Standing just inside the building, you get a good first view looking straight down the length of the nave and choir to the modern towering altar. This stunning setting has contributed to memorials such as the funerals of Admiral Lord Nelson in 1806 and Winston Churchill in 1965; to celebrations such as Queen Victoria's Diamond Jubilee in 1897, the Queen's Silver Jubilee in 1977, and the marriage of Prince Charles and Lady Diana Spencer in 1981.

Dome & Crossing: The crossing is irresistible. Sit beneath it and rest as you look up at the dome. It is supported on eight huge arches. Corinthian columns rise up to the dome, where the grisaille frescoes of the life of St. Paul by Sir James Thornhill, painted 1716–1719, are the only original decorations. The mosaics in the spandrels—the prophets by Alfred Stevens and the evangelists by G. F. Watts—were added in the 19th century, after a visit by Queen Victoria, who criticized the building as dreary and uncolorful.

The Crypt: The crypt, reached from the south transept, includes the Oculus (a multiscreen presentation on the cathedral's history) and Wren's own tomb, inscribed *"Lector, si monumentum requiris, circumspice—* Reader, if you seek his monument, look around you," words repeated on the floor beneath the dome. Adm. Nelson and the Duke of Wellington lie here, and near Wren lie the artists Joshua Reynolds and J. M. W. Turner.

The Nave: The monuments in the nave are a roll call of British heroes of the 19th and 20th centuries. Francis Bird's font of 1727 stands in the north transept, and Jean Tijou's wrought-iron gates close off the sanctuary; the **American Memorial Chapel** is behind the altar. Near it is the monument to poet John Donne (1571–1631), who was dean of St. Paul's and the greatest preacher of his day (see sidebar p. 60). In the south transept is Holman Hunt's painting "The Light of the World," the artist's copy of his original version (in Keble College, Oxford).

Galleries: Part of the building's massive restoration project

---

EXPERIENCE:
Hear Music in Wren's Churches

Take a respite from your day's travels with classical music recitals and choral services in the tranquil settings of Wren's City of London churches.

St. Paul's Cathedral's 50-voice choir sings hour-long Evensong services at 5 p.m. Monday through Saturday and at 3:15 p.m. on Sundays.

St. Lawrence Jewry hosts organ recitals at 1 p.m. on Tuesdays and classical piano concerts at the same time on Mondays. There are also organ recitals at **St. Stephen Walbrook** at 12:30 p.m. on Fridays; **St. Margaret Lothbury** at 1:10 p.m. on Thursdays; and **St. Mary-at-Hill** on Tuesdays at 1:15 p.m. (See p. 62 for addresses.)

John Donne

A poet, lawyer, Member of Parliament, and preacher, John Donne (1572–1631) had a career both impressive and eclectic, rising to dean of St. Paul's Cathedral in 1621, a position he held for the last ten years of his life.

He was admitted to the bar in 1592 at Lincoln's Inn where, for centuries, a somber tradition was in place: Whenever a senior member of the bar died, the chapel bells would ring out. Messengers were sent to find out who had passed away. This practice became the subject of the poet's most famous work, "Meditation 17" of his *Devotions Upon Emergent Occasions*, which he wrote in 1624 as he recovered from a near-fatal illness:

"Any man's death diminishes me, because I am involved in mankind; and therefore never send to know for whom the bell tolls; it tolls for thee." Donne is buried in St. Paul's Cathedral.

included the re-opening of the **Triforium,** a level above the main floor, which features a 300-year-old library and the Trophy Room containing Sir Christopher Wren's yardstick and death mask, as well as a huge model of the church.

Wren's several early designs for St. Paul's are also on display in the Triforium. After the 1666 fire, Wren was appointed Surveyor General in 1669 and was already designing new City churches when he produced his first model for St. Paul's in 1670. This was judged to be too modest; his Great Model of 1673–1674 showed his ideal design of a Greek cross with an extended nave. When this was rejected by the church commissioners as "not enough of a cathedral fashion," Wren made a new design that included a spire. Once the clergy had approved it and he had received the king's warrant to go ahead in 1675, he enlarged the dome, removed the spire, raised the nave walls, and chopped off three bays—thus returning as closely as he dared to his Great Model design. All the foundations were laid out at the start so that no changes could be forced upon him at a later stage. The Triforium can currently be visited only as part of a highly recommended guided tour; there's no timetable yet for when it will open to the public.

St. Dunstan's Chapel

West Portico

The 560 steps leading to the other galleries begin with a gentle climb to the **Whispering Gallery.** Unless you arrive early, there will not be enough peace and quiet for the whispers to carry around the gallery. Steeper steps, with views of the cone supporting the lantern, lead to the wide outside **Stone Gallery,** resting on the dome's drum. From here, you can see how the second story of the screen around the building is blind, with nothing behind it. Finally, a spiral staircase leads up to the **Golden Gallery,** narrow and not for the fainthearted, but giving stupendous views of the City, the twisting Thames, and Parliament's many spires a couple of miles away at Westminster. ■

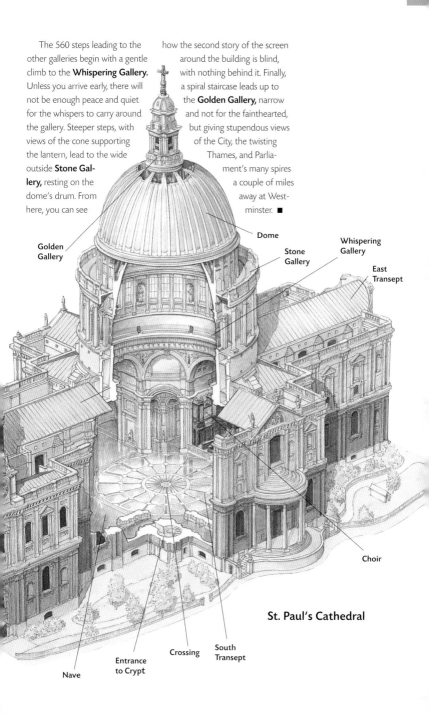

Golden Gallery

Dome

Stone Gallery

Whispering Gallery

East Transept

Choir

Nave

Entrance to Crypt

Crossing

South Transept

St. Paul's Cathedral

WREN'S CITY CHURCHES

The double disaster of the Great Plague of 1665 and the Great Fire of 1666 changed the City forever. The wealthy left, sparking the development of the elite residential area of St. James's. The rebuilt City was safer, with wider streets and better-constructed houses. Markets, shops, and other suppliers moved west, toward their customers. Sir Christopher Wren's new cathedral and churches gave a cohesive architectural character to the City that can still be felt today.

NOTE: Most City churches gear their opening times to coincide with the schedules of City workers and are therefore closed on weekends. Check individual websites for opening times.

Wren's 51 City churches, built from 1670 onward, made a huge impact. Today, 23 churches remain—19 were destroyed in World War II bombing, and nine have been lost at other times.

Their designs vary considerably. They include the domed and centralized **St. Mary-at-Hill** (*Lovat Lane, EC3, tel 020 7626 4184, stmary-at-hill.org*) and **St. Stephen**

■ St. Bride's on Fleet Street is one of Wren's grander post-fire structures.

Walbrook (*39 Walbrook, EC4, tel 020 7626 9000, ststephenwalbrook.net*), the grandly baroque **St. Bride's** (*Fleet St., EC4, tel 020 7427 0133, stbrides.com*), and **St. Lawrence Jewry** (*Guildhall Yard, EC2, tel 020 7600 9478, stlawrencejewry.org.uk*), whose facade is based on Wren's great model for St. Paul's Cathedral. **St. Magnus the Martyr** (*Lower Thames St., EC3, tel 020 7626 4481, stmagnusmartyr.org.uk*) is a good one to visit for its classic design and sumptuous interior, described in T. S. Eliot's *The Waste Land* (1922) as "inexplicable splendour of Ionian white and gold." He refers to the colonnades supporting the tunnel vaulting of the nave, which leads to the finely carved original reredos. Among the baroque statues and gilded sword rests, do not miss two other original features: the font and the organ case. The steeple, added in 1705, is one of Wren's best; his other notable ones surviving today are on St. Bride's and St. Mary-le-Bow.

Some of Wren's interiors have their original—or another, older or ruined church's—fittings. **St. Margaret Lothbury** (*Lothbury, EC2, tel 020 7726 4878, stml.org.uk*) fulfills both criteria. Outside, Wren has perched his obelisk tower on a domed base. Inside, the rectangular nave's magnificent furnishings include Wren's design for the finely carved tester and screen, whose barleystick columns and soaring eagle were originally built for All Hallows-the-Great (demolished in 1876).

Almost every Wren church has something special about it. For the interior of his very pretty **St. Mary Abchurch** (Abchurch Lane, EC4, tel 020 7626 1555, london-city-churches.org.uk), Wren gathered a team of talented friends, and their work remains almost unaltered. Beneath William Snow's paintings on the dome, some of the City's finest 17th-century wood carving survives, all retaining its original oxblood stain. There are William Emmett's door cases, font cover, and rails, Christopher Kempster's font, William Gray's pulpit, and—the church's glory—Grinling

---

INSIDER TIP:

Stay at the Andaz Liverpool Street [see Travelwise p. 243] and ask to see the Grecian-style Masonic Temple that lies beneath it.

—SIMON HORSFORD
Sunday Telegraph travel writer

Gibbons's reredos, the City's only authenticated piece by him.

St. Margaret Pattens (Rood Lane Eastcheap, EC3, tel 020 7623 6630, stmargaretpattens.org), so-called because wooden clogs, or pattens, were made nearby in the 13th century, also has a special interior. Here are some of

St. Bride's

St. Bride's, tucked off the south side of Fleet Street, near Ludgate Hill, has more than one claim to fame. In addition to being a handsome example of one of Sir Christopher Wren's post-fire churches, and containing ancient Roman ruins in its basement, St. Bride's also holds itself dear to wedding planners around the world. Whether apocryphal or not, the story goes that an 18th-century London baker, William Rich, based the shape of his daughter's wedding cake on the multitiered steeple of the church. The design apparently caught on, earning the 225-foot (69 m) spire the moniker "wedding-cake steeple" and locking cakesmiths into the pattern for centuries to come.

London's few remaining canopied pews, and the one carved with "CW 1686" is thought to have been Wren's own. There is also a punishment bench for the parish miscreants and, in the side chapel, hooks on which gentlemen hung their wigs on hot days. One of Wren's slender lead steeples rises above another fine interior, that of **St. Martin-within-Ludgate** (40 Ludgate Hill, EC4, tel 020 7248 6054, www.stmartin-within-ludgate.org.uk). The altarpiece, pulpit, font, and organ are magnificent examples of late 17th-century carving.

Finally, a visit to **St. Mary Aldermary** (Bow Lane., EC4, tel 020 7248 9902, www.achurchnearyou.com/st-mary-aldermary) takes you to Wren's only Gothic-style church. The fan vaulting, the only work of its kind made in the City in the 17th century, was probably Wren's interpretation of the pre-fire church. ∎

A CITY WALK

This walk gives a good idea of the dense, medieval compactness of the City and its range of fine buildings of all periods. Go on a weekday for liveliness, on weekends for quiet.

From Monument Tube station, walk down Monument Street to the **Monument ❶** *(themonument.info, $)*, which commemorates the Great Fire of 1666. Turn right onto Fish Street Hill. Facing you at the bottom of the hill is Wren's glorious church **St. Magnus the Martyr** (see p. 62). Turn left onto busy Lower Thames Street for a couple of hundred yards before turning left up St. Mary at Hill. Detour right onto St. Dunstan's Lane to the peaceful remains of **St. Dunstan-in-the-East**—a Wren tower and a garden.

Beyond St. Margaret Pattens (see p. 63) and the "Walkie Talkie" *(20 Fenchurch St.)* skyscraper, turn left at Fenchurch Street, then right onto Lime Street to find the arches of **Leadenhall Market,** the City's food market, opened in 1881. Continue on Lime Street past Richard Rogers's **Lloyd's building ❷** of 1978–1986 on the left.

Cross Leadenhall onto St. Mary Axe to inspect the vast egg-shaped building at **No. 30 ❸** (nicknamed the "Gherkin") before turning left to find medieval **St. Helen's Bishopsgate.**

From St. Helen's churchyard, turn left onto Bishopsgate and right onto Threadneedle Street. Cut through Finch Lane, and proceed across Cornhill and into the narrow court opposite to find **St. Michael Cornhill,** where Wren and Hawksmoor added to the medieval tower.

Now go right, onto Lombard Street, whose banking signs evoke medieval origins. Hawksmoor's **St. Mary Woolnoth ❹** of 1716–1727 faces onto Mansion House Square,

the core of financial London: the **Mansion House** of 1739–1753, the Lord Mayor's official residence, and the Bank of England. Walk around the **Bank of England museum** on Bartholomew Lane, then turn left on Lothbury to find **St. Margaret Lothbury** (see pp. 62–63).

Lothbury runs into Gresham Street, where **St. Lawrence Jewry** (see p. 62) stands in front of the **Guildhall ❺** on Aldermanbury, the seat of the City's government. The medieval crypt

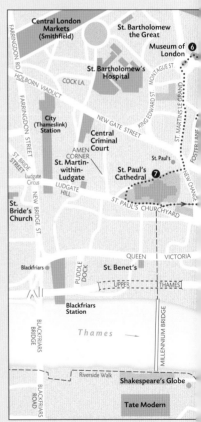

NOT TO BE MISSED:
St. Dunstan-in-the-East • Guildhall Art Gallery • Museum of London

Central London Markets (Smithfield)

St. Bartholomew the Great

Museum of London ❻

FARRINGDON RD

HOLBORN VIADUCT

COCK LA.

St. Bartholomew's Hospital

MONTAGUE ST.

NEW GATE STREET

KING EDWARD ST.

ST. MARTINS LE GRAND

FARRINGDON STREET

City (Thameslink) Station

Central Criminal Court

AMEN CORNER

St. Martin-within-Ludgate

FOSTER LANE

St. Paul's

NEW CHANGE

ST. BRIDE STREET

Ludgate Circus

LUDGATE HILL

St. Paul's Cathedral ❼

NEW BRIDGE ST.

St. Bride's Church

ST. PAUL'S CHURCHYARD

QUEEN   VICTORIA

Blackfriars

PUDDLE DOCK

St. Benet's

St. Benet's

UPPER   THAMES

Blackfriars Station

BLACKFRIARS BRIDGE

Thames

MILLENNIUM BRIDGE

Riverside Walk

Shakespeare's Globe

BLACKFRIARS ROAD

Tate Modern

is open to the public. You can visit the fine hall and also the **Guildhall Art Gallery** (*Guildhall Yard, EC2, tel 020 7332 3700, www.cityoflondon. gov*), which displays the City's art collection and incorporates a section of Roman London's amphitheater (see sidebar p. 69). Farther along Gresham Street, the Goldsmiths' Company has its hall on Foster Lane. Pewterers Hall is up Staining Lane, and there is a chunk of Roman wall on Noble Street. A bridge across London Wall road leads to the **Museum of London ❻** (see pp. 68–69).

Now walk down St. Martin's le Grand to **St. Paul's Cathedral ❼** (see pp. 58–61). Head east along Watling Street to Bow Lane, with

St. Mary-le-Bow at the top. Turn left up Queen Victoria Street. St. Stephen Walbrook and the Roman **Temple of Mithras ❽** (see sidebar p. 69) stand behind Mansion House, off Bucklersbury, while **St. Mary Abchurch ❾** (see p. 63) is set in a square down Abchurch Lane. Cannon Street leads back to Monument station.

🅰	Inside front cover F4
🚇	Monument Tube station
⤢	3.75 miles (6 km)
🕐	3 hours if just walking, a day with visits
➤	Monument Tube station

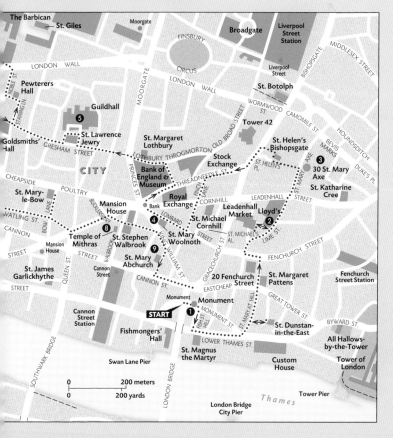

SMITHFIELD & CLERKENWELL

These two early spillovers from the crowded medieval City survived as a north London backwater while fashionable London moved west. Today, rapidly up-and-coming Clerkenwell has more medieval buildings than any other district, and London's only wholesale food market, Smithfield Meat Market, has been glamorously restored.

▪ The Smithfield Meat Market is a carnivore's dream.

**Smithfield &
Clerkenwell**

🅰 Map pp. 56–57

**Smithfield Meat
Market**

🅰 Map p. 57

🕒 Closed Sat.–Sun.

🚇 Tube: Barbican,
Farringdon

**smithfieldmarket
.com**

The 12th-century horse market on "Smooth field" (Smithfield) grew into a full-scale livestock market—the scene of terrific noise, brawls, and blood from slaughtered animals. It was moved to Islington in 1855 when the sale and slaughter of live animals was banned; only the magnificent **Smithfield Meat Market,** built in 1851–1866, survives. The original open space was the scene of major events, including the Bartholomew Fair, held annually from 1133 to 1855. Around the edges, seek out the medieval St. Bartholomew the Great (see opposite), Cloth Fair (see sidebar opposite), and beautiful **St. Etheldreda Church** (1300), tucked into Ely Place, off Charterhouse Street, just past the tiny alley leading to one of London's oldest pubs, **Ye Olde Mitre.**

Charterhouse Square is northeast of the market, with cobbles, gates, 18th-century houses, and, at the back, the substantial remains of **Charterhouse Monastery's** *(tel 0203 818 8873, thecharterhouse.org, several tours weekly by appt.)* cloisters and washhouse, once used by Carthusian monks. In St. John's Square, off St. John Street, stands the grand **St. John's Gate** of 1504. With the church's crypt and chancel, it was part of the Priory of St. John of Jerusalem and now houses a small museum *(tel 020 7324 4005, museumstjohn.org.uk).*

Clerkenwell was a refuge for monks and for craftsmen fleeing restrictions imposed by the City's guilds. The village center was the Green, a focus for jewelers and metalworkers. Little of St. Mary's Nunnery survives, but **St. James Clerkenwell** church *(Clerkenwell Close, EC1, tel 020 7251 1190, inspiresaintjames.org),* built in 1791 to replace the nunnery, has a fine organ. ∎

ST. BARTHOLOMEW THE GREAT

Medieval piety and pilgrimages had a profound effect on London. Henry I's court jester Rahere, having been cured of malaria caught during his pilgrimage to Rome, became an Augustinian monk and, in 1123, founded St. Bartholomew's Hospital and Priory. Both were funded by tolls from the annual Bartholomew Fair. What remains of this foundation today is London's oldest church, its only 12th-century monastic church, and its best piece of Romanesque building.

The Priory

The evocative priory church of St. Bartholomew the Great, built in 1123, was restored in 1880–1890 by Sir Aston Webb. It is reached through a 13th-century stone arch, originally the entrance to the nave. The striking half-timbered Tudor gatehouse is post-Dissolution (1559). The path to the church's door runs past what was once the ten-bay nave, and the cloisters were on the right.

Inside, Rahere's choir, ambulatory, and Lady Chapel survive, showing the full magnificence of medieval London's wealthy religious houses. The honey-colored walls, squat columns, unmolded arches, and simple decoration create an atmosphere for contemplation far from the city's bustle.

Rahere was buried here in 1143; his tomb (of a later date) is beside the altar. William Bolton, one of the last priors, gave the Tudor Window in 1515. Soon after, Sir Richard Rich acquired the dissolved priory, destroyed most of it, and lived in the Lady Chapel, which is found through Webb's wrought-iron screen. It later became a printer's office—Benjamin Franklin worked here as a young man in 1725.

The Hospital

St. Bartholomew's *(West Smithfield, EC1, tel 020 3465 5798, www.bartshealth.nhs.uk/ st-bartholomews)* was London's first hospital, built on land given by King Henry I. After the Dissolution, it became secular. It acquired buildings by James Gibbs in 1730–1759, and two murals by Hogarth. Inigo Jones, the architect, was born nearby in 1573 and baptized in the hospital church. There is an interesting museum on-site *(closed Sat.–Mon.)* accessible via the Henry VIII Gate. ∎

St. Bartholomew the Great

- Map p. 57
- West Smithfield, EC1
- 020 7600 0440
- Tube: Barbican

greatstbarts.com

Cloth Fair

The tiny lanes and alleys around Cloth Fair, next to St. Bartholomew the Great, are wonderfully atmospheric. A walk around this neighborhood, especially on a misty evening, can transport you back to the medieval days when the city's clothiers hosted their annual fair in the area.

Cloth Fair, the little street that gives the area its name, wends its way from West Smithfield (and the 21st century), passing 17th-century houses, jettied upper stories, faux gaslights, and the stone exterior wall of St. Bartholomew. Two interesting pubs are the Victorian **Rising Sun** *(38 Cloth Fair, EC1, tel 020 7726 6671)* and the **Hand & Shears** *(1 Middle St., EC1, tel 020 7600 0257)*, in business since 1537.

MUSEUM OF LONDON

The astounding collection at the Museum of London tells the story of the capital of Britain from prehistoric times to the present. Treasures range from a wealthy Roman's floor mosaic to an 18th-century dollhouse and dresses made of Spitalfields silk. London's glories, atrocities, and failures are all represented here in ten permanent galleries. Above all, the impression is one of Londoners speaking to us across the centuries.

The Layout

The museum, impressively renovated and expanded recently, opened in 1976. The core collection is an amalgamation of the Guildhall Museum, founded in 1826 for City-related objects, and the London Museum at Kensington Palace, which focused on London's cultural history, especially costume. London's frantic rebuilding during the 1980s and '90s, and developers' willingness to halt work while archaeologists excavated, extended the collection beyond manageable limits. Only a portion is on display; more can be seen in the Museum of London Docklands (see p. 214) and at the Museum of London Archaeological Archive—the world's largest such archive—in Hackney, which can be visited via guided tour.

Five of the permanent galleries were reorganized and reopened in 2010 to tell the story of modern London (from 1666 to the present). It is always worth visiting the temporary exhibitions.

Your Visit

The visit can begin with the prehistoric gallery, **"London Before London,"** and the remains of the Shepperton Woman, one of the oldest skeletons ever found in the London area.

Next is the Roman gallery, **"Roman London,"** where you'll find detailed models of the port and the forum. The models become even more impressive when you see the nearby recreations of some of the settings, with mosaic floors, kitchens complete with herbs and spices, an elegant dining room, and sculptures from the Temple of Mithras (see sidebar p. 69).

The gallery dedicated to the Middle Ages, **"Medieval London,"** covers the period up to the coronation of Elizabeth I (1558). The coins and pottery in the Saxon galleries and the arms abandoned after the Viking raids are evidence that London by no means came to a standstill when the Romans left. The collection, which also narrates another side of London, includes pilgrims' badges, Black Death crosses, a merchant's trunk, and high fashion, pointed-toe shoes as well.

You can see the splendor of the Tudor period in the remains of Henry VIII's Nonsuch Palace and in a model of St. Paul's Cathedral, before 1666, whereas grisly information about superstitions, food, and plumbing will give you an idea of the era's darker side.

EXPERIENCE: Discovering Roman London

Remnants of the old Roman city wall and other ancient ruins are scattered around and underneath the City of London's streets. The **Museum of London** offers excellent walking tours, often with working archaeologists, to these sites and many other hidden gems. Check out *museumoflondon.org.uk.*

One of the most impressive sections of Roman wall stands in gardens just south of the Tower Hill Tube stop. A hundred yards or so north of there, another lengthy section of Roman wall (with bonus medieval add-ons) can be found somewhat incongruously at the back of the parking lot fronting the Grange City Hotel on Cooper's Row.

In 1954, British construction workers digging a building foundation on Walbrook unearthed another Roman ruin, the third-century A.D. **Temple of Mithras,** dedicated to the Persian god of light and sun. The ancient temple was uprooted and moved nearby so that construction could continue—today, sixty years later, it has been moved back to its original location. Recently opened, the temple is viewable in situ in an exhibition space within the new Bloomberg London development on Walbrook *(londonmithraeum.com).*

"**War, Fire and Plague**" takes you back in time to Elizabethan and early Stuart London, narrating the instability of civil war, with one monarch put to death and another restored to the throne. The collection includes Charles I memorial medallions, Oliver Cromwell's death mask, and an amazing sight and sound display that allows you to experience the Great Fire of 1666.

Downstairs, in "**The Expanding City**" gallery, 18th-century newspapers, trade cards, and pottery bring life to the Georgian era. The displays in the 19th-century galleries chronicle the transportation, construction, public services, and entertainment of the times, while the "**Victorian Walk**" recreates a stroll down a shop-lined street where a barbershop, a pub, a tailor's shop, and a pawnbroker convincingly evoke the London of 1900.

London's continued growth in the 20th century is reflected in the "**People's City,**" a gallery that showcases an art deco elevator from Selfridges and an interactive map of poverty, and narrates the history of the British suffragette movement.

The "**World City**" gallery uses multimedia displays to explore the city from the 1950s to the present, narrating how, after facing war and poverty, London became the vibrant, multicultural city of today. The last stop of your visit is at the "**City Gallery,**" where some of London's icons are on display. Be sure to see the Lord Mayor's coach, which is still used for his November procession. Before you leave the museum, take a moment to admire the enormous copper and steel Olympic Cauldron that was lit during the 2012 Olympics. ∎

Museum of London

🗺 Map p. 57

✉ 150 London Wall, EC2

☎ 020 7001 9844

💲 Charge for some special exhibitions

🚇 Tube: Barbican, St. Paul's, Moorgate, Bank

museumoflondon .org.uk

Museum of London Archaeological Archive

✉ Mortimer Wheeler House, Eagle Wharf Rd., N1

💲 Charge for tours

🚇 Tube: Old Street, Angel

museumoflondon .org.uk

ISLINGTON

Up the hill from the City, Islington has long been associated with fun. Some aristocrats set up house here after the Dissolution of the Monasteries in the 16th century, but it was as an 18th-century spa that Islington's importance was established. Although Georgian houses were soon surrounded by a patchwork of Victorian squares, Islington is still synonymous with entertainment—theaters, markets, restaurants, pubs—and has a strong community spirit of its own.

Camden Passage
✉ Off Upper St., N1
☎ 020 7359 0190
🕒 Stalls: Open Wed., Sat., & Sun. Book market: Open Thurs.
🚇 Tube: Angel

camdenpassage
islington.co.uk

London Canal Museum
✉ 12–13 New Wharf Rd., N1
☎ 020 7713 0836
🕒 Closed Mon.
💲 $
🚇 Tube: King's Cross, St. Pancras

canalmuseum.org.uk

Two contrasting markets capture the spirit of Islington: traditional **Chapel Market,** on a street of the same name just northwest of the Angel Tube stop, where locals buy their food (the market is renowned for its fish) and other goods; and sophisticated, international **Camden Passage** (see sidebar below), saved from developers in the 1960s. (Don't confuse Camden Passage with the much larger Camden Lock Market a couple of miles west.) Duncan Street and Charlton Place lead from Camden Passage to the grand Georgian houses of Duncan Terrace.

Upper Street, reputed to have more restaurants than any other European street, has the landmark **St. Mary's Church** (tel 020 7226 3400, stmaryislington.org)

INSIDER TIP:

Take time for the often overlooked, charming little London Canal Museum, north of King's Cross just west of Islington.

—DEREK LAMBERTON
National Geographic contributor

of 1751–1754, with a fine steeple. Three of the many Islington's theaters are close by: the **King's Head** pub-theater (115 Upper St., tel pub: 0207 226 4443, tel theater box office: 0207 226 8561, kingsheadtheatrepub.co.uk); the **Little Angel Theatre** for children (14 Dagmar Passage, tel 020 7226 1787, littleangeltheatre.com), near handsome Cross Street; and the avant-garde **Almeida Theatre** (tel 020 7359 4404, almeida.co.uk) on Almeida Street.

Canonbury, to the northeast, is a delight to walk through: rows of late Georgian terraces, now desirable houses. Pretty Compton Terrace leads to Canonbury Square, with the grand Canonbury House of 1780 nearby. Barnsbury, to the west, has a string of Victorian squares, the next wave of building for City business people. ∎

Camden Passage

One of the densest concentrations of antique dealers in Britain crams into this narrow Islington lane, paved with York flagstones. Serious specialist shops line the passage, devoted to vintage clothes, clocks, prints, antiquarian books, and other items. Arcades have been squeezed in wherever possible, and you can find art nouveau objects, Staffordshire figures, Bakelite, enamelware, and more. Go early on Wednesday, Saturday, or Sunday, when stalls fill every inch, goods are piled on the ground, and every last fish fork has its price.

The grandeur of Westminster Abbey, the Houses of Parliament, and Buckingham Palace, enriched by chapels and parks

WESTMINSTER

The Changing of the Guard at Buckingham Palace

WESTMINSTER

Westminster, the nation's political and royal hub, has a totally different atmosphere from that of the commercial City. Lying 2 miles (3.2 km) upstream from it, London's second city was born a thousand years later, on a very different type of riverbank and for different reasons. This is an area of palaces and large open spaces, of public buildings and public spectacle rather than secret deals; of unfenced royal estates instead of a protected, walled port.

Origins of Westminster

Westminster was born beside the Thames, on boggy land watered by the Tyburn River. This unlikely spot is believed to be where Sebert, king of the East Saxons, founded the Church of St. Peter, possibly in A.D. 604.

Whatever its cloudy origins, Westminster quickly received royal blessings. Saxon kings gave land and relics; St. Dunstan, Bishop of London, contributed a dozen monks in 960; but it was Edward the Confessor who put it firmly on the map. His dream, inspired by royal foundations on the Continent, was to build a new palace, an extensive monastery, and an abbey church fit for royal burial. William the Conqueror and all subsequent sovereigns have reinforced Westminster's royal, religious, and political role in England's life.

NOT TO BE MISSED:

Westminster Today

The riverside Palace of Westminster, better known as the Houses of Parliament, has long dominated the day-to-day life of the area. Parliament's offices have spilled into neighboring buildings, including Michael Hopkins's fortresslike gray-black Portcullis House.

Westminster Abbey is the area's second focus and it is the abbey's magnificent building, and its role in Britain's history, that attracts visitors today. Members of Parliament (MPs) have worshipped at the parish church of Westminster, St. Margaret's, in preference to the much grander abbey next door, ever since the Puritan Speaker of the House of Commons worshipped there on Palm Sunday, 1614.

Wallace Collection

MANCHESTER SQUARE

BAKER ST.

WIGMORE ST.

ORCHARD ST.

JAMES ST.

Marble Arch

OXFORD STREET

Marble Arch

GROSVENOR SQUARE

❶

PARK LANE

MAYFAIR

PARK LANE

Apsley House

Hyde Park Corner

PARK

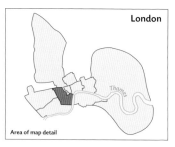

London

Thames

Area of map detail

Westminster Bridge, beside Parliament, was opened in 1750 and rebuilt in 1852–1862. Today, it is a departure point for pleasure boats on the river (see pp. 52–54). The Archbishop of Canterbury's London palace, Lambeth, is across the river.

Parliament's offices on Whitehall—a street lined with grand buildings—would have obliterated all memory of the glorious Whitehall Palace had Inigo Jones's Banqueting House and John Vardy's Horse Guards not survived.

As Victorian London grew increasingly polluted, England's monarchs left Whitehall Palace for Kensington Palace and Hampton Court, but they always kept court at St. James's Palace. When George III bought Buckingham House in 1761, he brought the London life of the sovereign back into Westminster. Buckingham Palace remains the monarch's London home, though St. James's Palace is the official court residence. ■

❶ U.S. Embassy ❷ Royal Mews ❸ Queen's Gallery ❹ Queen Victoria Memorial ❺ Spencer House ❻ Lancaster House ❼ Clarence House ❽ Queen's Chapel ❾ Marlborough House ❿ Churchill War Rooms & Churchill Museum ⓫ Methodist Central Hall ⓬ St. Margaret's ⓭ Cenotaph

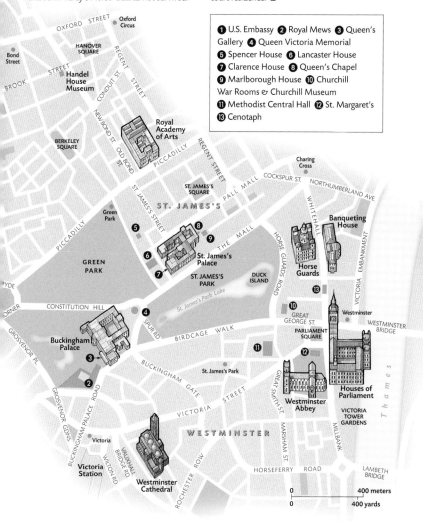

WESTMINSTER ABBEY

It is always worth pausing in front of a great building before entering, and this is particularly true of Westminster Abbey. Today, it takes a leap of the imagination to envisage the impact on medieval London of this soaring church—it is the tallest Gothic church in the country—and of its extensive abbey buildings and grounds.

■ Complete with crown, Elizabeth I's effigy lies in state in Westminster Abbey's Lady Chapel. Her half sister, Mary Tudor, is buried with her in the tomb.

Westminster Abbey

🗺 Map p. 73

✉ Chapter Office 20 Dean's Yard, SW1

☎ 020 7222 5152

🕐 Closed Sun. except for services. Last admission 3:30 p.m., except 1 p.m. on Sat.

💲 $$$

westminster-abbey .org

This is not the original abbey church. No evidence has been found of the first church built on this spot, dedicated to St. Peter. Edward the Confessor's, begun in 1050, is gone too. So is the Norman church of 1110–1150, which was gradually demolished to make way for Henry III's church. Today's abbey is largely the result of Henry's devout and expensive building program, begun in 1245. It was he who built the Gothic chancel, transepts, and crossing, and the first five bays of the nave.

Henry was close to the French Court and his architect, Henry of Reynes, may very well have been French. Several basic elements are clearly French-inspired: the polygonal apse with its radiating chapels, the first of its kind to be built in Britain; its amazing height; and its lavish decoration.

Imagine just the chancel, pinned on to the Norman nave. That is how it was for a century. Then, in 1375, Richard II had the Norman nave pulled down so Henry Yevele could begin the new one. The nave was completed in the 1390s, and the great west window was added in the prevailing perpendicular style. The west towers, designed by Nicholas Hawksmoor, were not added until the 18th century.

Henry VII used the leanest possible perpendicular style when he added his chapel to the east end in 1503–1512. It is well worth viewing from the outside. The great outer piers carrying the buttresses that support the weight of the roof—and so enable the windows to be huge—are folded and paneled.

When Henry VIII dissolved the monasteries, he took the rich Abbey of Westminster for himself in 1534, closed it in 1540, and later sold off two-thirds of its extensive lands. There was a brief reprieve under Mary I, then Elizabeth I sealed the abbey's fate and it became the Collegiate Church of St. Peter at Westminster.

The Interior

The first impression is one of extreme richness, in decoration and in monuments. But it was not always so. Imagine the interior empty of all monuments, with a delicate chancel screen whose function was to divide the monks from the worshippers. Today's rich but heavy Gothic Revival screen in the nave, made in 1839, is by Edward Blore; he also designed the elaborate choir stalls, in place by 1848. When pilgrims flocked to see the Confessor's shrine and the cloisters were filled with Benedictine monks, multicolored light would have streamed through the stained-glass windows onto the whitewashed interior walls,

and only the carved decoration would have been seen.

Your Visit

So rich are the abbey's monuments that you should join a tour. Try to arrive early to attend a service in St. Faith's Chapel, or come in the afternoon for Evensong.

Visitors are directed through the abbey on a one-way circuit, though the route has changed several times in recent years. Entrance is currently through the **Great North Door,** underneath James Thornhill's beautiful stained-glass rose window in the north transept.

INSIDER TIP:

Evensong at 5 p.m. in Westminster Abbey, with young choristers from the Choir School, is sublime.

—MARY LAMBERTON
National Geographic contributor

At the crossing see Sir George Gilbert Scott's high altar of 1868, incorporating Salviati's mosaic of the Last Supper. It is here that the monarch is crowned; for the coronation of Elizabeth II in 1952, nine processions lasted over four hours in a service based on King Edgar's coronation at Bath in 973.

Royal Tombs

The Royal Tombs are some of the abbey's most impressive monuments. The ancient tomb of Edward the Confessor is at the heart of the building—though,

Henry VII's Chapel

Rose Window

North Entrance

unless you're part of the verger tour *(times vary, $)*, it is off-limits to visitors. Edward's tomb is surrounded by other kings: Henry III, Edward I, Edward III, Richard II, and Henry V.

Henry VII's Chapel (also called The Lady Chapel) is arrestingly beautiful. London's finest late perpendicular building, its centerpiece is the poignant tomb of Henry VII, who lies next to his beloved queen. The huge windows, together with the cobweb-fine fan vaulting, create a delicate, decorative lightness. The statuary, as elsewhere, was at one time painted and gilded; the choir stalls have richly carved misericords (or mercy seats); the banners belong to knights of the ancient Order of the Bath.

The Nave

Wandering the nave is like being in an overstocked museum of sculptures and reliefs. The 1731 monument to Sir Isaac Newton, designed by William Kent, is flanked by physicist Stephen Hawking's grave (2018). Michael Rysbrack sculpted Newton's figure and those of Ben Jonson and John Milton, both in **Poets' Corner.** The symbolic **Tomb of the Unknown Warrior** is that of an unidentified soldier from World War I. The **Coronation Chair** is found just to the side of the tomb, by the West Entrance.

Poets' Corner

Poets' Corner, by no means restricted to memorials to poets, is in the South Transept. Here, with patience, you can find not only Geoffrey Chaucer and Edmund Spenser, but also novelists Jane Austen and George Eliot, composer George Frederick Handel, and actor David Garrick. The walls are decorated with 13th-century wall paintings. Behind lies the quiet, magical St. Faith's Chapel (reserved for private prayer), with a 14th-century wall painting.

Other Abbey Buildings

Where the south transept joins the nave, a door leads to the **Abbey Cloisters,** which give a good idea of the atmosphere in London's medieval monasteries. Surrounding the cloisters are several abbey buildings. The **Chapter House** of 1250–1253

Shrine of Edward the Confessor

South Transept

Chapter House

West Towers

High Altar

North Transept

Choir

Choir Stalls

Nave

West Window

West Entrance (Services Only)

Westminster Abbey

is where the abbot would give daily instructions to his monks, and it was here that Parliament met in the later 13th and 14th centuries. The **Pyx Chamber** of 1065–1090 and the **Undercroft Museum,** once monks' dormitories, now house wax effigies made for funeral processions:

Charles II's is the oldest. More buildings lie outside: In **Broad Sanctuary,** an arch leads into Dean's Yard, where Westminster School is found. Look for the College Hall of the 1360s. ∎

PALACE OF WESTMINSTER

Commonly known as the Houses of Parliament, this Victorian Gothic riverside palace, with its landmark Big Ben clock tower, is London's newest palace, built on the foundations of its oldest. On October 16, 1834, a fire destroyed the rambling old palace, which had been the principal London royal residence from William the Conqueror to Henry VIII. Even after Henry moved to Whitehall Palace in 1530, Westminster remained the seat of government—as it does today.

The Palace of Westminster, housing Parliament, dates primarily from the 19th century.

Palace of Westminster (Houses of Parliament)

- Map p. 73
- Parliament Square, SW1
- 020 7219 3000
- $$$
- Tube: Westminster

parliament.uk

Little survived the 1834 fire: William II's Westminster Hall, the cloisters and crypt of St. Stephen's Chapel, and the 14th-century **Jewel Tower,** possibly built as a giant safe for Edward III's jewels, furs, and gold. A visit to the Jewel Tower, the only old part easily accessible, makes a good start.

There were 97 entries in the competition for the new building— all designs had to be in the fashionable Gothic or Elizabethan Revival styles. Architects Charles Barry and Augustus Welby Pugin won. Their great building had 1,200 rooms, 2 miles (3.2 km) of corridor, 11 courtyards, 100 staircases, and a river facade 320 yards (293 m) long. Almost complete by 1847, this was the symbol of the Mother of Parliaments as the British Empire enjoyed its apogee.

The Exterior

There are two ways of enjoying the river facade: from nearby Westminster Bridge or from

Churchill War Rooms & Churchill Museum

This maze of underground rooms served as the headquarters for the government's War Cabinet from August 1939 until September 1945. They are decorated and furnished as they were then, and it is easy to imagine the secret information arriving, the meetings and planning sessions, the transatlantic telephone calls—and Sir Winston Churchill catching a few hours' sleep in his small bedroom. Beside them, the Churchill Museum illuminates the man and his period. A branch of the Imperial War Museum, this fascinating time capsule is very much recommended.

Lambeth Palace across the river.

The view from the river is fairy tale. Pugin, an ardent Gothicist, coated the classicist Barry's order with a riot of decoration. Statues of British sovereigns from William the Conqueror to Victoria cover the facade, while gilded pinnacles catch any sunlight. Such sumptuousness was matched on the inside.

The Elizabeth Tower, known by the name of its bell, **Big Ben,** symbolizes British government. If Parliament sits at night, a light shines on top. The tower was completed in 1858, and the clock, with a bell cast in Whitechapel (see p. 209), started in 1859. Its dials are 23 feet (7 m) wide, its hour hand 9 feet (2.7 m) long, and the minute hand 14 feet (4.2 m) long.

The Interior

On the southern end of the palace is **Victoria Tower,** over which the Union Jack flies. Completed in 1860, the tower houses a copy of every Act of Parliament since 1497. The interior of this end of the building, devoted to the House of Lords, is decorated in red. The Lords' function is to review, question, revise, and amend proposed legislation. Their Peers' Lobby leads to the Central Lobby. To the right is the Members' Lobby, where non-Members (Strangers) can come to meet their Member of Parliament (MP) or watch debates from the Strangers' Gallery. Farther north, the House of Commons (St. Stephen's Hall) is clad in somber green. It is built on the site of the original royal chapel and is where Parliament met from 1547 to 1834. The 19th-century building kept to the chapel layout, as did the rebuilding that took place after World War II bombing: The Speaker's chair is in the center, where the altar had been, the party in government on his/her right, the Opposition on the left. ■

Jewel Tower

- ✉ Abingdon St., SW1
- ☎ 020 7222 2219
- 💲 $
- 🚇 Tube: Westminster

www.english-heritage.org.uk

Churchill War Rooms & Churchill Museum

- 🗺 Map p. 73
- ✉ Clive Steps, King Charles St., SW1
- ☎ 020 7930 6961
- 💲 $$$
- 🚇 Tube: Westminster, St. James's Park

iwm.org.uk

EXPERIENCE:
Attend a Parliamentary Debate

You can get a feel for government in action by attending a debate whenever Parliament is in session (Mon.–Thurs. & some Fri.): Just join the line at the Cromwell Green visitor entrance (the wait can be an hour or more). To go on a highly recommended 90-minute guided tour (Sat., if Parliament is not in session, $$$), prepurchase a ticket (tel 020 7219 4114, Ticket Office, ticketmaster.co.uk or parliament.uk).

A WESTMINSTER WALK

The streets on this half-day walk are full of monuments that were and, in part still are, the seat of Britain's political power, both parliamentary and monarchic.

From **Westminster Bridge ❶**, enjoy the river facade of the Palace of Westminster. On the north end of the bridge, Thomas Thornycroft's bronze, unveiled in 1902, shows **Queen Boudicca** and her daughters hurtling toward London in their chariot.

Walk past **Big Ben**'s Elizabeth Tower ❷ (see p. 79), then left around the Palace of Westminster, passing first an 1899 statue of Parliamentarian leader Oliver Cromwell (1599–1658), then the Crusader Richard I (r. 1189–1199). **St. Margaret's Church, Westminster Abbey,** and the **Jewel Tower ❸** (see p. 78) stand across the road. Continue straight to **Victoria Tower Gardens** to find two memorials—to the suffragette Emmeline Pankhurst (1858–1928) and to the emancipation of slaves in 1833—and Rodin's sculpture, "The Burghers of Calais."

Continue along Millbank. Elegant 18th-century Westminster is found down Dean Bradley Street, in Smith Square, where

EXPERIENCE:
Rent a Deck Chair

After a long day walking London's streets, there are few sights as appealing as the comfortable canvas deck chairs clustered in several of London's parks from spring through fall. The best known site is at the northern tip of **Green Park,** though chairs are also set up in **Kensington Gardens, St. James's Park,** and **Hyde Park** (by both the Serpentine and Speaker's Corner).

But this restorative respite isn't free. Expect to pay up to £2 ($3) to soak up an hour of English sunshine. A beleaguered civic employee has the thankless job of walking around to ask payment from the grumbling patrons.

NOT TO BE MISSED:

Parliament Square ● Banqueting House ● Downing Street ● St. James's Park

St. John's Church ❹, now a concert hall, often has lunchtime concerts. Walk straight past the fine houses of Lord North Street, left down Cowley and right onto Dean Barton Streets to Great College Street. Turn left. An arch on the right side of the street leads into Dean's Yard. At the far end of the yard, another arch opens into Broad Sanctuary, beside the west door of **Westminster Abbey** (see pp. 74–77). Opposite, the domed Methodist Central Hall of 1905–1911 and the Middlesex Guildhall of the same date stand on either side of Powell Moya and Partners' **Queen Elizabeth II Conference Centre ❺**, opened in 1986.

Parliament Square, down Broad Sanctuary to the right, is a political sculpture court. Statues include those of Abraham Lincoln, statesman Lord Beaconsfield (born Benjamin Disraeli, 1804–1881), and the old, bearlike Sir Winston Churchill. Sir George Gilbert Scott's Foreign Office (Old Treasury), built in 1868–1873, fills the north side of the square.

Go straight past Big Ben again to find two annexes for MPs: new Portcullis House on the left and, after turning left onto Victoria Embankment, Richard Norman Shaw's striped 1880s building. Farther along Victoria Embankment, turn left on Horse Guards Avenue toward Whitehall; the **Banqueting House** (see p. 82) stands on the corner on the left. Whitehall has four monuments in the road: Sir Edwin Lutyens's **Cenotaph,** a 2005 statue honoring the women of World War II, and equestrian

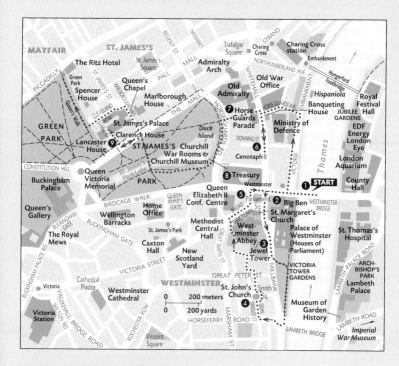

statues to Field Marshals Earl Haig (1861–1928) and the 2nd Duke of Cambridge (1819–1904).

Downing Street 6 lies across Whitehall and to the left, behind its great gates on the right. The prime minister's official residence is at No. 10. Back up Whitehall, William Kent and John Vardy's **Horse Guards** was built in 1745–1755. The guard is changed twice daily. Go through to **Horse Guards Parade 7** to see the building's park facade, the backdrop to royal pageantry such as Trooping the Colour.

St. James's Park lies ahead. To the far left, past the memorial statue to Earl Mountbatten and near the statue of Clive of India (1725–1774), are the **Churchill War Rooms & Churchill Museum 8** (see sidebar p. 79). Farther into St. James's Park, the bridge over the lake gives fine views back toward Whitehall and leads to the Mall. From here look left, up past the Queen Victoria Memorial to Buckingham Palace. **Clarence House 9**, to the left, formerly

⬛ Inside front cover D3
➤ Westminster Tube station
🕒 3 hours
↔ 3 miles (4.8 km)
➤ Green Park Tube station

the Queen Mother's home, is now refurbished as the Prince of Wales's London home (*prince ofwales.gov.uk*). Its reception rooms are open to the public (*tel 020 7766 7303, royalcollection.org .uk*) via Stable Yard for a month during the summer, usually around August. Backtracking, Marlborough Road runs north of the Mall and leads to **St. James's Palace,** whose Queen's Chapel is to the right. Walk around the palace, turning into Cleveland Row, which leads to Green Park. Turn right on Queen's Walk and past **Spencer House** (the 18th-century ancestral home of Princess Diana's family) up to the Green Park Tube station.

BANQUETING HOUSE

More a grand room with a basement than a house, this huge, double-cube space, lit by floor-to-ceiling windows on the Whitehall side, has its entire ceiling painted by Peter Paul Rubens and is perhaps London's most beautiful room.

Banqueting House

- Map p. 73
- Whitehall, SW1
- 020 3166 6000
- Closed Sun. & for government functions
- $. Recorded tour included
- Tube: Westminster, Charing Cross, Embankment

hrp.org.uk

James I built it between 1619 and 1622, employing architect Inigo Jones, who was already working on Queen's House at Greenwich (see p. 218). Later Jones designed Queen's Chapel for St. James's Palace and Covent Garden's St. Paul's as well as the Piazza (see p. 124). The king wanted to rebuild all of Henry VIII's rambling, brick Whitehall Palace, but this was the only part to be completed. The Banqueting House survived the fire of 1698, when the rest of the palace was destroyed. London's first building to be partly encased in Portland stone, it set a new design tone, inspired by Andrea Palladio.

The crypt was for the king's informal parties. The grand room upstairs was for masques, banquets,

court ceremonies, and diplomatic functions. On entering the room, the visitor would see the decoration of two orders, Ionic below and Corinthian above, mirroring the building's exterior. Ranks of courtiers standing on both sides led the visitor to the enthroned king, ahead. Looking up, he or she would see Rubens's panels, painted in 1634 for Charles I for £3,000 (about $4,800). For these paintings, which honored Charles's father, James I, as the symbol of the union of England and Scotland and celebrated the benefits of wise rule, Charles bestowed a knighthood on Rubens.

Later events were to put Rubens's allegory into question. Charles I was beheaded on a scaffold mounted right outside on the facing street on January 30, 1649; but in 1660, it was here that Charles II celebrated his own restoration to the throne. ∎

Maundy Thursday

British monarchs long observed Maundy Thursday by washing the feet of paupers, a reference to Jesus' washing his disciples' feet at the Last Supper. You won't find bare toes and suds at a modern Royal Maundy Service, but the queen's attendants sport towels over their clothes, and her fragrant floral bouquet hints at the tradition's malodorous history. At the event, the queen gives elderly citizens purses of special coins; the monarch's age determines the number of recipients. The Banqueting House hosted the service, its name based on the Latin for "command," for centuries, but the venue now changes annually.

WESTMINSTER CATHEDRAL

Begin in the cathedral's piazza, off Victoria Street. Here, the red and white bulk of London's last cathedral rises uninterrupted. The Roman Catholic hierarchy was not reestablished in England and Wales until 1850, 300 years after the Reformation. In 1894, Archbishop Vaughan chose John Bentley to design a cathedral on two conditions: that it have a wide nave for big congregations, and that it look nothing like nearby (Protestant) Westminster Abbey.

The Blessed Sacrament Chapel of Westminster Cathedral

Bentley had been working in the Gothic style. This simply would not do, being too similar to the abbey. So he toured Italy, Greece, and Constantinople (Istanbul), and returned to create a church that mixed Byzantine and Romanesque ideas using red brick and white Portland stone.

Climb the 273-foot (83 m) **Campanile** for views toward Big Ben, Nelson's Column, and Buckingham Palace. The cross on top of the Campanile is said to contain a relic of the True Cross.

Inside the cathedral, incense perfumes the air, mosaics in chapel domes reflect the lights of votive candles, and a great gold cross hangs above the huge nave. Marble lines the walls, while the domes and apse are held together by bridges supported on columns inspired by Ravenna's seventh-century churches. Eric Gill's **"Stations of the Cross,"** made in 1914–1918, are on the nave piers. A permanent exhibit ($) displays relics, an architectural model, chalices, and other cathedral treasures. ∎

Westminster Cathedral

🅰 Map p. 73

✉ 42 Francis St., SW (off Victoria St.)

☎ 020 7798 9055

🕐 Campanile: Mon.–Fri. 9:30 a.m.–5 p.m., Sat.–Sun. 9:30 a.m.–4 p.m.

💲 Donation; Campanile: $

🚇 Tube/Rail: Victoria

westminster cathedral.org.uk

ST. JAMES'S PALACE

A visit to St. James's Palace should begin in Friary Court on Marlborough Road, watching the old guard during the Changing of the Guard ceremony (see p. 89). The original palace, which had four courts, was built in the 1530s by Henry VIII as part of a lavish building program. Despite fires and rebuilding, much of the exterior survives.

St. James's Palace

- 🗺 Map p. 73
- ✉ Cleveland Row, Marlborough Gate, SW1
- 🕐 Palace closed to the public
- 🚇 Tube: Green Park

The name of one of the courts, Friary Court, betrays the origins of the palace. A medieval Augustinian friary, it became a women's leper hospital dedicated to St. James the Less. Henry VIII bought the hospital and grounds, built the palace, and enclosed 300 acres (121 ha) of land (now St. James's Park).

After the Whitehall Palace fire of 1698, St. James's became the sovereign's principal London residence. After George III's move to Buckingham Palace in 1762, St. James's remained the official royal residence. Today, new sovereigns are proclaimed and make their first speeches here. Foreign ambassadors are now appointed to the Court of St. James's, and they ride from here in a glass coach to make their first courtesy call on the queen.

Opposite Friary Court stands **Queen's Chapel** *(Sun. services Easter–July)*. Built in 1623 for Charles I's Catholic wife, Henrietta Maria, it was England's first Italian-inspired classical church. Inigo Jones designed it and, as at Banqueting House, made the interior a simple double cube.

Henry's four-story **Gatehouse,** with its clock, octagonal towers, and linenfold-paneled doors, gives an idea of what fairy-tale palaces Tudor Whitehall and Greenwich must have been. It is sometimes possible to peek into Ambassadors Court and, on some Sundays, to visit the **Chapel Royal** *(Sun. services Oct.–Easter)*, whose painted roof may have been done by Holbein. The rest was lavishly redecorated in the 1830s.

It was at St. James's Palace that the court custom of having a poet laureate as an official part of the royal household began. John Dryden was the first. Carol Ann Duffy held the title until 2019. ∎

◾ The Tudor Gatehouse of St. James's Palace

BUCKINGHAM PALACE

The Duke of Buckingham's relatively modest mansion, built in 1705, is now lost behind successive additions of regal rooms, splendid art, and an imposing facade. Outside the railings, people gather on momentous occasions to cheer the queen and the royal family, who come out onto the balcony between the great central columns. The sovereign's London home is a focal point of the capital.

■ A detachment of the Queen's Guard marches in front of Buckingham Palace.

The View

The best view of Buckingham Palace is from the Mall, near Sir Aston Webb's "Queen Victoria Memorial," created in 1901–1913. Thomas Brock's marble statue of the queen looks up the Mall, surrounded by allegorical figures of such Victorian virtues as Charity, Truth, Progress, and Manufacture; a gold-leaf Victory figure soars high above. The circular **Memorial Gardens** that surround the statue, symbolizing the British Empire, have gates donated by Canada, South Africa, and Australia.

Straight ahead, across the parade ground where the Changing of the Guard ceremony takes place, the palace's Portland stone facade seen today was constructed by Sir Aston Webb in just three months in 1913. Before that, Buckingham Palace and its surroundings had been far less imposing. John Sheffield, Duke of Buckingham, built a country house here in 1705. After George III bought it in 1761

Buckingham Palace

- 🗺 Map p. 73
- ✉ The Mall, SW1
- ☎ 020 7766 7300
  Royal Mews:
  020 7766 7302
- 🕐 Open Aug.–Sep.
- 💲 $$$$
- 🚇 Tube: Green Park, Victoria, or St. James's Park

rct.org.uk

for his wife, Queen Charlotte of Mecklenburgh-Strelitz, Sir William Chambers remodeled it, retaining its private character; ceremonial functions continued to take place at St. James's Palace.

The Building

It was George IV who began aggrandizing the house in 1826. He instructed John Nash to transform it into an appropriately grand palace where he could hold court and official ceremonies. The elderly Nash, hampered by inadequate funds and the need to incorporate the old building, added a string of new rooms along the garden side, with State Rooms up on the first floor. Nash's Bath stone garden facade is particularly delightful in its light, French neoclassical style, but his Mall facade was obscured by Edward Blore's east wing, added in 1847–1850 to provide more space for Queen Victoria—nurseries, bedrooms, kitchens, and a huge ballroom 123 feet (37 m) long.

The Interior

In all, the palace has 600 rooms, including 19 State Rooms, 52 royal and guest bedrooms, 188 staff bedrooms, and 78 bathrooms. More than 400 people work here, and each year more than 40,000 are entertained in the palace. Used for state ceremonies, official entertaining, and royal garden parties, it is one of the world's few remaining working royal palaces.

While the queen keeps a mere dozen rooms overlooking Green Park for herself, visitors can enjoy the scale and lavish furnishings of the State Rooms. George IV's taste for opulence is displayed in sculpted panels, elaborate ceilings, and bright colors. The Blue, White,

■ The palace's White Drawing Room is open to the public in August and September.

Royal Parks

London's nine royal parks were once private possessions of the sovereign, used for hunting and other pastimes. Gradually, under pressure, they were opened to the public, beginning with St. James's Park in the 1660s.

The parks have various origins. Henry VIII took Hyde Park in exchange for land in Berkshire. Primrose Hill was an exchange with Eton College. Richmond Park was a series of farms bought by Charles I. William and Mary added Kensington Gardens to Nottingham House.

Today, an informal atmosphere is preserved, though park law and regulations are enforced by a parks security force. Gardeners maintain a labor-intensive but impressive style—40,000 tulips are planted annually in front of Buckingham Palace, 250,000 more at Hampton Court. Naturalists look after the animals, trees, and lakes. You can walk through nearly 2 miles (3.2 km) of parkland—from Westminster to Notting Hill—through St. James's, Green, and Hyde Parks to Kensington Gardens.

and Green Drawing Rooms, the Music Room, and the Throne Room are some of the grandest.

The palace is a treasure house of art; the Royal Collection is one of the world's finest. When George V and Queen Mary came to the throne in 1910, they employed Sir Aston Webb to improve the exterior while they arranged the contents. Queen Mary's organized approach resulted in furniture being reassembled from all over the royal residences and restored.

The Tour

Today, in summer, it is possible to visit some of the **State Rooms,** a move initiated to raise funds after Windsor Castle's 1992 fire (see sidebar p. 223). Visitors enter Buckingham Palace through the **Ambassadors Entrance,** where Nash's facade is visible past the Grand Quadrangle. Go up the grand Carrara marble staircase to see the **Green Drawing Room** and the red **Throne**

Room. Next is the **Picture Gallery,** where 50 major paintings from the Royal Collection hang in the 165-foot-long (50 m), top-lit room. The **Silk Tapestry Room** leads into the **East Gallery,** then the **ballroom** and the rooms overlooking the 30 acres (12 ha) of gardens. The **State Dining Room** is first, then the **Blue Drawing Room,** the **Music Room** with its great bow window, and the **White Drawing Room.** You leave down the Ministers' Staircase, past the portraits and sculptures of the **Marble Hall,** and out to the gardens.

Other Palace Areas

You can see more of the Royal Collection at the **Queen's Gallery** (rebuilt and enlarged in 2002). Here, changing exhibitions display a selection of the queen's own art, one of the world's finest private collections. The nearby **Royal Mews** on Buckingham Palace Road, are home to the Royal Family's state coaches and cars. ∎

ROYAL LONDON

London is full of contradictions. Although a democratically elected government sits at Westminster, with the sovereign merely a figurehead, the royal presence is strongly felt. At a time when the very existence of a royal family is under question, the capital is littered with royal reminders.

Queen Elizabeth II rides in a state carriage along The Mall, a route of exactly 0.5 nautical mile (0.9 km).

It was Edward the Confessor, King of England from 1042 to 1066, who first made Westminster his capital. Queen Elizabeth II traces her blood-descent back to Egbert of Wessex, king of the English from 829. London's palaces, pageantry, statues, and symbols result from this history.

Homes & Gardens

The choice of royal homes to visit in London begins with Buckingham Palace (see pp. 85–87), followed by Clarence House (see p. 81), both lived in today. Then there are Whitehall Palace's surviving Banqueting House (see p. 82), Westminster's Jewel Tower (see p. 78), Kensington Palace (see pp. 158–159), and the fortress-palace, the Tower of London (see pp. 204–207). Farther afield, magnificent Hampton Court Palace (see pp. 197–200) lies upriver, beyond Kew Palace (see p. 192) and Marble Hill House (see p. 194). Greenwich (see pp. 215–218) is downstream, while the riches of Windsor Castle (see pp. 222–223) are a 40-minute train ride west. On Sundays, the Chapels Royal at St. James's, Hampton Court, the

By Appointment

More than 800 shops in Britain have a royal coat of arms above the door. This indicates that the business holds a royal warrant to supply "By Appointment" to the queen, Duke of Edinburgh, or the Prince of Wales. Dating from the Middle Ages, the tradition remains strong today. The highest concentration of these suppliers, who use the position to promote their goods' quality, is in St. James's and Mayfair.

Tower, and the Queen's Chapel are occasionally open to worshippers. St. James's Palace, Westminster Hall, and Marlborough House can be enjoyed just from the outside, but only tantalizing fragments remain of Richmond, Rotherhithe, and other lost palaces.

The royal parks were once royal hunting grounds. Garden lovers should not miss Queen Mary's Garden in Regent's Park, the Tudor and Privy Garden at Hampton Court, the Rose Garden in Hyde Park, or the Royal Botanic Gardens at Kew.

Pageantry

Despite some recent scaling down of royal pageantry, there is still plenty to see.

The colorful Changing of the Guard takes place at Buckingham and St. James's Palaces at about 11:30 a.m. every day from April to June, and on alternate days the rest of the year. (Arrive early if you want a good view.) You can also watch the mounted Queen's Life Guard change guard at Horse Guards Parade at 11 a.m. Monday to Friday, and at 10 a.m. on Sundays.

The Ceremony of the Keys, the ritual locking of the Tower of London's gates, has been performed every night, without fail, for over 700 years. The ceremony, conducted by the Chief Yeoman Warder, takes place at exactly 9:53 p.m. and lasts for seven minutes; after the two guards lock the gates of the tower for the night, sentries call out, asking who goes there. When they reply that they are the Queen's keys, they are allowed to pass. Be sure to reserve your tickets to the ceremony well in advance at *hrp.org.uk* on the page dedicated to the Ceremony of the Keys, or reserve in person at the Ceremony of the Keys Office *(Tower of London, London, EC3N 4AB)*.

Another colorful bit of public pageantry is the annual Trooping the Colour ceremony in June that marks the official celebration of the queen's birthday (though her actual birthday is April 21). The queen proceeds in a carriage from Buckingham Palace to Horse Guards Parade, where she inspects her troops. The event began in the early 1700s, when it was a practical event for soldiers to be shown the flags ("colors") of their battalions so that they could easily recognize and rally behind them in battle. It's free to watch the procession; check *royal.gov.uk* for information on getting seats.

Other annual events include Beating the Retreat in the summer and the State Opening of Parliament in November. The queen still follows the Court Year and entertains visiting heads of state in April, July, and November.

A formal procession attends the State Opening of Parliament each November.

ST. JAMES'S, MAYFAIR, &
PICCADILLY

The heart of aristocratic London has enjoyed a reputation for exclusiveness since its development by the aristocrats themselves, when they moved westward from the City and leased land to speculative builders.

St. James's

Today, St. James's Square, laid out by Henry Jermyn in the 1660s, is home to the discerning bibliophiles' refuge, the **London Library** *(tel 020 7766 4700, londonlibraryco.uk)* at No. 14. Founded by Thomas Carlyle in 1841, the library is a private collection of more than 1,000,000 titles, some dating back to the 16th century. Membership is open to all; overseas members have access to a rapidly growing electronic library.

Christie's *(tel 020 7839 9060, christies.com)*, the international art auctioneers founded in 1766, is on nearby King Street. Auctions take place daily; visit the website to register as a bidder or to view the catalog. Christie's is surrounded by art dealers who break from their shops to lunch at their exclusive clubs (see sidebar p. 92) or shop on Jermyn Street (see sidebar opposite). Guests of the Ritz, Stafford, and Duke's hotels echo the luxurious lifestyle once enjoyed in such mansions as **Spencer House,** ancestral home of Princess Diana, painstakingly restored by Lord Rothschild *(tel 020 7514 1958, www.spencerhouse.co.uk)*.

Mayfair

Essentially a development of six great estates, Mayfair's residential grandeur is enhanced by deluxe hotels: the Dorchester, Claridge's, and the Connaught.

■ Burlington Arcade in Piccadilly

The home of composer George Frideric Handel from 1723 to 1759 is now **Handel House Museum** (*25 Brook St., W1, tel 020 7495 1685, handelhouse.org*). **Sotheby's** (*34–35 New Bond St., W1, tel 020 7293 5000 sothebys. com/en*), Mayfair's art focus, is worth a visit if only for the fascinating sculpture that sits inconspicuously atop its doors. Bought by a collector from Sotheby's in the 1880s for £40 ($64), it's London's oldest outdoor statue: a superb 1320 B.C. depiction of the Egyptian lion-goddess Sekhmet. The piece was never picked up by the buyers and has been the auction house's symbol ever since.

INSIDER TIP:

In business for more than a century, the chocolatier Prestat, in Princes Arcade, Piccadilly, makes some of the best truffles you'll ever eat.

—JANE SUNDERLAND
National Geographic contributor

Sotheby's is on the most stylish shopping strip, New and Old Bond Streets, where Asprey's, Gucci, Prada, Dior, Rolex, Tiffany, Cartier, Bulgari, Louis Vuitton, and Chopard jewelers create dazzling shop windows to lure spenders. Savile Row runs parallel to lower New Bond Street to the east and is

---

EXPERIENCE:
Take Home a Custom-Made Shirt

Jermyn Street is known for its bespoke (an English term denoting "custom-made") shirtmakers serving the classy, discerning male dresser since the 18th century.

The purchase process begins by selecting a fabric, which can be a more daunting proposition than it sounds—**Turnbull & Asser** (*71–72 Jermyn St., SW1, tel 020 7808 3000, turnbullandasser.co.uk*), for example, boasts of having more than 1,000 options on hand. Then comes the fitting, the off-site cutting and stitching, and your one-shirt test period. The entire process, accompanied by the advice of highly professional staff, can take up to six weeks, but it can be done by mail once the original fitting is complete. There's usually a six-shirt minimum per order; expect to spend up to £200 ($320) per shirt.

---

the place to go—as it has been for centuries—for custom-made suits.

Piccadilly

Dividing the districts of Mayfair and St. James's, Piccadilly runs from Piccadilly Circus to Hyde Park Corner. The Duke of Wellington's **Apsley House** at Hyde Park Corner is a rare survivor of Mayfair's mansions, with Adam fireplaces and pictures by Goya and Velázquez. Quality pleasures line the street's core: the Ritz hotel and Hatchard's bookshop on one side; the **Royal Academy of Arts** and **Burlington Arcade** on the other.

The academy was founded in 1768, with George III as its patron and Sir Joshua Reynolds its first

Spencer House

- ⬛ Map p. 73
- ✉ 27 St. James's Place, SW1
- ☎ 020 7514 1958
- 🕐 Open Sun. only. Closed Aug.
- 💲 $$
- Ⓜ Tube: Green Park

spencerhouse.co.uk

Gentlemen's Clubs

The 18th-century coffeehouses and gambling clubs of Mayfair and St. James's developed into somber gentlemen's clubs. Large clubhouses along Pall Mall and St. James's Street became homes-away-from-home for members who tended to share the same interests. On Pall Mall, the **Athenaeum** *(tel 020 7930 4843, athenaeumclub.co.uk)* is known for academics and bishops, while the **Reform Club** *(tel 020 7930 9374, reformclub.com)* attracts liberal thinkers (it was the first to give full membership to women). On St. James's Street, the **Carlton** *(tel 020 7493 1164, carlton club.co.uk)* is for Tories, **Brooks's** *(tel 020 7493 4411, brooksclub.org)* is more liberal, and **White's** *(tel 020 7493 6671)* is for the very grand. Several of the clubs enjoy reciprocal membership arrangements with private clubs in the United States.

Apsley House

- Map p. 72
- 149 Piccadilly, SW1
- 020 7499 5676
- Closed Mon.– Tues. Apr.–Oct. & Mon.–Fri. Nov.–Mar.
- $
- Tube: Hyde Park Corner

english-heritage .org.uk

Royal Academy of Arts

- Map p. 73
- Burlington House, Piccadilly, W1
- 020 7300 8090
- Cost varies with the exhibition
- Tube: Green Park, Piccadilly Circus

royalacademy.org.uk

president. Gainsborough was a founding member; Constable and Turner were students. The tradition of newly elected academicians presenting one work to the academy began early and is the origin of the great annual Summer Exhibitions, when Royal Academicians exhibit their work alongside amateur and professional artists who enter in competition.

In 2013, the academy opened **The Keeper's House** *(keepershouse.org.uk)*, a social space (including a café, bar, and art displays) for both artists and art aficionados. Located in the academy's courtyard, the Keeper's House is open to the public every evening except Sunday.

Burlington Arcade runs alongside the academy. Samuel Ware's covered shopping arcade, completed in 1819, was a Continental idea welcomed by fashionable, often rain-drenched London. Piccadilly, Royal Opera, Princes, and Royal Arcades are all in this area, each containing boutiques. ■

Savile Row tailors cut their cloth for bespoke men's garments.

EXPERIENCE: Enjoying a Cuppa (Tea)

Never mind that tea wasn't introduced to Britain until the mid-17th century or that coffee actually preceded it to the scepter'd isle: The image of an English afternoon tea is practically synonymous with refined British culture.

A visit to London wouldn't be complete without enjoying an afternoon tea. Nearly all services offer an eclectic choice of teas—ranging from Indian black teas (Indian and Chinese) to English or Irish Breakfast, Earl Grey, and Lapsang Suchong. These fine brews are accompanied by sandwiches, then scones with clotted cream and jam, and pastries to finish.

A traditional British afternoon tea includes not only tea, but finger foods such as small sandwiches, scones, and pastries.

Hotels

Most major hotels in the city offer an afternoon tea. The experience won't come cheap; the hotel teas below average about £35–£45 ($56–$72) per person. Dress is usually smart casual (i.e., no shorts or sandals), and reservations are highly recommended.

Tea in the **Ritz's** Palm Court *(150 Piccadilly, W1, tel 020 7493 8181 & toll-free from the U.S. 877-748-9536, www.theritzlondon.com)* is the classic experience. Men need to wear a tie and jacket, and photos are not allowed. Reserve at least one month in advance for a weekday and four months in advance for a weekend. It is best to book the last sitting, so you do not have to rush.

The **Dorchester** *(45, Park Lane, W1, tel 020 7493 4545, thedorchester.com)* offers many timed seatings in two separate restaurants.

Brown's Hotel *(Albemarle St., W1, tel 020 7493 6020, www.roccofortehotels.com)* has a tea sommelier in its English Tea Room.

Other excellent afternoon teas are served at the Park Room at **Grosvenor House,** a JW Marriott Hotel *(Park Lane, W1, reservations 020 7499 6363, marriott. co.uk);* at **Claridge's** *(Brook St., W1, tel 020 7629 8860, claridges.co.uk);* at the **Lanesborough** *(Hyde Park Corner, SW1, tel 020 7259 5599, lanesborough.com);* and at the **Landmark** *(222 Marylebone Rd., NW1, tel 020 7631 8000, landmarklondon. co.uk).*

Department Stores

Harrods *(87–135 Brompton Rd., SW1, tel (0)20 3626 7020, harrods.com)* was founded in 1849 by tea merchants, so it would be fitting to visit the beautiful Harrods Tea Rooms for a traditional tea. Nearby, the Fifth Floor Restaurant at **Harvey Nichols** *(109–125 Knightsbridge, SW1, tel 020 7235 5000, harveynichols .com)* is less expensive than other options at £22.50 ($36). In Mayfair, the St. James's Restaurant at **Fortnum & Mason** *(181 Piccadilly, W1, 020 7734 8040, fortnum andmason.com)* offers a variety of tea services, including a signature Estate High Tea.

WALLACE COLLECTION

One of the capital's finest private art collections is found at Hertford House, a palatial 18th-century mansion just north of Mayfair and Oxford Street in Manchester Square.

The Wallace Collection includes a first-class assembly of paintings.

Wallace Collection

Map p. 72

Hertford House, Manchester Square, W1

020 7593 9500

Tube: Bond Street, Marble Arch

wallacecollection .org

The house was built for the Duke of Manchester in 1777. But it was four generations of the art-loving Hertford family who created the collection. The 1st Marquess supplied Canalettos and the 2nd Gainsboroughs. The 3rd added Sèvres porcelain and Dutch canvases, and the 4th bought Fragonards, Watteaus, and Bouchers, plus furniture, and installed the Parisian staircase. As a postscript, the 4th Marquess's illegitimate son and inheritor, Richard Wallace, renovated the house and added his Italian majolica and Renaissance armor, bronzes, and gold. His widow gave both house and collection to the nation.

Hertford House is a joy for art lovers, with a collection that includes a series of masterpieces. Many of the mansion's twenty-eight rooms were renovated with elaborate bronzes, gold, and silk tapestries. The collection includes 18th century French paintings, furnishings, and porcelain, much of which once belonged to Madame de Pompadour and to Marie Antoinette, as well as canvases by Titian, Canaletto, Guardi, Rembrandt, and Gainsborough. Considered the finest collection of French paintings outside France, it also includes Frans Hals's "The Laughing Cavalier" (1624) and Fragonard's "The Swing" (1767).

The mansion is also home to an extraordinary collection of armors and Renaissance treasures as well as elaborate clocks, Limoges porcelain, and Venetian glass. A lavish staircase leads to the upper floor, where you can admire the paintings of Boucher. ∎

Great views and great entertainment: museums, concert halls, theaters, and restaurants

SOUTH BANK

Marine life surrounds visitors at the Sea Life London Aquarium.

SOUTH BANK

The serious core of London—Westminster and the City—sits on the north bank of the Thames; the south bank is a solid strip of entertainment. Here, museums for design, modern art, war, and underwater life are interspersed with theaters, concert halls, restaurants, and a fine cathedral. The seeds for development were sown when Puritan City government banned theaters from the City in 1574 and they went over the river, making Southwark a refuge for actor-managers. Today, bridges old and new, plus the Jubilee Tube line, make access to this vibrant area easy.

This stretch of the Thames between Tower and Westminster Bridges sits directly opposite the City and Westminster, filling the space inside the river's broad curve. According to recent archaeological discoveries, Southwark developed early as an entertainment

area for Roman London directly opposite, linked by the one bridge across the tidal Thames. Over the centuries, as London expanded, the south bank developed—and the bridges multiplied to six for road traffic, three for rail, and one for pedestrians. And the revival of the south bank is

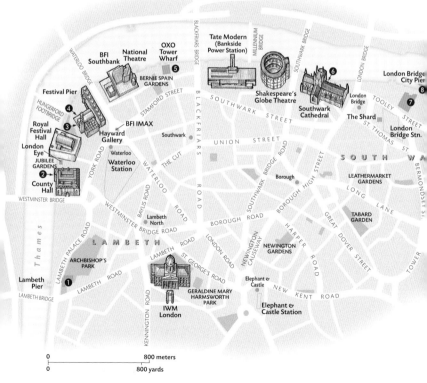

still going on. A nearly continuous river walkway provides stunning views of City and Westminster landmarks.

The Jubilee Line extension runs along the south bank from Westminster to the O_2 arena. Its Bermondsey station is a short walk from Cherry Garden Pier. Nearby, the Angel pub is where Captain Cook planned his trips and James McNeill Whistler painted London views.

Beyond Butler's Wharf and Tower Bridge is London Bridge City. Here, Goodhart-Rendel's striking art deco St. Olaf's House and Hay's Wharf have been restored. H.M.S. *Belfast* (see

---

NOT TO BE MISSED:

Taking in a play at the National Theatre   99

Enjoying the stellar views across London from the Shard or the London Eye   97, 99

Warplanes and the First World War exhibit at the IWM London   101

The Old Operating Theatre and Herb Garret—a chilling plunge into Victorian-era medicine   102

Seeing a Shakespeare play at the rebuilt Globe Theatre   103

---

❶ Lambeth Palace ❷ Sea Life London Aquarium and the London Dungeon ❸ Purcell Room ❹ Queen Elizabeth Hall ❺ OXO Tower ❻ Clink Prison Museum ❼ Hays Galleria ❽ H.M.S. *Belfast* ❾ City Hall ❿ Design Museum

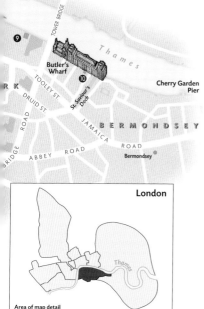

sidebar p. 106), moored in the Thames nearby, is a WWII cruiser and fixture on the riverfront.

Southwark occupies the area between London and Blackfriars Bridges. Its great cathedral is almost smothered by railway lines, and Borough Market's bustling food stalls (see p. 164) lie in its shadow.

Nearby, off Borough High Street, the towering 95-story Shard building (1,017 ft/310 m) dominates the skyline. Designed by Renzo Piano and opened in 2012, the viewing platforms on the 68th through 72nd floors offer 40-mile (64 km) vistas in clear weather. The riverside west is more open, a fine setting for the rebuilt Globe Theatre and its museum, which evoke memories of Tudor entertainment. Here, too, is Tate Modern at Bankside.

West of Blackfriars Bridge and the OXO Tower, the South Bank Centre fills the riverside with street entertainers and plenty of tourists. In the heart of this major entertainment area is Nicholas Grimshaw's heroic, 400-yard-long (365 m), curved and glazed Waterloo International Terminal (1991–1993). Finally, the Sea Life London Aquarium and the London Dungeon fright show fill the County Hall building. Beyond it, steps lead onto Westminster Bridge, one of the best viewpoints for the Houses of Parliament across the river. ■

SOUTHBANK CENTRE & AROUND

Southbank Centre is the focal point for the lively arts and entertainment district across the Thames from Westminster. Events run from morning until late at night and range from informal jazz to highest Shakespearean tragedy. Meanwhile, the embankment between the London Eye and Southbank Centre is a popular tourist hangout that attracts an array of food vendors and street entertainers.

■ The Thameside London Eye provides stellar views of the city.

Southbank Centre

✉ Belvedere Road, SE1

☎ 020 3879 9555

💲 Free–$$$$, depending on the event

🚇 Tube: Waterloo, Westminster, Embankment, or Charing Cross

southbankcentre .co.uk

Southbank Centre

Built for the 1951 Festival of Britain—a government-sponsored extravaganza held to cheer up the British people during post-war austerity—Southbank Centre is now Western Europe's largest arts complex. A new generation of architects built a miniature wonderland showing off Britain's modern achievements in science, art, and sociology. There was a Dome of Discovery, itself destined to inspire the Millennium Dome (now the O₂ arena), as well as sculptures by Reg Butler and Henry Moore, and the Festival Hall.

Now called the **Royal Festival Hall,** this concert hall built in 1951 was extended in 1962 and is the only building to survive from the festival. The 2,700-seat hall replaced Queen's Hall (bombed during WWII) and was entirely renovated in 2007. With its Le Corbusier inspiration, clean lines, and egglike auditorium nestling in a forest of columns and glazed galleries, this was London's first modern public building.

In 1964–1967, the **Queen Elizabeth Hall** and the **Purcell Room,** smaller concert halls, were built, together with the **Hayward Gallery,** whose glowing sculpture on the roof changes according to the wind The upper level, often windy walkways, anonymous entrances, and concrete walls are not inviting—but compensation is found in the glorious music and art inside. These three entertainment venues have been renovated and reopened to the public in 2018.

National Theatre

Sir Denys Lasdun's National Theatre, known by Londoners as the "National" or the "NT," was the culmination of an old dream. Back in the 18th century, actor-manager David Garrick suggested a national theater. The campaign was taken up by H. Granville-Barker, George Bernard Shaw, Laurence Olivier, and others, and the theater finally opened in 1977. It has three auditoriums. The Olivier's open stage lends itself to epic productions; the smaller Lyttelton has a conventional layout; and the flexible little Dorfman has a shell that can be made into any shape at all. Foyer spaces are also used for music, the theaters for pre-performance talks, and the backstage tour is one of London's best. The night-time panorama from the terraces is breathtaking—stretching from St. Paul's to Westminster.

British Film Institute

The British Film Institute (BFI; see sidebar p. 46) is tucked next to the NT beneath Waterloo Bridge, where secondhand bookstalls are set up daily on the towpath beneath the bridge arches. The BFI's huge program ranges from old classics to the latest avant-garde foreign films. It also runs the annual London Film Festival.

Nearby, the distinctive circular **BFI IMAX** cinema *(tel 333 0144 501, odeon.co.uk)* shows films on the largest screen in Britain.

The Shard

The distinctive pyramid shape makes The Shard immediately recognizable and has distinguished the city skyline since 2012. Designed by Renzo Piano, a famous Italian architect, it is one of the tallest skyscrapers in Europe. It is a building conceived to be a real vertical city, and in fact it houses private residences, offices of international companies, first-class bars and restaurants, an exclusive hotel, recreational spaces and the best viewing point in London: **The View from The Shard** *(Joiner Street, SE1, tel 0844 499 7111, €€€–€€€€, www.theviewfromtheshard.com)*. From the windows of the 68th, 69th, and 72nd floors, the view extends 360 degrees, for miles, giving breathtaking views, especially at sunset. Tickets for the visit are subject to availability; it is recommended to buy them in advance from the website.

The London Eye

The London Eye opened in 2000 opposite the Houses of Parliament and quickly established itself as one of the capital's best run attractions. Passengers ride a complete circle in one of 32 enclosed capsules. Breathtaking views are enjoyed morning to late evening, weather permitting. ∎

National Theatre

- 🅰 Map p. 96
- ✉ South Bank, SE1
- ☎ Information: 020 7452 3000 Reservations: 020 7452 3000
- 🕐 Closed Sun.
- 💲 Free–$$$$, depending on the event
- 🚇 Same as Southbank Centre

nationaltheatre .org.uk

British Film Institute (BFI)

- 🅰 Map p. 96
- ✉ Belvedere Rd., Lambeth, SE1
- ☎ 020 7928 3232
- 💲 $
- 🚇 Same as Southbank Centre

bfi.org.uk

The Shard

- 🅰 Map p. 96
- ✉ 32 London Bridge Street, SE1
- 🚇 London Bridge

www.the-shard.com

The London Eye

- 🅰 Map p. 96
- ✉ Lambeth, SE1
- ☎ 870 990 8881
- 💲 $$$$. Book a timed ticket in advance to beat the lines.
- 🚇 Tube: Waterloo, Westminster

londoneye.com

SEA LIFE LONDON AQUARIUM

Down in the bowels of County Hall lurks the capital's biggest, darkest, and most fascinating maze; its glass walls are windows onto softly lit underwater habitats from around the world. Thousands of fish live here, from shoals of tiny, turquoise fish, zipping along in formation, to smooth hound sharks. After a visit, the desire to put an end to the destruction and pollution of the world's waters takes on a new urgency.

Sea Life London Aquarium

🗺 Map p. 96
✉ County Hall, Riverside Building, Westminster Bridge Rd., SE1
☎ 0871 663 1678
💲 $$$$
Ⓜ Tube: Westminster, Waterloo

visitsealife.com

First opened in 1997, the London Aquarium was purchased in 2008 by Merlin Entertainments, the owner of such mega-popular London sites as the London Eye and Madame Tussauds. After an extensive £5 million ($8 million) refurbishment, the aquarium reopened to visitors in 2009 as one of Sea Life's network of 49 sea sanctuaries in around 20 countries.

The new layout offers a one-way route over three floors, exhibiting more than 500 species in 60 displays. The one-way system ensures you won't miss anything important, but it also can cause bottlenecks at popular displays.

The aquarium's tanks are arranged along themed zones,

with touch pools and plenty of clear descriptions. They start with displays of sea creatures from the depths of the Atlantic Ocean and move on to illustrate life in a tidal zone, a Pacific Ocean shipwreck, coral reefs, rain forests, and even the Thames River.

Special exhibits feature penguins of the Antarctic and crabs— but the coup de grâce is the Shark Walk, which takes you over a huge tank that is home to more than a dozen sharks.

Free talks by the resident aquarists and interactive feedings add to the fascination. What is needed is time: To stand watching one tank for several minutes is much more rewarding than rushing from one to another. ∎

London's Other Aquariums

While the Sea Life London Aquarium is certainly the granddaddy of the genre, two other good aquariums in London are also well worth visiting.

Take the train from London Bridge to Forest Hill to visit the **Horniman Museum & Gardens** (100 London Rd., Forest Hill, SE23, tel 020 8699 1872, horniman.ac.uk), home to a well-regarded aquarium with displays of jellyfish, sea horses, and coral and tropical fish. Entrance to the museum and gardens is free, except for the aquarium, which

costs £4 ($5.20; children under 3 free).

The aquarium at the **ZSL London Zoo** (Outer Circle, Regent's Park, NW1, tickets 0344 225 1826, zsl.org, $$$) was the world's first, established in 1853. The very term "aquarium" was coined here, shortening the "aquatic vivarium" name then in use. The current building, divided in three areas, dates from 1924 and highlights coral reefs, Amazonian fish, and conservation and breeding programs for endangered species (including Thames fish and eels).

IWM LONDON

Britain's national museum of 20th- and 21st-century war is not only about tanks and guns. In fact, they form just a tiny fraction of a large and fascinating collection that covers every aspect of war, civil or military, political, social, or cultural.

The museum first opened as the Imperial War Museum in 1917, moving to its current site—the former Bethlem Royal Hospital, or "Bedlam," for the treatment of mental illness—in 1936. In addition to the wide-ranging displays, special exhibitions draw on the museum's 10,000 or so quality posters and paintings. The museum continues to send official war artists to places of conflict around the world.

Reopened in 2014 after an extensive refurbishment, the IWM's new atrium features fighter planes (including a classic Spitfire), a Soviet T-34 tank, and a giant V2 rocket similar to those that rained down on London toward the end of WWII—these instruments of war contrast with the displays that graphically demonstrate the human damage caused by war.

The extensive new **First World War Galleries,** opened on the centenary of the war's outbreak in 1914, include a re-creation of a wartime trench, artifacts from the famous Christmas Truce, and exhibits on the Red Baron and other WWI flying aces.

An impressive but harrowing **Holocaust Exhibition** examines the persecution and murder of European Jews and other groups from 1933 to 1945. The exhibition begins on the third floor and

■ The IWM London focuses on modern warfare, including the weaponry of World War II.

exits on the second, next to the gallery that features IWM's contemporary art collection.

The **Secret War Gallery,** upstairs, justifies the money and expertise spent on government spying, artificial intelligence, and undercover espionage, with accounts of Special Air Services (SAS) operations in the Gulf Wars.

The gallery focusing on conflicts since 1945 has a slice of the Berlin Wall and General Schwarzkopf's Gulf War uniform. The **Lord Ashcroft Gallery** displays Victoria Crosses (for members of the military) and George Crosses (for civilians) and tells the stories of heroism that earned them. ■

IWM London

- Map p. 96
- Lambeth Rd., SE1
- 020 7416 5000
- Tube: Lambeth North, then 5-minute walk, or Elephant & Castle

iwm.org.uk

SOUTHWARK CATHEDRAL

Medieval Southwark's liberal reputation was encouraged by its priory church, St. Mary Overie, which belonged to the diocese of Winchester, in Hampshire. Prostitutes, known as Winchester Geese, were rife, and assorted rough entertainment included bull- and bearbaiting and gambling. The arrival of the theaters sealed the area's position as the Tudor and Stuart entertainment center. All this is evoked in the Clink Prison Museum (see sidebar below), on the site of its namesake jail, which began as a dungeon for disobedient clerics beneath the bishop's palace.

Southwark Cathedral

🗺 Map p. 96

✉ Southwark Cathedral, London Bridge, SE1

☎ 020 7367 6700 Tours: 020 7367 6734

💲 Donation

🚇 Tube/Rail: London Bridge

southwarkcathedral .org.uk

After warehouses, railways, and a new bridge destroyed much of the Southwark of the 19th century, renovation work has restored the cathedral and its surrounding cobbled streets and old warehouses. Borough Market next door attracts thousands of hungry browsers (see p. 164).

The cathedral began as the Augustinian Priory of St. Mary Overie, founded in 1106. In 1212 the priory burned down; of the Gothic church, only the choir and retrochoir survived. The choir was then renovated (a fine Tudor stone screen was added), but after the Reformation it was used as a bakery and pigsty. In the 19th century, it lost its east-end chapel to the London Bridge approach, and was substantially restored—the tower and retrochoir in 1822, the nave in 1838 and again in 1890 by Sir Arthur Blomfield. In 1905 the church of St. Mary was made a cathedral.

The Harvard Memorial Chapel's 12th-century walls mark the location of the 1607 baptism of John Harvard, founder of Harvard University. And Christopher Webb's stained-glass Shakespeare Window of 1953, installed on the cathedral's south side to replace windows destroyed in WWII bombings, depicts numerous scenes from the Bard's plays. ∎

Ghoulish London

South Bank has proclaimed itself London's theme park for the macabre.

It all started in 1974 with the **London Dungeon** (Wesminster Bridge Road, Lambeth, SE1, tel 020 76540809, thedungeons.com, $$$), which has rides and realistic depictions of medieval torture, disease, poverty, and despair . . . perfect for a family holiday. Live actors lead shows that inform, entertain, and occasionally torment.

West of Southwark Cathedral you'll find the **Clink Prison Museum** (1 Clink St., SE1, tel 020 7403 0900, clink.co.uk, $), located on the site of the old jail. Less a scare show than a real educational museum, it nonetheless uses guides in period costumes and a creepy atmosphere to grab its visitors' attention.

For a look at some real-life terror, visit the **Old Operating Theatre and Herb Garret** (9a St. Thomas St., SE1, tel 020 7188 2679, oldoperatingtheatre.com, $), just off Borough High Street. This operating theater for women was in use from 1822 until 1862. The theater and its medical museum depict the nature of surgery in the bad old days before anesthesia or proper hygiene.

SHAKESPEARE'S GLOBE THEATRE

When American actor Sam Wanamaker came to London in 1949, he began searching for the site of the original Globe Theatre, first built in 1599, closed in 1642, and later destroyed. In 1970 Wanamaker began to re-create what he believed was the most important public theater ever built. Although he died in 1993, as did the theater's architect, Theo Crosby, in the following year, the project to reconstruct the Elizabethan theater continued to completion.

A standing audience surrounds actors performing *Henry VIII* at the Globe Theatre.

The site of the theater, 200 yards (183 m) from the original location, was cleared in 1987. Pentagram Design used contemporary illustrations and archaeological evidence, together with traditional materials and techniques, to re-create the Tudor theater: a polygonal building of 20 three-story wooden bays. Audience capacity is around 1,400, including 500 standing places. In 1994 the theater's walls were constructed as Britain's largest lime plastering project, and thatching began of the first new thatched building in central London since the Great Fire of 1666.

On May 27, 1997, the theater opened for its first season of 17th-century plays with Shakespeare's *Henry V* and *The Winter's Tale*, Middleton's *A Chaste Maid in Cheapside*, and Beaumont & Fletcher's *The Maid's Tragedy*. Since then it has all been hugely successful, apart from the difficulty of hearing the actors if it is raining.

Actors report experiencing a new closeness with their audience and each season has brought the acting company more acclaim. Shakespeare addicts should reserve time for the interactive challenges in the exhibition. ∎

Shakespeare's Globe Theatre

🅰 Map p. 96

✉ New Globe Walk, Bankside, SE1

☎ Theater: 020 7902 1400
Exhibition: 020 7902 1500

💲 Exhibition: $$$

🚇 Tube: Southwark, London Bridge. Blackfriars Rail: London Bridge

shakespearesglobe .com

TATE MODERN

As if to put the final stamp of approval on the revived South Bank, Tate's collection of international modern art opened in May 2000 in Sir Giles Gilbert Scott's Bankside Power Station. Now a major London landmark, Tate Modern has revitalized its surroundings and generated the first new Thames bridge in over a century—the pedestrian-only Millennium Bridge, which opened in June 2000.

Both building and site are sensational. Scott's cathedral-like, brick power station stands on a wide riverside terrace looking across to St. Paul's Cathedral. Sir Christopher Wren lived nearby and came here to enjoy the best view of his masterpiece. Completed in 1963 to replace an older power station, the Bankside structure's most valuable asset is the Turbine Hall, about 100 feet (30 m) high and 500 feet (152 m) long, running the width of the building.

Herzog & de Meuron, a Swiss architectural firm, won the international competition to make the transformation, which has been praised for its originality and use of space and light. Visitors enter the building on a ramp and descend into the Turbine Hall. They then proceed through a series of top- and side-lit galleries into the other areas of the building. There are activity spaces, an auditorium, shops, and education programs. Eating areas include pleasant garden and riverside outlooks; the roof bar-restaurant has spectacular views over London.

2016 Extension

As part of a major expansion project, a new tower, also by Herzog & de Meuron, was

■ **The wide, open space of Tate Modern's Turbine Hall offers room for reflection and encourages exhibits of daring scale.**

opened on the south side in 2016. The addition, 11 levels tall, increases the museum's collection space by 60 percent for displaying Tate's increasingly diverse art media.

The Collection

In 1916 Tate was given the responsibility of forming a collection of international modern art, encompassing painting and sculpture from 1900 and after.
The recent growth of the collection, together with a huge increase in its popularity, meant the Millbank site was too small. Tate outposts opened in Liverpool in 1987 and St. Ives in Cornwall in 1993. Then the modern collection gained its own vast space in 2000.

INSIDER TIP:

Don't miss the repurposed underground oil tanks (level 0) for performance and installation artworks.

—MARLENA SERVISS
National Geographic contributor

As the number of works has doubled since 1950, the collection is now acknowledged as one of the world's four most important collections of modern art, competing with New York's MoMA and Solomon R. Guggenheim Museum, and Paris's Musée National d'Art Moderne.

Movements especially well represented include surrealism, abstract expressionism, pop

art, and conceptual art. Many masterpieces by influential artists seen only rarely are regularly rotated among the four suites of permanent galleries (on levels 2, 3, and 4). These include Salvador Dalí's "The Metamorphosis of Narcissus" (1937), Pablo Picasso's "The Three Dancers" (1925), and Andy Warhol's "Camouflage" (1986).

The same is true for major British artists. There is now more opportunity to see great works such as Francis Bacon's "Study for Portrait on Folding Bed" (1963), Henry Moore's "Helmet Head No. 1" (1950), and Stanley Spencer's "The Centurion's Servant" (1914).

In addition, a special suite of galleries hosts five loan exhibitions per year. The permanent galleries explore different themes: "Nature," "Objects," "People," "Society," "Abstraction," and "Feelings, Concepts and Ideas." ■

Tate Modern

- 🅰 Map p. 96
- ✉ Bankside, SE1
- ☎ 020 7887 8888
- 💲 Donation
- 🚇 Tube: Southwark, London Bridge, or Mansion House and walk across the Millennium Bridge

tate.org.uk

EXPERIENCE:
Take the Ferry From Tate to Tate

Art fans can shuttle back and forth between Tate Modern and Tate Britain on the Tate Boat service run by **Thames Clippers** (*tel 020 7001 2200, thamesclippers .com, $$*). Boats depart every 40 minutes from both Bankside Pier (at Tate Modern) and Millbank Pier, home of Tate Britain (see pp. 186–188). Getting there is half the fun: The 15-minute ride between the museums presents superb views of St. Paul's, the City, Somerset House, and Westminster on the north bank, and the arts venues of the south bank.

BUTLER'S WHARF

London's principal wharves were the "legal quays" on the north bank, while the south bank's "suffrance wharves" eased the volume of 19th-century shipping. After the docks closed, Londoners treated these testimonies to their city's wealth in different ways.

Butler's Wharf
🅐 Map p. 97

Design Museum
🅐 Map p. 97
✉ 224–238 Kensington High Street, W8
☎ 020 3862 5900
💲 Free or donation
🚇 Tube: Holland Park, West Kensington. Rail: Kensington Olympia
designmuseum.org

City Hall
🅐 Map p. 97
✉ The Queen's Walk, SE1
🕐 Closed Sat.–Sun.
🚇 Tube: London Bridge, Tower Gateway
www.london.gov.uk

Two vistas reveal the dramatic differences. One is from Butler's Wharf to the unforgiving Guoman Hotel, out of sympathy with St. Katharine Dock and the riverside in scale, shape, and materials. The other is of Butler's Wharf from the north bank. Here, the sensitive mix of renovated warehouse building and interesting, well-proportioned new structures maintains London's riverside history while equipping it to be a lively neighborhood for the 21st century.

The hero of Butler's Wharf is Sir Terence Conran. As a small boy, he came here with his father, a dealer in gum copal resin, and watched the freighters unloading. He saw the Bermondsey area's decline, then boldly stepped in to revive it. In 1984, his company, Conran Roche, acquired the south bank site and its 17 historic buildings.

Conran opened up the quayside and converted the central, massive Butler's Wharf Building (1871–1873) into apartments, shops, and a string of restaurants. His pet project was the **Design Museum,** opened in 1989 to display provocative and classic examples and thus stimulate design awareness. Its restaurant offers panoramic views.

Designer and stylist Zandra Rhodes is the energy behind the **Fashion & Textile Museum** *(83 Bermondsey St., tel 020 7407 8664, ftmlondon.org),* which displays Rhodes's own collection along with other contemporary designers. Atmospheric **Shad Thames** street, a historic remnant of an old Victorian warehouse district, runs west from just behind the Fashion Museum toward Tower Bridge.

As if to confirm Conran's revival, the mayor of London, Ken Livingstone, chose this area, just west of Tower Bridge, for **City Hall,** his egg-shaped headquarters designed by Foster and Partners (2002). You can access it to admire its unique architecture on weekdays and during exhibitions and events. On the 9th floor, the *London's Living Room* is open only during the Open House London festival *(openhouselondon. org.uk).* ∎

H.M.S. *Belfast*

Docked near London Bridge, the H.M.S. *Belfast* (The Queen's Walk at Morgan's Lane, Tooley St., SE1, tel 020 7940 6300, iwm.org .uk, $$$$) was one of the most powerful light cruisers ever built. In 1944, the warship—now an official branch of the Imperial War Museum—was among the first to open fire against the Germans on D-Day. In 1971 the ship's decks opened to the public. Wear comfortable shoes—tours include climbing ladders.

Two major national galleries, theaters, restaurants, first-run cinemas, and state-of-the-art amusements

TRAFALGAR SQUARE & SOHO

Bright lights at Piccadilly Circus

TRAFALGAR SQUARE & SOHO

This small area of uncompromisingly commercial, secular London, far from the river and parks, has few great public buildings. It is, nevertheless, a microcosm of the capital's reaction to Londoners' demands for change over the centuries.

In Tudor times, farms, fields, and woods— the possessions of various monasteries—lay north of royal Westminster. To improve his hunting around Whitehall Palace, whose stables until the 19th century covered much of today's Trafalgar Square, Henry VIII appropriated the land that would later become Soho. The focus for London's commercial entertainment was thus established.

Shaftesbury Avenue, completed in 1886, divides Soho into two distinct halves. The narrow streets to the north have in the 20th century been home to newly arrived Greeks, mainland Italians, and Sicilians, creating a slightly exotic and friendly Continental atmosphere. Today, many of the area's seedy clubs have been turned into chic bars and restaurants, and there are plans to pedestrianize some of the narrow streets. To the south, a handful of streets makes up Tong Yan Kai (Chinese Street), as one of London's newest immigrant populations calls it. The Chinese, fleeing poverty in Hong Kong, arrived here from the 1950s onward and quickly created an atmospheric Chinatown. Tucked down Leicester Place is Notre-Dame-de-France, a Roman Catholic church—once an entertainment venue but converted in 1865 by art nouveau pioneer Auguste Boileau. In 1960, Jean Cocteau added some frescoes.

Moving farther south, 19th-century Leicester Square had transformed from residential square to entertainment center by the 1950s, with Turkish baths and a full-scale circus. And when the picture palaces arrived from America, several great halls offered their clients the cheap but gloriously escapist Hollywood dreams. Nightclubs soon abounded, where Noël Coward, Gloria Swanson, and Marlene Dietrich encouraged the inter-war fashionable set to dance fast and forget the looming clouds of social change and the onset of another war. Today, cinemas still dominate the square.

Trafalgar Square, to the southeast, makes an uneasy transfer from entertainment center to more somber London districts. James Gibbs's St. Martin-in-the-Fields, 1721, was the blueprint for colonial churches, especially in

Oxford Circus

REGENT STREET

NOT TO BE MISSED:

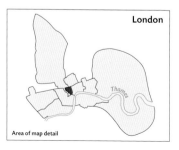

London

Thames

Area of map detail

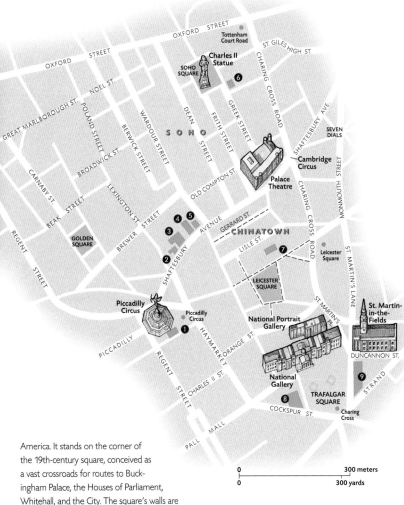

America. It stands on the corner of the 19th-century square, conceived as a vast crossroads for routes to Buckingham Palace, the Houses of Parliament, Whitehall, and the City. The square's walls are Smirke's porticoed Canada House, Baker's fine South Africa House, and William Wilkins's National Gallery, which was built in 1832–1838; Sainsbury Wing was added between 1988 and 1991. In the center of the square, Horatio, Viscount Nelson, the hero of the Battle of Trafalgar in 1805, looks down on a timeless London scene of statues, fountains, and eager visitors. ∎

❶ Criterion Theatre ❷ Lyric Theatre
❸ Apollo Theatre ❹ Gielgud Theatre
❺ Queen's Theatre ❻ House of
St. Barnabas ❼ Notre-Dame-de-France
❽ Canada House ❾ South Africa House

NATIONAL GALLERY

This is one of the world's most impressive national galleries. Indeed, the National Gallery's collection of more than 2,300 paintings is a succession of masterpieces that tells the story of European painting from the 13th to the early 20th century. Because the collection is relatively small and the rooms compact, the visitor can stroll through all the galleries, pick out some highlights, and choose areas to return to on another day for an in-depth look.

■ Thousands of European paintings from past centuries crowd the walls of the National Gallery.

National Gallery
- Map p. 109
- Trafalgar Square, WC2
- 020 7747 2885
- Charge for some special exhibitions
- Tube: Charing Cross, Embankment, Leicester Square

nationalgallery
.org.uk

It was George IV who, observing the enlightened progress of public art galleries in Paris and elsewhere, suggested to a government reluctant to fund the arts that there should be a National Gallery of England. Fortunately, prompted by the promised gift of a fine collection, it stumped up £57,000 ($91,200) in 1824 to pay for the 38 pictures left by John Julius Angerstein, a Russian-born financier living in London. At first, his pictures were exhibited in his Pall Mall house; then in 1838 they were moved into William Wilkins's building overlooking Trafalgar Square. Exhibition space increased in more recent years with the building of the North Wing in 1975 and the 1991 opening of the Sainsbury Wing extension.

Overview

At least 85 percent of the paintings in the impressive

collection—unless on loan or in restoration—are on display. If a room is closed, its contents will usually be displayed elsewhere; simply ask. The 66 galleries are divided into four sections: 13th- to 15th-century (1200s–1500s) paintings in the Sainsbury Wing; 16th-century (1500s–1600s) paintings in the West Wing; 17th-century (1600s–1700s) paintings in the North Wing; and 18th- to early 20th-century (1700s–1930s) paintings in the East Wing. (The official website enables visitors to choose and print their favorite tour.) More recent 20th- and 21st-century art is displayed at Bankside's Tate Modern (see pp. 104– 105), while most of the British paintings are at Tate Britain (see pp. 186–188) in Pimlico.

1200s–1500s Paintings (Rooms 51–66)

The place to start is the Sains- bury Wing. The gallery's earliest Renaissance paintings are hung here, a mixture of northern and southern European works. One of the earliest is Giotto's "The Pentecost" (1306–1312), in Room 51. With his murals in Florence and Padua, this work marks the beginning of a new artistic era, one in which painting became realistic, three- dimensional, and dramatic. Rooms 52–56 illustrate this fur- ther, notably with "The Wilton Diptych" (1395–1399), possibly commissioned by Richard II of England for his private devo- tions; Paolo Uccello's "Battle of San Romano" (circa 1440),

showing a Florentine victory over the Sienese; and Rogier van der Weyden's almost sur- real naturalistic "The Magdalen Reading" (before 1438). There are the groundbreaking por- traits by Robert Campin and Jan van Eyck's "The Arnolfini Por- trait" (both from the 1430s).

INSIDER TIP:

Take a behind-the- scenes tour before your visit: Watch the DVD of Frederick Wiseman's 2014 documentary *National Gallery.*

—JUSTIN KAVANAGH
*National Geographic
Travel Books editor*

Rooms 57–60 contain more complex technical challenges, such as Leonardo de Vinci's "The Virgin of the Rocks" (circa 1491–1507) in Room 57. Bot- ticelli's "Venus and Mars" (1480– 1490) in Room 58 is one of the Florentine artist's few secular

Downstairs in Room A

Room A, below the main gallery, reopened in 2014 after a major renovation. The space now displays 220 works in approximate chronological order from the 14th to the late 19th century, providing an overview of European painting during this period. The retrospective begins with "St Romulus" (circa 1423) by Fra Angelico and proceeds in approximately chronological order to "Land- scape with Poplars" by Cézanne (1885–87). Room A is open on Wednesdays and the first Sunday of each month.

works, still decorative, but achieving a wonderfully translucent gown for Venus.

Rooms 61–66, at the end of this section, contain a number of familiar Renaissance paintings. From the Veneto, there is Andrea Mantegna's "The Agony in the Garden" (circa 1460) and his brother-in-law Giovanni Bell-

■ **Georges-Pierre Seurat's "Bathers at Asnières" (1884)**

ini's picture of the same subject, painted five years later. Portraits grow in number and refinement in this section—for instance, Bellini's "Doge Leonardo Loredan" (circa 1501). Finally, don't miss the two Piero della Francesca panels, "The Baptism of Christ" from the 1450s and "Nativity" (1470–1475).

1500s–1600s Paintings (Rooms 2–14)

The High Renaissance artists represented here include Raphael, Michelangelo, Bronzino, and Correggio. Inspired by Bellini, Venetian artists such as Titian explored

color and worked increasingly in oil paints on canvas. Subject matter broadened to include bigger portraits, mythological compositions, still lifes, and landscapes. The age of collectors began, and the artist's skills were valued as much as his subject matter.

Two Italian artists featured in Room 8 demonstrate these changes: Correggio in "The School of Love" (1525) and Parmigianino in his "Madonna and Child with Saints" (both circa 1520). Room 8 also contains paintings by some of the leading artists of 1500–1550: Michelangelo's "The Entombment"; Sebastiano del Piombo's "The Raising of Lazarus"; Bronzino's "An Allegory With Venus and Cupid"; and Raphael's "Portrait of Pope Julius II," created in 1511 during the phase late in the painter's short life when he perfected his skills as a portrait artist.

Venetian color dominates in Rooms 9 and 10, with Titian's "The Vendramin Family" (1543–1547) and Paolo Veronese's "The Family of Darius before Alexander" (1565–1567).

Other notable works in this section include Titian's "Bacchus and Ariadne" (1520–1523) in Room 2 and the Holbeins in Room 4 that include "The Ambassadors" (1533), an early portrait of two full-length figures.

1600s–1700s Paintings (Rooms 15–32)

The richness of 17th-century painting fills the next 19 rooms. Landscape had become a

INSIDER TIP:

The National Gallery is quietest on Monday mornings, a fine time to linger at your favorite works. It's also open until 9 p.m. every Friday.

—NEIL SHEA
*National Geographic
magazine writer*

favorite subject of collectors and patrons, and northern artists such as Cuyp, Ruisdael, and Rubens produced some of the most sublime canvases. Under the influence of northern artists, Italians reduced the size of pictures, while Italy's classical art and southern light inspired such northerners as Poussin, Claude Lorrain, and Rubens. Van Dyck, Velázquez, and Rembrandt took the portrait tradition a step further, and the most innovative painting schools were the Spanish and Dutch, typified by these last two painters.

Claude Lorrain's landscapes in Rooms 15, such as "Seaport with the Embarkation of the Queen of Sheba" (1648), were hugely influential in 18th-century English painting and landscape gardening. The Turner pictures in Room 15 are proof of this. French paintings in Rooms 18 and 19 include Philippe de Champaigne's magnificent 1637 portrait of Cardinal Richelieu and Nicholas Poussin's golden-lit "The Adoration of the Golden Calf" (1634). The Dutch pictures in Rooms 21–28 include Aelbert Cuyp's pastoral "River Landscape with Horseman and

EXPERIENCE: Events in the Gallery

The National Gallery offers an array of excellent, free programs (in English) for both adults and families.

Children under five can take part in the **Magic Carpet Storytelling** program *(half-hour sessions offered at 10:30 a.m. and 11:30 a.m. every Sunday),* where stories are told in front of one of the gallery's paintings. There is no need to reserve in advance but space is limited and the number of participants allowed is established thirty minutes before the beginning of each session. To participate, go to the lobby of the Pigott Education Centre, accessible via Orange Street at the back of the museum.

A popular program for adults that may bring out the inner portrait painter in every participant is **Talk & Draw,** which takes place every Friday from 1 to 3 p.m. A brief lesson about painting is held in the gallery, after which visitors try their hand at reproducing one of the masterpieces on display. No experience is necessary and all materials are furnished on site.

At lunchtime each weekday and on every Friday afternoon, you can listen to a lecture about one of the pieces in the collection. Lunchtime lectures last 35 minutes and Friday mini-lectures last 10 minutes.

The educational programs are endless; you can follow art history courses, participate in workshops, learn using audio-guided tours or smartphone apps, and attend free concerts. Guided visits are also available for the hearing and vision impaired.

Dulwich Picture Gallery

Before the National Gallery came into existence, Sir John Soane's custom-designed neoclassical gallery, opened in 1814, was England's first public art museum. Located about 15 minutes by train from Victoria or London Bridge Stations, it owes its astounding collection to the failure of the British government to accept the offer of 400 pictures collected by art dealer Noel Desenfans. The collection was intended for the projected National Gallery of Poland in Warsaw, but when the Polish king was forced to abdicate in 1795, Desenfans offered it to Britain. The government declined the offer. Desenfans then gave the paintings to Sir Francis Bourgeois, who bequeathed them to Dulwich College, already the owners of a good art collection. Wandering the dozen top-lit rooms today, you can enjoy what might have been exhibited in Trafalgar Square: Rembrandt's "Girl at a Window," sketches by Rubens, and several Gainsboroughs.

Dulwich Picture Gallery

✉ Gallery Rd., SE21

☎ 020 8693 5254

🕐 Closed Mon.

💲 $$

🚉 Regular trains from Victoria and London Bridge Stations to North Dulwich or West Dulwich

dulwichpicture gallery.org.uk

Peasants" (circa 1660); a collection of Rembrandts, such as "Self-Portrait at the Age of 34" (1640) and "A Woman Bathing in a Stream" (1655); and Vermeer's especially intimate "A Young Woman Standing at a Virginal" (1670–1672).

Equally stunning is Room 29, a collection of Rubens canvases that range from the allegorical "Peace and War" (1629–1630) to his powerful "Samson and Delilah" of 1609. Royal portraits reach new grandeur in rooms 30–31 with Velázquez's "Philip IV of Spain in Brown and Silver" (1631–1632) and Van Dyck's "Equestrian Portrait of Charles I" (1637–1638).

1700s–1930s Paintings (Rooms 33–46)

The subject matter of 18th- and 19th-century painting is both colorful and accessible—beach scenes, flowerpots, the writing of a letter. It retains many traditional genres, such as portrait, landscape, still life, domestic scenes, and narrative.

British paintings fill Rooms 34–36. Portraits are especially strong and include Sir Joshua Reynolds's "Lady Cockburn and Her Three Eldest Sons" (1773), Thomas Gainsborough's "The Morning Walk" (1785), and Sir Thomas Lawrence's aging, delicate Queen Charlotte, painted four years later.

Turner's "The Fighting Temeraire" (1839) takes landscape painting into new territory. Spanish portraits in Room 39 includes Francisco de Goya's "The Duke of Wellington" (1812–1814), and French paintings in Room 41 feature Ingres's sumptuous "Madame Moitessier" (1856). Lyrical Impressionist paintings fill Rooms 43 and 44, including Claude Monet's "The Beach at Trouville" (1870), Pierre-Auguste Renoir's "The Skiff" (1875), and Georges Seurat's "Bathers at Asnières" (1884).

The collection ends in Rooms 45 and 46 with such masterpieces as Vincent van Gogh's "Sunflowers" (1888). ■

NATIONAL PORTRAIT GALLERY

This is where you can put faces to familiar names, from a Tudor king to the inventor of the steam engine or a favorite novelist. Here you can see the faces of the personalities who have influenced all facets of British history. From top to bottom, this is a chronological parade of the brilliant, talented, or high-achieving, of the beautiful and ugly, of the good and devious. Each is fascinating, and the clear labeling helps explain the significance of those people who may not be so familiar. The collection makes an excellent, visual skip through the island's history.

Founded in 1856 in the Victorian spirit of idealism, heroism, and didactic hopes of education by example, the collection's aim was to assemble and display portraits of the British great and good as an inspiration to others. The portraits moved around London until they came to rest here in 1896, in Ewan Christian's building behind the National Gallery.

At first, a person had to be dead to be eligible for inclusion here, allowing time to assess his or her worthiness. Today, that rule has been broken, and living inspirations include athletes, actors, businesspeople, playwrights, artists, and scientists; visitors renting the audio/visual guide can hear some of these contemporary sitters and artists talking frankly about their portraits. More than 11,000 portraits are in the collection, although only about 10 percent of that number are on display at any one time. (Note that the portraits rotate, so it's possible some of the works described here may not be on display when you visit.) Even allowing for the fact that some people have more than one image, that is still a considerable number of significant people, and a wide enough selection for visitors to find their ideal hero.

Your Visit

Because the portraits are arranged chronologically, with the earliest at the top of the building, the best way to visit the gallery is to start on the second floor and walk down. Here in Rooms 1–20, personalities run from the 16th to the early 19th century. On the first floor in Rooms 21–32, you'll find portraits of people who lived in the 19th and 20th

National Portrait Gallery

▲ Map p. 109
✉ St. Martin's Place, WC2
☎ 020 7306 0055
💲 Charge for some special exhibitions, $
🚇 Tube: Charing Cross, Leicester Square

npg.org.uk

■ The portrait of William Shakespeare (circa 1600–1610)

centuries; members of the current royal family are either in Room 32 or on the ground floor. The rest of the ground floor is a daring selection of recent and contemporary contributors to British society, both painted and photographed. Special exhibitions in the Wolfson Gallery, also on the ground floor, include the annual BP Portrait Award in summer. The Photography Gallery meanwhile displays the annual wintertime Taylor Wessing Photographic Portrait Prize.

The gallery's Ondaatje wing extension opened in 2000 and includes an atmospheric new Tudor room, a downstairs theater, and the rooftop Portrait Restaurant with spectacular panoramic views across London.

Second Floor: Here are a few stars to look out for. The Tudor Galleries include Rowland Lockey's (copied partly from Holbein) great portrait of Sir Thomas More and his family in their Chelsea home.

Worth seeking out is William Scrots's anamorphic portrait, "Edward VI" (1546), meaning that it has been painted to be viewed from a sharp angle to correct the perspective. Elizabeth I portraits include one by Marcus Gheeraerts the Younger to mark her visit to Ditchley Park, near Oxford—her feet are planted on Oxfordshire. The portrait of Shakespeare is the only known contemporary portrait of the playwright and was the gallery's first acquisition. Do not miss the case of exquisite miniatures of Tudor aristocracy—including Catherine of Aragon, Mary, Queen of Scots, and Robert Dudley, Earl of Leicester—by Nicholas Hilliard and others. "Star players" in the English Civil War (Oliver Cromwell) and Restoration (Charles II) hang near the diarist Samuel Pepys, who is painted in a rented Indian outfit and holding

EXPERIENCE: Make Your Own Brass Rubbing

There was a time when a visit to any church or abbey in London would include the sight of people on their knees, rubbing wax on construction paper pulled tight over raised brass tomb reliefs to create a semi-magical pictorial representation of the artwork underneath.

But the realization that this was damaging the medieval and Victorian reliefs has stopped this practice, so today the only spot in London where you can discover the simple and engaging craft of brass rubbing is the **London Brass Rubbing Centre** (*Trafalgar Square, tel 020 7766 1100, stmartin-in-the-fields.org, $ or*

more), located in the basement crypt of St. Martin-in-the-Fields church, just across from the National Portrait Gallery.

While the brasses are replicas, the range of subjects is impressive. With some time and just a little skill, you can take home a monochromatic or multicolored depiction of a regal lord or lady, William Shakespeare, a Celtic circle, St. George and the dragon, or Zodiac signs.

A small rubbing can be created in about 20 minutes, while a quality larger image can take an hour or two to make. Ready-rubbed drawings can also be purchased at the center's shop.

a music score he composed.

Britain's dynamic 18th century produced a host of exceptional figures. You can find Jonathan Swift, Sir Christopher Wren, Sir Joshua Reynolds, and Dr. Johnson, not forgetting explorer Capt. James Cook and Adm. Lord Nelson. The Romantic poets John Keats, Samuel Taylor Coleridge, and a contemplative William Wordsworth are here, too, as well as Patrick Miller, designer of the first steam-propelled boat, and other heroes of the industrial revolution. Lawrence's portrait of George IV nicely captures that king's decadent elegance.

First Floor: Victorian and Edwardian personalities start with early Victorians such as the Brontë sisters, who were painted by their brother, Patrick Branwell. (Patrick initially included himself in the portrait, but later painted himself out underneath a white pillar; however, his ghostly image has reappeared over time.) Heroes of the empire include linguist and explorer Sir Richard Burton, painted by Leighton. Prince Albert, Queen Victoria's consort, epitomizes 19th-century cultural-scientific advances, whereas Thomas Carlyle and Benjamin Disraeli are proponents of later Victorian culture. For the Edwardian arts, you can discover what Rudyard Kipling, George Bernard Shaw, and Edward Elgar looked like.

Architect Piers Gough has refurbished Rooms 30–31; the vista down this great space is retained by hanging the early 20th-century portraits on glass panels. Near here, a splendid picture by John Lavery of George V, Queen Mary, and their family at Buckingham Palace in 1913 is usually on display.

Ground Floor: These rooms are some of the most exciting, for they contain images of living

 ■ **Patrick Branwell Brontë's portrait of the Brontë sisters**

people. In addition to the annual BP Portrait Award exhibition, special exhibits and rotating selections of contemporary paintings and photographs are on display here. A half flight up from the ground floor brings you to the "Portrait Explorer," a space where you can search online for specific portraits in the entire collection. ■

SOHO

Until Westminster Council began its crackdown in June 1986, Soho was one of London's raunchiest areas. It appeared to the outsider never to sleep. The maze of narrow streets, passages, and courts was the haunt of prostitutes; seedy bars lurked on the corners; basements housed peep shows, striptease clubs, and pornography bookshops. Collectively, it was known as the Vice, and the council decided to do away with it. As each lease expired, its renewal was refused and the property sold off, usually to become a restaurant, office, or flat.

Although mainstay Madame JoJo's, a longtime cabaret/burlesque hall, closed in 2014, new restaurants and sleek bars have helped maintain Soho's round-the-clock liveliness and make it an excellent area to wander.

Piccadilly Circus
Piccadilly Circus is the hub of Soho's amusements. It was laid

Sidewalk diners enjoy a cappuccino in Soho.

out by Nash in 1819 as part of the Prince Regent's dream to link Carlton House and Regent's Park (see p. 147). This busy intersection of streets, with Eros in its center, was transformed when Shaftesbury Avenue was built in the 1880s. When the **Eros statue** was added in 1893, its nudity outraged Victorian sensibilities, but it quickly became a symbol for London.

Alfred Gilbert's aluminum figure in fact portrays not Eros the god of love, but Anteros (Eros's brother) the Angel of Christian Charity. It commemorates Anthony Ashley Cooper, 7th Earl of Shaftesbury, 1801–1885, a philanthropist and statesman who fought hard to improve conditions for factory and colliery workers, chimney sweeps, and the insane.

Such was the significance of Piccadilly Circus that London's first illuminated advertisements blazed here in the 1890s. More theaters arrived, including one right beside Eros, the basement **Criterion.** This theater, decorated with Thomas Verity's beautiful mosaics and tiles, and its street-level restaurant are well worth a look.

To the east of Piccadilly Circus, travelers of the world meet in lively, pedestrianized **Leicester Square.**

Shaftesbury Avenue
The backbone of London's commercial theaterland, Shaftesbury Avenue was driven through the Soho slums, necessitating the rehousing of 3,000 people.

EXPERIENCE: Having a Pint in a Historic Pub

A visit to London wouldn't be complete without having a traditional ale (or two) in one or two of the city's renowned and historic watering holes.

Historic Pubs

London is a city brimming with history, and many surviving pubs have served as silent witnesses. In Soho, French expatriates during World War II gathered at the **French House** (49 Dean St., W1, tel 020 7437 2477, french housesoho.com, $$–$$$), a bohemian enclave—Charles de Gaulle is said to have planned resistance strategies from the upstairs bar. South of the Thames, the Tudor **George Inn** (77 Borough High St., SE1, tel 020 7407 2056, national trust.org.uk/george-inn, $$–$$$) is London's last remaining two-storied coaching inn. Bougainvillea and half-timbering set the mood.

In Smithfield, the **Hand & Shears** (1 Middle St., EC1, tel 020 7600 0257, $) stands on the site of a 12th-century alehouse. Condemned prisoners from Newgate Gaol were known to stop there for their last drink. In nearby Clerkenwell, the **Jerusalem Tavern** (55 Britton St., EC1, tel 020 7490 4281, www.stpeters brewery.co.uk/london-pub, $) has been in business since the 14th century; the current building dates from 1720 and offers traditional craft beers from St. Peter's Brewery.

The **White Hart** (191 Drury Lane, WC2, tel 020 7242 2317, whitehartdrury lane.co.uk, $$–$$$) in Holborn is believed to have been originally licensed in 1216

The City's Black Friar pub, on Queen Victoria Street, built in 1875

(the year after the Magna Carta was signed). **Ye Olde Cheshire Cheese** (145 Fleet St., EC4, tel 020 7353 6170, $$–$$$), north of Inner Temple, dates from 1667 and was a favorite of Dickens. And, hidden down an alleyway off Hatton Garden in Holborn, **Ye Olde Mitre** (1 Ely Ct., EC1, tel 020 7405 4751, yeoldemitreholborn. co.uk, closed weekends, $–$$) was mentioned by Shakespeare in both Richard II and in Richard III. The current structure was built in 1772.

Victorian Gin Palaces

These extravagant 19th-century pubs—no longer serving just gin—often have beautiful frosted and etched glass and mirrors, ornate furnishings, rich wood paneling, and interesting features such as snugs (small, semi-private bar-parlors designed

for ladies—and for flirting) and snob screens (frosted-glass bricks that divide the snugs from the perceived riffraff tending the bar).

Some worthy examples: the **Argyll Arms** (18 Argyll St., W1, tel 020 7734 6117, nicholsonspubs.co.uk, $$–$$$), off Oxford Circus; Holborn's 1872 **Princess Louise** (208 High Holborn, WC1, tel 020 7405 8816, princesslouisepub .co.uk, $); in Little Venice, the **Prince Alfred** (5a Formosa St., W9, tel 020 7286 3287, theprincealfred.com) with tiny doors to stoop under as you venture from snug to snug; and, just up the street, the **Warrington Hotel** (93 Warrington Crescent, W9, tel 020 7286 8282, the warrington.co, $$–$$$), a grand 1857 pub that has recently renovated five of its original hotel rooms.

Opened to traffic in 1886, it quickly attracted theatrical impresarios who built theaters suitable for staging fashionable musical farces. In 1983, the impresario Andrew Lloyd Webber bought and restored to glory the **Palace Theatre,** originally designed by Collcutt and Holloway in 1888–1891.

A cluster of theaters down the street begins with **Queen's**

INSIDER TIP:

For discounted theater tickets, join the line at the TKTS booth in Leicester Square. You can reserve same-day or advance seats.

—LARRY PORGES
National Geographic
Travel Books editor

Theatre of 1907, subsequently rebuilt, and the **Gielgud Theatre,** built in 1906. The French Renaissance **Apollo** rose five years earlier, while the **Lyric,** one of the first theaters on the street, was built in 1888 with profits from a hit musical playing in Leicester Square.

North of Shaftesbury Avenue

At the west end of the grid of streets north of Shaftesbury Avenue, the stallholders of **Berwick Street's** fruit and vegetable market stand in front of pretty 18th-century houses. On Old Compton Street, once the heart of French London, more recent

Italian immigrants run **I Camisa & Son** deli and grocery and the Sicilian bakery, **Patisserie Valerie.** Italians left their mark on Dean Street, too, at P. G. Leoni's **Quo Vadis** restaurant, which opened in 1926, and on Frith Street, where **Bar Italia** serves up perfect cappuccinos. Across from Bar Italia, **Ronnie Scott's** hosts top jazz stars, while the plain facade of the 1746 **House of St. Barnabas,** on Greek Street, belies a magnificent interior. Beside it, Charles II's statue in **Soho Square** testifies to Soho's noble beginnings.

Chinese Soho

Almost all the tall, narrow houses of London's Chinatown have a shop or restaurant at street level. There are Chinese traditional medical shops, newsagents selling Chinese papers, and many more. But mostly, there are restaurants. In addition to stir-fried or steamed Cantonese food, specialties include dim sum snacks. In Soho the Chinese have succeeded in keeping alive their mother tongue, and the atmosphere is enhanced by Chinese-style telephone booths, benches, colorful lanterns, and red-and-gold gateways on either end of **Gerrard Street** and on **Macclesfield Street** toward Shaftesbury Avenue.

Tucked down Leicester Place you'll find the distinctly non-Chinese **Notre-Dame-de-France**—once a theater but converted into a church in 1865 by Auguste Boileau. ∎

Courts of law, theaters, shops, markets, and entertainments between the City and Westminster

COVENT GARDEN TO LUDGATE HILL

Window-shopping in Covent Garden

COVENT GARDEN TO LUDGATE HILL

Hugging the curve of the Thames, this part of London fills the space between the capital's two cities: Westminster and the City. Ancient buildings such as Temple Church and Lincoln's Inn Gateway, Covent Garden's restored market, the Adelphi Theatre, and the Royal Opera House show how this area has changed continuously to keep pace with its customers.

When Westminster became the seat of royal and political power, a riverside path linked it to the merchants' City of London. The sweep of the Strand, so called because it ran close to the north bank of the Thames, and Fleet Street, named after the river it crossed, became a favorite address for medieval bishops. Later, after the Dissolution of the Monasteries, the area took on a slightly different character.

Along either side of Fleet Street, toward St. Paul's Cathedral, some bishops' houses evolved into barristers' inns of court, while early printers and booksellers established themselves around the churches of St. Bride and St. Dunstan. Newspaper presses thundered on Fleet

Street from 1702 until the 1980s. The printers have gone, but the law remains. Lawyers defend their clients in the great courts, while their pupils hurry through the streets with armfuls of files.

Along the Strand, Tudor and Stuart rulers presented the bishops' former houses and waterside gardens to favored courtiers. George Villiers, a favorite of both James I and Charles I, enlarged the palace of the bishops of Norwich to include a water gate, which survives today in Embankment Gardens, testifying to both the grandeur of these residences and the pre-Embankment width of the Thames River.

The Savoy Theatre reflects the changing roles of the Strand down the centuries. The first building on the site, the sumptuous 14th-century Savoy House, fashionably faced the River. In Covent Garden's 17th-century heyday, the Strand was a smart promenade, but by the late 19th century it had degenerated into a seedy mixture of prostitutes, coffeehouses, and cheap theaters. When Richard D'Oyly Carte built his Savoy Theatre in 1881, he put the entrance on the newly built, clean, and smart Embankment rather than on the Strand. Later, in 1929, the entrance was turned to face a much improved Strand; the Aldwych crescent had replaced a swath of slums in 1905.

Today, the heart of the area is again Covent Garden. Originally the garden of a convent attached to Westminster Abbey, it was given to the Earl of Bedford after the Dissolution of the Monasteries. Covent Garden Piazza, laid out in 1631, became the blueprint residential London

NOT TO BE MISSED:

ENDELL ST

MONMOUTH ST.

ST. MARTIN'S LANE

square. Half a dozen others followed nearby, including Lincoln's Inn Fields, to house the gentry who were moving out of the City after the Great Fire of 1666. When society moved farther west, the aristocratic tone of the piazza changed to a commercial one with the arrival of the main London fruit and vegetable market, coffeehouses, and gambling dens. When the market moved to south London in 1974, the area was cleaned up and became a lively mixture of shops, restaurants, and museums encircled by a dozen theaters. ■

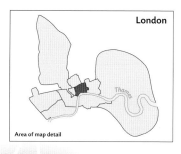

London

Area of map detail

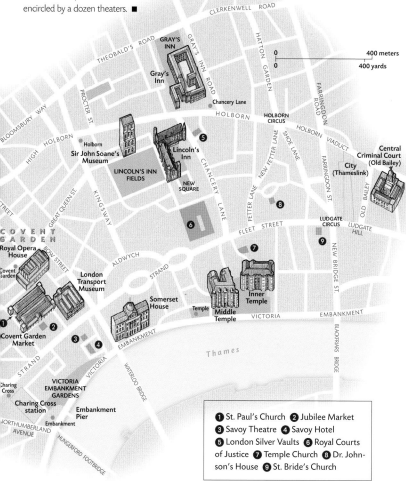

1 St. Paul's Church 2 Jubilee Market
3 Savoy Theatre 4 Savoy Hotel
5 London Silver Vaults 6 Royal Courts
of Justice 7 Temple Church 8 Dr. Johnson's House 9 St. Bride's Church

COVENT GARDEN

The restored market buildings, chic shops, and entertainers in the piazza typify this much changed area, bordered by the Strand, Kingsway, High Holborn, and Charing Cross Road.

Covent Garden Market hosts a variety of shops and cafés.

London Transport Museum

🅰 Map p. 123

✉ Covent Garden Piazza, WC2

☎ 020 7379 6344

💲 $$

🚇 Tube: Covent Garden

ltmuseum.co.uk

The 1st Earl of Bedford acquired this land in 1552, after Westminster Abbey was dissolved. But it was the 4th earl who laid out London's first residential square of high-society houses. When the aristocrats moved west, the 5th earl won a license for a fruit and vegetable market in 1671. Traders, prostitutes, and literary types, including Richard Sheridan and James Boswell, met here. Stalls selling everything from lavender to birdcages sprawled over the square.

Order of a sort began in 1831, with the building of the Central Market. Floral Hall (1860), the Flower Market (1870–1872), and the Jubilee Market (1904) followed. This was the Covent Garden of George Bernard Shaw's

Pygmalion: of "low life" in the piazza but high life in the Royal Opera House, first built in 1732.

When the market moved in 1974, the buildings were restored, not demolished, and the area has been revitalized. The **main market** is full of shops and restaurants. Street entertainers perform in the traffic-free piazza. **Jubilee Market,** on the south side of the piazza, has stalls selling antiques on Mondays, art and crafts on the weekends, and a general market the rest of the week. Next door, the excellent **London Transport Museum** occupies part of the old Flower Market. In the northeast corner of the piazza, the refurbished **Royal Opera House** (tel 020 7304 4000, roh.org.uk) has food, bars, and quality daily entertainment. ∎

SOMERSET HOUSE

An extraordinary art collection and a large public piazza that is a fountain in summer and an ice rink in winter have reawakened Sir William Chambers's sumptuous palace, built in 1776–1786 for government bureaucrats.

One of central London's most successful arts complexes is in the 16th-century palace of Edward Seymour, Protector of Somerset, which was later the domain of various Tudor and Stuart royals, but was demolished on the orders of George III to make way for London's most impressive 18th-century public building. The Navy Board, Inland Revenue, the Register General of Births, Deaths, and Marriages, and a handful of learned societies enjoyed luxurious offices here until 1989. Today, the courtyard draws visitors to enjoy ice-skating in winter and water-jet fountains in summer. The River Terrace has a café and excellent views over the Thames. Inside, the **Courtauld Institute**

Galleries *(tel 020 7848 2526, courtauld.ac.uk, $$)* are closed until 2021 for work on Courtauld Connects, a project that will improve their accessibility. Samuel Courtauld, industrialist and art patron, founded the Institute in 1932, aiming to help art history students experience great paintings in fine settings. His French Impressionist and Postimpressionist canvases were later joined by the Rubens, Tiepolo, and Van Dyck paintings of the Princes Gates Collection; by the Botticellis, Goyas, and Gainsboroughs of the Lee Collection; and by more than 7,000 old-master prints and drawings. Here you can enjoy works by Manet, Turner, van Gogh, Matisse, and Degas. ∎

Somerset House

▲ Map p. 123
✉ Strand, WC2
☎ 020 7845 4600
🚇 Tube: Temple, Embankment, Covent Garden

somersethouse.org.uk

Ice rink
💲 $$
🕐 Closed mid-Jan.–mid-Nov.

EXPERIENCE: Skate Among the Monuments

Visiting London in the winter? Join the locals for one of the coolest activities in town: outdoor ice-skating at some of the city's most impressive and historic locales.

The summertime fountain in the courtyard at **Somerset House** turns into a skating rink from mid-November until the end of January each year *(tickets from Ticketmaster, tel 0844 844 0444 or via somersethouse.org.uk/ice_rink, $$)*, with the 18th-century mansion making a stunning backdrop. Skating lessons, DJ nights, and live music on Tuesdays are all part of the fun on the spacious 9,700-square-foot (900 sq m) rink. Both day and night, the Somerset House ice rink never ceases

to charm Londoners and tourists alike. Other temporary rinks are located amid the wonderfully scenic settings at the **Tower of London** *(www.toweroflondon icerink.com, tel 844 4827 777, $$$)* and Knightsbridge's **Natural History Museum** *(nhm.ac.uk, $$$)*. London's largest open-air rink is at **Hyde Park's Winter Wonderland** *(hydeparkwinter wonderland.com/rink.html, tel 020 7402 7259, $$)*. A rink overlooks the Thames at **Canary Wharf** in Docklands *(icerink canarywharf.co.uk, tel 08456 531 431, $$)*; another resides at Tudor **Hampton Court Palace** *(hrp.org.uk, tel 020 3166 6000, $$–$$$)*.

INNS OF COURT & OLD BAILEY

London has four Inns of Court. Each one is an independent society governed by Benchers who call their students, known as pupils, to the Bar—hence the word barristers. Such orders were gradually established after Edward I's Ordinance of 1292 put all men of law under the judges' control, thus ending the clergy's position as lawyers and reducing their power.

■ The Royal Courts of Justice building was built in the Victorian era.

Royal Courts of Justice (Law Courts)

🏛 Map p. 123
✉ Strand, WC2
☎ 020 7947 6000
💲 $$
🕐 Closed Sat.–Sun.
🚇 Tube: Temple, Chancery Lane

theroyalcourts ofjustice.com

NOTE: No cameras or children under 14 are allowed in the courts.

The Inns have records going back to the 15th and 16th centuries. Each was originally a great mansion, where students and barristers lived. In Tudor times, when litigation was as popular as the arts, lawyers trained at the Inns of Court sat at courts throughout London but enjoyed a high life back at their halls and chambers. Members of Middle Temple treated Elizabeth I to a performance of Shakespeare's *Twelfth Night* in their magnificent hall.

Gray's Inn (*8 South Square, WC1, tel 020 7458 7800, www.*

graysinn.org.uk), whose students were established in Reginald de Grey's mansion by 1370, is the farthest north and has a Tudor screen in its hall. The garden walks are open to visitors from noon to 2:30 p.m. in the summer. Early lawyers of **Lincoln's Inn** (*Lincoln's Inn, WC2, tel 020 7405 1393, lincolnsinn.org.uk)* lived on the property of the Earl of Lincoln in the surviving Old Hall, built in 1490–1492; later lawyers included Oliver Cromwell.

Inner Temple (*Inner Temple, EC4, tel 020 7797 8250, innertemple. org.uk)* and **Middle Temple** (*Middle*

Temple, EC4, tel 020 7427 4800, middletemple.org.uk), just off the Strand and Fleet Street, derive their names from the Knights Templar, a brotherhood whose members protected pilgrims bound for Jerusalem. At the Dissolution of the Monasteries, their lands became crown property, which the Benchers leased in perpetuity in 1608. Today, their labyrinth of courts and buildings includes a fine Elizabethan **Hall** *(Middle Temple Lane, always open),* the Inner Temple gateway of 1611, and Wren's King's Bench Walk of 1678. The **Temple Church** *(Inner Temple Lane, EC4, tel 020 7353 3470, templechurch.com),* originally a round Norman building with a nave added later, has effigies of 13th-century Templars. When the Embankment's land reclamation provided the barristers with Inner Temple Gardens, they hosted the Royal Horticultural Society's annual flower show, now held at Chelsea (see sidebar p. 181).

In the 19th century, interest in legal education forced barristers to use their inns more for work than for pleasure. The courts were centralized in the **Royal Courts of Justice,** and today the inns are sandwiched between these courts and the Central Criminal Court, known as the **Old Bailey** after the street beside it. ■

Central Criminal Court (Old Bailey)

- 🅐 Map p. 123
- ✉ Old Bailey, EC4
- ☎ 020 7192 2739
- 🕐 Closed Sat.–Sun.
- Ⓜ Tube: St. Paul's

cityoflondon.gov.uk

NOTE: A list of the day's programs is noted by the main door. No children under 14 admitted. No electronics, bags, food, or drinks are allowed in the building.

Fleet Street Printing

The Law Courts mark the beginning of Fleet Street, which until recently has been synonymous with the printing industry. After the death of William Caxton, who published the first book printed in England in 1477, his commercially acute pupil Wynkyn de Worde moved the presses from Westminster to Fleet Street. De Worde set up England's first press with movable type near St. Bride's Church (see p. 63), close to his clergy customers. Between 1500 and 1535, he published about 800 books. Printers, bookbinders, booksellers, and writers soon filled the lanes off Fleet Street. Dr. Samuel Johnson lived in one (see p. 128) and patronized the coffeehouses and pubs around it.

On March 11, 1702, Fleet Street added to its ecclesiastical, literary, scientific, and political output by publishing its first newspaper, *The Daily Courant.* But the newspaper industry did not really take off until Alfred Harmsworth, pioneer of popular journalism, bought the *Daily Mail* in 1896 and pushed its circulation up to a million. He later founded the *Daily Mirror* with his brother.

Fleet Street remained the hub of the national newspapers until the 1980s. Then international press baron Rupert Murdoch pushed through the technological revolution that resulted in all newspapers leaving Fleet Street for offices linked to their presses, or to websites, by computer.

A WALK THROUGH LEGAL LONDON & COVENT GARDEN

This walk is best done on a weekday, when activity in legal London adds atmosphere; but Covent Garden, although busy on a weekday, is at its most bubbly on Saturday, with entertainers and markets. The walk begins at Temple and ends at Covent Garden Tube stations. The first part is a loop, which could be a walk in itself, or which could be omitted.

In & Around the Strand

From the Temple Tube station, walk up to the Strand and turn left past Somerset House containing the Courtauld Institute (see p. 125). Turn left again onto **Waterloo Bridge ❶**, where there are good views east to the City towers and south toward Westminster.

Return to the Strand and turn left. The **Savoy Hotel** (now re-opened after a massive £100 million/$160 million restoration) and **Theatre ❷** are on their own lane to the left. Richard D'Oyly Carte built the theater in 1881, where Gilbert and Sullivan's operas, including the successful *Mikado,* financed the adjoining deluxe hotel as well as Claridge's. Both buildings later benefited from work by the art deco architect Basil Ionides.

Along the Strand, turn left by the Coal Hole pub, with its rich Edwardian interior, and go down Carting Lane to Victoria Embankment Gardens. Inside the gardens, turn right at the statue of Robert Raikes. At the end of the paths is York Watergate on the right, a survivor from grand riverside York Mansion of 1626.

Backtrack through the gardens past the statue of composer Sir Arthur Sullivan (1842–1900). Leave the gardens at the far end, cut up Savoy Street, then turn right to return past Aldwych. **St. Mary le Strand ❸** stands mid-road, James Gibb's first London church (1714–1717). This was the first of 50 churches Queen Anne planned (she achieved 12) for the capital's growing population. **St. Clement Danes,** another church, lies beyond. The Strand ends with the magnificent **Royal Courts of Justice ❹** (see p. 127) on the left, and Thomas Twining's tea store, established in 1706, at No.

> ### NOT TO BE MISSED:
>
> Inner and Middle Temples
> • Temple Church • Dr. Johnson's House • Gray's Inn • Lincoln's Inn • Covent Garden Piazza

216, and the 1882–1883 Lloyd's Bank banking hall, lined with Doulton tiled panels made at Lambeth, on the right.

The Law Courts & Covent Garden

At the start of Fleet Street, a mid-road memorial topped by a griffin rampant marks the ever tense boundary between the Cities of London and Westminster—between the monarchy and its source of finance. Opposite Chancery Lane, an archway leads into **Inner** and **Middle Temples ❺** (see pp. 126–127). Going straight ahead, then right, find Fountain Court and Middle Temple's Hall (another court); going straight, then left, find **Temple Church** (1160–1185 and 1220–1240) (see p. 127) with effigies of Knights Templar; the Inner Temple Gardens; and Wren's King's Bench Walk, 1677–1678. An opening here leads to Bouverie Street and back to Fleet Street.

Just to the right across the road, both Bolt and Hind Courts lead into Gough Square, a patch of 17th-century alleys and houses. Dr. Samuel Johnson lived and compiled his dictionary here from 1749 to 1759. Now it is a simple, atmospheric museum, **Dr. Johnson's House ❻** (*17 Gough Square, EC4, tel 020 7353 3745, closed Sun., drjohnsonshouse.org, $$*).

At the back of the square, turn left on

Pemberton Row to go to Fetter Lane, then along Norwich and Furnival Streets to High Holborn. Staple Inn's half-timbered houses are to the left. The way into **Gray's Inn 7** (see p. 126) is 100 yards (91 m) farther along, its narrow entrance next to the Cittie of Yorke Pub; squares lead to the grassy Walks (gardens). Down Chancery Lane, dozens of silver shops make up the **London Silver Vaults** (tel 020 7242 3844, silvervaultslondon.com, closed Sun.). Farther down, the Gatehouse (1518) leads into **Lincoln's Inn 8** (see p. 126). Here New Square leads into Lincoln's Inn Fields and so to **Sir John Soane's Museum** (see p. 130).

From here, Remnant Street and Great Queen Street lead across Kingsway to Bow Street, home of the **Royal Opera House** (see p. 124). Russell Street, on the right, goes into **Covent Garden Piazza 9** (see p. 124). The **London Transport Museum** (see p. 124), with fine displays including complete trams and buses, is on the left; the **main market** (see p. 124) is straight ahead.

On the far side of the piazza, go along Henrietta Street and turn right on Bedford Street. Inigo Jones's classical **St. Paul's Church** (1631–1633) has memorials to actors. Garrick Street, where the Garrick Club honors actor David Garrick, leads to Long Acre and Covent Garden Tube station. Long Acre and parallel Shelton Street and Shorts Gardens are good for shopping.

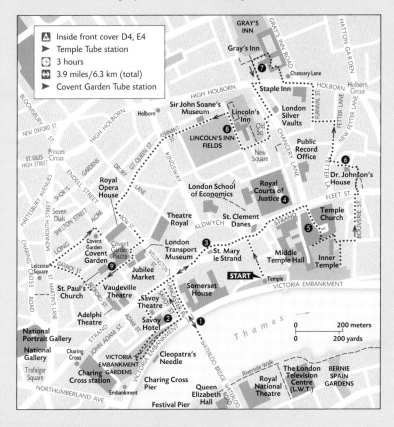

SIR JOHN SOANE'S MUSEUM

One of London's more eccentric and atmospheric house-museums, this was where architect Sir John Soane lived from 1813 until his death in 1837. It is still redolent of his personality. Soane designed No. 12 Lincoln's Inn Fields for himself in 1792; later he bought No. 13 and rebuilt it as a timeless, intensely personal home for his collection. In 1823 Soane expanded to No. 14, which today houses the museum's Picture Room and the Monk's Parlour.

■ The library of Sir John Soane's Museum

Sir John Soane's Museum

🗺 Map p. 123

✉ 13 Lincoln's Inn Fields, WC2

☎ 020 7405 2107

🕐 Closed Mon.–Tues.

💲 Donation. Free guided tours. Tour with a staff expert: £50

🚇 Tube: Holborn

soane.org

NOTE: Appointment required *(tel 020 7440 4263)* for private tours for six people or more.

The best way to arrive is to walk around Lincoln's Inn Fields, a large square laid out in the 1630s, go through the gardens to the north side, and ring the bell at No. 13.

On the ground floor, above the library fireplace, are John Flaxman's reliefs "The Silver Age" and "The Golden Age," two fine pieces of Soane's rich collection of English sculpture. Through the corridor, lined with antique marbles, lies the Picture Room. In this tiny room Hogarth's paintings "The Rake's Progress" and "The Election" series are

stored against the walls in layers that unfold to reveal the works.

Down in the basement crypt, the "Sepulchral Chamber" contains the sarcophagus of Pharaoh Seti I, made in 1300 B.C. and found in the Valley of the Kings, as well as a nearly pristine early 17th-century bronze cast of the Roman god Pluto.

The museum has undergone major expansion works, inaugurated in September 2016, which have provided for the restoration and opening of many parts

INSIDER TIP:

Go early to Sir John Soane's Museum to reserve your place on the guided tour, or go for a candlelit opening on the first Tuesday evening of each month.

—SIMON HORSFORD
Sunday Telegraph *travel writer*

of the original house, including domestic rooms and bedrooms. A new museum shop has also been opened and the flow of visitors along this maze-like exhibition has been better regulated. ■

Eighteenth-century squares, the British Museum, and a handful
of fascinating individual small collections for special interests

BLOOMSBURY

■ The exterior of the British Museum's
reading room

BLOOMSBURY

Bloomsbury's air is filled with calm contemplation and wonder, a mood set by the presence of the University of London and the venerable British Museum, plus their satellite institutions. It is hard to believe that Soho's bars, Covent Garden's entertainment, and the bustle of north London's busy railway stations are all but a five-minute walk away.

Like much of central London, Bloomsbury has agricultural, monastic, and aristocratic chapters in its book. The Domesday Book, William the Conqueror's 11th-century inventory of his English possessions, records a wood for 100 pigs and vineyards here. Later, Edward III gave the land to the Charterhouse monks. After the Dissolution, Henry VIII gave it to his Lord Chancellor, the Earl of Southampton. The 4th Earl of Southampton laid out the square that is now Bloomsbury Square in 1660. A clever marriage linked the Southampton family with the Bedfords. The 4th Duke of Bedford's widow built Bedford Square in the 1770s, while her son was a minor. After he became the 5th Duke, he recognized the area's potential and, around 1800, began building Bloomsbury.

Land was parceled off to developers, principally James Burton, an ambitious Scot. He was succeeded by his architect son, Decimus Burton, and Thomas Cubitt (see sidebar p. 183). The sequence of elegant squares then progressed rapidly: Bloomsbury Square was redeveloped, Russell Square was begun in 1800, Tavistock in 1806, Gordon in 1820, and Woburn in 1825.

Meanwhile, in 1823 work began on replacing Montague House, the British Museum since 1759, with a specially built museum. Soon after, in 1836, England's first nondenominational university, the University of London, was founded in Bloomsbury. East of the patchwork are Brunswick and Mecklenburgh Squares, laid out in the 1790s by the governors of the Thomas Coram Foundation for Children (now the Foundling Museum; see sidebar p. 139), a hospice for abandoned children founded by Captain Coram in 1732 and endowed by Hogarth, Gainsborough, Handel, and others. It overlooked the hospital's land, now Coram's Fields, and set a different tone from nearby streets—Queen Square, Great James Street, and Lamb's Conduit Street. Handsome Doughty Street was completed in 1812; later Charles Dickens lived here. West, across Tottenham Court Road, Fitzroy Square was laid out by the Adam brothers in the 1790s. ∎

HAMPSTEAD RD

ROAD

EUSTON

Warren Street

FITZROY SQUARE

FITZROY STREET

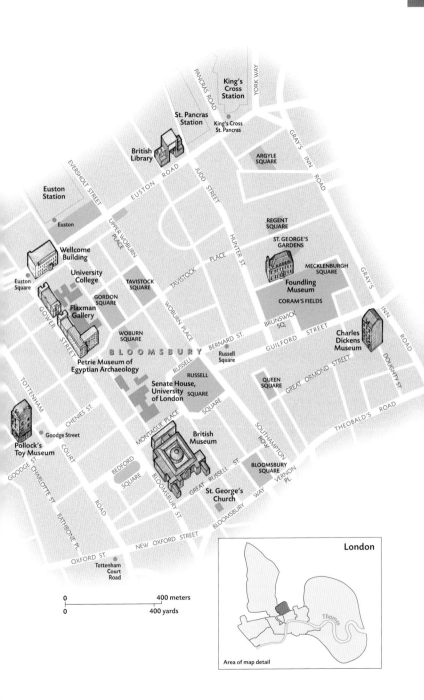

King's Cross Station

PANCRAS ROAD

YORK WAY

St. Pancras Station

King's Cross St. Pancras

British Library

EVERSHOLT STREET

EUSTON ROAD

JUDD STREET

ARGYLE SQUARE

GRAY'S INN ROAD

Euston Station

Euston

UPPER WOBURN PLACE

REGENT SQUARE

HUNTER ST.

ST. GEORGE'S GARDENS

Wellcome Building

TAVISTOCK PLACE

MECKLENBURGH SQUARE

University College

TAVISTOCK SQUARE

Foundling Museum

Euston Square

GOWER STREET

GORDON SQUARE

Flaxman Gallery

WOBURN PLACE

CORAM'S FIELDS

BRUNSWICK SQ.

GUILFORD STREET

GRAY'S INN ROAD

Charles Dickens Museum

B L O O M S B U R Y

WOBURN SQUARE

BERNARD ST.

RUSSELL

Petrie Museum of Egyptian Archaeology

Russell Square

DOUGHTY ST.

RUSSELL SQUARE

QUEEN SQUARE

Senate House, University of London

GREAT ORMOND STREET

TOTTENHAM COURT ROAD

CHENIES ST.

SOUTHAMPTON ROW

THEOBALD'S ROAD

MONTAGUE PLACE

Goodge Street

Pollock's Toy Museum

GOODGE ST.

BEDFORD SQUARE

British Museum

GREAT RUSSELL ST.

BLOOMSBURY SQUARE

VERNON PL.

GOODGE STREET

CHARLOTTE ST.

RATHBONE PL.

BLOOMSBURY ST.

St. George's Church

BLOOMSBURY WAY

NEW OXFORD STREET

OXFORD ST.

Tottenham Court Road

0 ————————— 400 meters
0 ————————— 400 yards

London

Thames

Area of map detail

BRITISH MUSEUM

Britain's largest museum is not to be taken on lightly. Its nine departments look after the national collection of archaeology and ethnography. It covers 13.5 acres (5.4 ha), employs 1,200 people, has almost six million visitors a year, and cares for more than eight million objects ranging from prehistoric bones to chunks of Athens's Parthenon, from whole Assyrian palace rooms to exquisite gold jewels. This is a living museum: It changes daily as different pieces are put on display, special exhibitions are held, and new discoveries change their fields.

■ The British Museum's famed collection of Egyptian antiquities includes coffins, portraits, sculptures, and masks, as well as mummies.

The Museum

This astounding treasure-house began as the simple idea of one man, Sir Hans Sloane. A physician who lived at nearby Bedford Place, he collected minerals, coins, books, and other objects with rare obsessiveness. On his death in 1753, he suggested the government buy all 80,000 bits and pieces, which they did. The same year, the British Museum Act was passed, creating London's first public museum. Money was raised, Montague House was bought, and the museum doors were opened in January 1759. Entry was by written application, but the curators were not interested in the public. Groups were escorted through the galleries in just half an hour and not permitted to linger or gaze at the objects.

The foundation collection also included the library and the finds of antiquarian Sir Robert Cotton and the manuscripts of politician Robert Harley. It expanded alarmingly fast. Even before the museum opened, in 1757 King George II donated most of the Royal Library's 12,000 volumes. The Hamilton antique vases, Townley classical sculptures, Elgin marbles, George III's extensive

---

INSIDER TIP:

Aficionados of Japanese history should not miss the spectacular suit of samurai armor on the upper floor.

—PATRICIA DANIELS
National Geographic contributor

---

library, Capt. James Cook's collections from his voyages, and the Bank of England's coins all came to Montague House.

The house overflowed. So Robert Smirke's great classical temple to learning was built around the house in 1823–1838. Then the house was demolished to make way for the entrance colonnade and portico, which closed the courtyard, known as the Great Court. The domed Reading Room was built in 1854–1857, and all remaining space was filled with galleries and book stacks. Even then, the museum overflowed. In 1881 the Natural History department went to South Kensington (see pp. 174–176); and in 1973 the Printed

Books and Manuscripts department went to the British Library, confusingly situated in a part of the museum.

By the latter part of the 20th century, a radical solution was needed. First, the British Library was given its own building at St. Pancras, just north of Bloomsbury. This released 40 percent of the museum's space, which, crucially, included the Great Court. A program of expansion and renewal was completed in 2003, the museum's 250th birthday. The centerpiece is the Great Court in the middle of the museum. Cleared of all but the Reading Room and roofed in glass, it is another light-filled public Bloomsbury square, this time a covered one. This is the information area for the museum's nearly 100 galleries, a central bureau for its educational events, and a space where visitors can rest, shop, refresh themselves, and cross from one part of the museum to another.

Galleries are organized around the Great Court. The suite of ethnography galleries exploring indigenous cultures is on the north side, and the Age of Enlightenment gallery fills the former King's Library on the east side.

Your Visit

Clearly, this is not a "do in a day" museum. Many visitors will pick up a map and seek out what they know they want to see. For others, the museum is overwhelming. In the Great Court, there is information and lists of the day's events. To help transform this into a

British Museum

- Map p. 133
- Great Russell St., WC2; rear entrance on Montague Place
- 020 7323 8195
- For some exhibitions
- Tube: Tottenham Court Road, Holborn, Russell Square

britishmuseum.org

British Museum

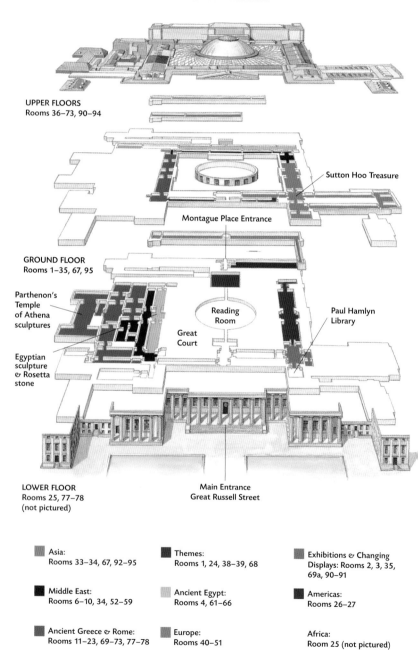

UPPER FLOORS
Rooms 36–73, 90–94

Sutton Hoo Treasure

Montague Place Entrance

GROUND FLOOR
Rooms 1–35, 67, 95

Parthenon's
Temple
of Athena
sculptures

Reading
Room

Paul Hamlyn
Library

Great
Court

Egyptian
sculpture
& Rosetta
stone

LOWER FLOOR
Rooms 25, 77–78
(not pictured)

Main Entrance
Great Russell Street

Asia:
Rooms 33–34, 67, 92–95

Themes:
Rooms 1, 24, 38–39, 68

Exhibitions & Changing
Displays: Rooms 2, 3, 35,
69a, 90–91

Middle East:
Rooms 6–10, 34, 52–59

Ancient Egypt:
Rooms 4, 61–66

Americas:
Rooms 26–27

Ancient Greece & Rome:
Rooms 11–23, 69–73, 77–78

Europe:
Rooms 40–51

Africa:
Room 25 (not pictured)

manageable, stimulating experience, here is a trail that focuses on just a few objects.

Egyptian Antiquities: First explore the rooms surrounding the Great Court, ending with the great, long gallery (Room 4, on the west side of the building) that contains the cream of the finest collection of Egyptian antiquities outside Egypt—many thousands of objects (a few more are displayed upstairs in Rooms 61–66). Sculpture fills this gallery, and among the heads of Rameses II, Amenophis II, and other ancient rulers is the small but ultra-significant **Rosetta stone** (see sidebar this page). The upstairs Egyptian galleries contain funerary models for the afterlife, painted mummies, books of the dead, and Coptic portraits.

Middle Eastern Pieces: Next to the Egyptian sculptures is the Middle East department in Rooms 6–10. This covers the civilizations that rose and fell in the huge area between Egypt and Pakistan. The **Assyrian friezes** are especially beautiful. Excavated last century, they have come from palaces built in the ninth century in the capitals of Nimrud, Khorsabad, and Nineveh. Rooms 7 and 8, the **Nimrud Gallery,** have some colossal, protective winged lions and narrative scenes of the king hunting, the army swimming across a river, and an attack on a town. Room 9, the **Nineveh Room,** tells the story of Assyrian military campaigns in southern Iraq.

Greek Antiquities: The remaining rooms in this part of the museum, Nos. 11–23, are mainly devoted to Greek antiquities. One of the world's finest collections, covering every aspect of life, it ranges from the early simplicity of Cycladic figures to the sophistication of Greek vase paintings. The sculpture is exceptional and includes pieces from some of the world's best known buildings.

Rosetta Stone

Carved in 196 B.C., when Egypt's pharaohs were dead and the Greek Ptolemaic kings ruled the land, the Rosetta stone—one of the British Museum's prized possessions—would, 2,000 years later, become the key that allowed scholars to unlock the secrets of ancient Egyptian hieroglyphics.

In 1799, Napoleon's soldiers found the stone and its long trilingual inscriptions while tearing down an ancient wall. Jean-François Champollion used the more familiar Greek words to decipher the two other sets of writing: the hieroglyphic and demotic scripts of the Egyptians.

Less than 4 feet high by 3 feet wide (1.2 m by 0.9 m), the stone heralds a decree from a council of priests.

Room 17 contains the **Nereid Monument,** the front of a tomb built like a miniature Greek temple. The other outstanding piece is in Room 18, which contains sculptures from the **Parthenon's Temple of Athena,** built in the fifth century B.C. as part of a plan to beautify Athens. Using money intended for the navy, the sculptor Phidias oversaw the decorative work on the most magnificent building from the

■ **Carved female figurines from predynastic Egypt are among the British Museum's millions of objects.**

golden age of ancient Greece. It remained perfect until gunpowder stored there exploded in 1687. In the early 19th century, Lord Elgin brought many of the surviving sculptures to London: the great frieze of the procession to celebrate Athena's birthday, plus sculptures from the pediments and metopes.

Upper Galleries: Go up the stairs to the upper levels. In Room 68, the **Citi Money Gallery** is a treasury displaying 2,000 years of British coinage in commerce, history, and portraiture.

Some precious and delicate objects from the **Medieval and Later Antiquities** department fill the corner Rooms 41–48. Several special treasures are worth seeking out here. In Room 41, early pieces include the **Sutton Hoo Treasure,** an Anglo-Saxon royal burial ship that survived intact in Suffolk and was excavated in 1939. Room 41 also includes Byzantine and Early Christian objects,

Celtic bowls, Merovingian coins, and high-quality locally made jewelry, all illustrating the diversity and sophistication of Anglo-Saxon high society. Room 40, one of the medieval rooms, contains the **Lewis Chessmen,** possibly carved in Scandinavia in the 12th century and found on the Hebridean island of Lewis in 1831.

Rooms 49–51 display the **Prehistoric and Romano–British Antiquities** spanning early history to the Christian period. There is a gold torque from Norfolk, a bronze mirror, and gaming pieces. In Room 49, a mosaic floor found in Dorset in 1963 contains the earliest known representation of Christ in a mosaic floor in the Roman empire.

Asian & Islamic Pieces: Now head to the North Wing. There are several levels here, connected by stairs and elevators. Rooms 91a on Level 4 and 92–94 on Level 5 are devoted to **Japanese art.** Room 95 on Level 2 houses the Sir Percival David collection of exquisite **Chinese porcelain.**

On the floor below them, Room 33 is the Joseph E. Hotung Gallery, which begins at the west end with some early **Indian Buddhist sculptures** and moves through the cultures of **Southeast Asia.** Beneath this, Room 34 contains the John Addis Gallery of **Islamic arts.**

The British Museum grows almost daily: Most British archaeological discoveries come here; bequests are frequent; and the museum continues to buy new pieces for its collection. ■

THE MUSEUM TRAIL

The British Museum is the inspiration for a host of other fascinating museums and historical sites scattered throughout Bloomsbury and around Covent Garden. Telephone the smaller ones to confirm opening times before visiting.

Start at the **British Library.** Edouard Paolozzi's sculpture of Newton in the courtyard introduces the headquarters of one of the world's most important library collections, composed of more than 150 million items—King George III's 65,000 volumes are housed in a magnificent six-story glass-walled tower. Galleries include the **Sir John Ritblat Gallery,** displaying rare treasures such as the Magna Carta. Other rooms include a philatelic gallery showcasing rare and important stamps.

From here, take in the dependably fascinating science exhibitions at the **Wellcome Collection** *(183 Euston Rd., NW1, tel 020 7611 2222, wellcomecollection.org, closed Mon., free).* More tricky to find, and visit, are several little museums at the University of London's University College. The UCL Art Museum

(ucl.ac.uk/museums) runs the **Flaxman Gallery,** under the dome of the Wilkins main library building, featuring full-size plaster models by neoclassical sculptor John Flaxman; and the **Flaxman Collection** *(UCL Art Museum, Wilkins Building South Cloisters, off Gower St., WC1, tel 020 7679 2540, closed weekends, free),* which displays some of Flaxman's drawings as well as works by Turner, Rembrandt, and Durer. On nearby Malet Place you'll find the **Petrie Museum of Egyptian Archaeology.** Finally, the School of Oriental and African Studies runs the **Brunei Gallery** *(Russell Square, WC1, tel 020 7898 4046, www.soas. ac.uk/gallery, closed Sun.–Mon., free).* A short detour leads you to the wonderful **Pollock's Toy Museum** *(1 Scala St., W1, tel 020 7636 3452, pollockstoys.com, closed Sun.),* two houses of childhood treasures.

The route now passes by the British Museum (see pp. 134–138). Drop into Nicholas Hawksmoor's restored Baroque masterpiece, **St. George's Church** (1716–1731; *stgeorgesbloomsbury.org.uk),* on Bloomsbury Way. East of Kingsway, the **Hunterian Museum**'s collection, closed until 2021, traces the development of surgery *(Royal College of Surgeons, 35–43 Lincoln's Inn Fields, WC2, tel 020 7405 3474, rcseng.ac.uk).* The trail ends at **Somerset House** (see p. 125) across the Strand. ∎

The Foundling Museum

Another route from the British Library to the British Museum takes you via the Foundling Museum (see p. 132), a grand refurbished house that offers a fine picture collection and galleries recounting the plight of London's abandoned children in the 18th century.

British Library

- Map p. 133
- 96 Euston Rd., NW1
- 01937 546 000
- Open daily. Reading Room closed Sun. Reservations recommended.
- Donation Events: $ Exhibitions: $$
- Tube/Rail: King's Cross, St. Pancras, Euston

bl.uk

Petrie Museum of Egyptian Archaeology

- Map p. 133
- University College, WC1, Malet Place entrance
- 020 7679 2884
- Closed Sun.–Mon.
- Free
- Tube: Euston Square

www.petrie.ucl.ac.uk

The Foundling Museum

- Map p. 133
- 40 Brunswick Square, WC1
- 020 7841 3600
- Closed Mon.
- $
- Tube: Russell Square

foundlingmuseum.org.uk

LONDON SQUARES

Bloomsbury's squares of flat-fronted, brick houses overlooking gardens of lawns, trees, and the odd statue have a rhythm that sets the tone for much of London. The London square is a very specific piece of urban design, which suited the English social system, love of gardens, and, once the Enlightenment took hold, its sense of order. Introduced in the 17th century, the square reached its peak of popularity in the 19th century. More than 150 of them are spread across central London.

■ Soho Square features a picturesque gardener's hut.

Inigo Jones, Charles I's favorite architect, laid out Covent Garden Piazza in 1631 for the Earl of Bedford. While the earl was inspired by Paris's Place des Vosges, Jones was remembering Palladio's work in Italy. The result was a handsome residential square whose houses, built behind a uniform facade, overlooked an airy central space. It was quite different from anything the tight-knit London City offered, and it was popular. By 1700, a dozen squares had been built for London's wealthy, including Lincoln's Inn Fields, Soho, Leicester, Bloomsbury, St. James's, and several in the Inns of Court.

The squares often proved to be nuclei for 18th-century development, the period when squares were given their most satisfactory sizes and proportions. This is the case in Mayfair, where the concept developed at St. James's Square leaped across Piccadilly to appear as Hanover, Berkeley, and Grosvenor Squares. More isolated gems were built, too, such as the Charterhouse (on the edge of the City) and Smith (in Westminster).

But it is Bedford Square, one of the early Bloomsbury squares, that reached near-perfection and survives complete. A daring piece of speculative development in the 1770s, Bedford was London's first square to be planned and built as a single architectural unit. Each side follows a simple design, a great palace facade with a pediment in the middle, overlooking a central oval garden.

Walking paths wind among plane trees in Portman Square Garden.

Originally, the square was gated and guarded to preserve residents' privacy. Only the residents had keys to the gardens—a practice still in use in many London squares. Tradesmen used the back entrances in the mews lanes behind the buildings, where the stables were. Coal was delivered to the front of the house, however, and poured down coal holes in the pavement, so that it reached the basement kitchens without dirtying the main house. You can still see the metal lids for these coal holes in some sidewalks.

During London's rampaging 19th-century expansion, developers constantly utilized the square. Islington's 18th-century terraces were joined first by Canonbury Square in around 1800, then by the unpretentious squares of Barnsbury. But a new scale of grandeur was introduced in the creation of Belgravia. Belgrave Square, the centerpiece for Thomas Cubitt's development (see pp. 182–183), begun in 1825, is huge and unashamedly pompous. Mansions mark each corner, each terrace is four stories high, and columns and pilasters are rampant. Working with George Basevi, Cubitt broke up the facades, giving individuality to the houses by varying the entrances, elevations, and decoration.

The break with the austere Georgian square was complete. Even today, every square still retains something that makes it peculiar. Eaton Square resembles a triumphal way; Chester Square, long and narrow, is surprisingly intimate; Ladbroke Square's Italianate houses overlook what is possibly London's largest private communal garden. Late 20th-century developments at Chelsea Harbour and Broadgate have kept the idea of the city square alive.

The Bloomsbury Group

At the beginning of the 20th century, a handful of artists and writers formed a clique devoted to the philosophy of G. E. Moore, which decreed that the most important things in life were the "pleasures of human intercourse and the enjoyment of beautiful objects. It is they that form the rational ultimate end of social progress." Most of the group had Cambridge connections, but they all gathered in Bloomsbury's Gordon Square, where in 1904 the Stephen family—Virginia (later Woolf), her sister Vanessa (later Bell), Toby, and Adrian—moved into No. 46. The economist John Maynard Keynes was part of the group, as were E. M. Forster, Lytton Strachey, Leonard Woolf (Virginia's husband), and Vanessa's husband, Clive Bell. So, too, was Roger Fry, the artist and critic who left his art collection to the Courtauld Institute. Paintings by him and another Bloomsbury artist, Duncan Grant, are in the Courtauld Institute Galleries (see p. 125).

CHARLES DICKENS MUSEUM

Charles Dickens had many London homes, but only this one survives. He, his wife, Catherine, and their young son Charles moved onto Doughty Street in 1837 and lived here for three key years. Dickens wrote the first of his great novels in this house.

Charles Dickens Museum

- 🅰 Map p. 133
- ✉ 48 Doughty St., WC1
- ☎ 020 7405 2127
- 🕐 Closed Mon.
- 💲 $
- 🚇 Tube: Russell Square, Chancery Lane

dickensmuseum.com

The house was well located: in a good residential area, yet close to the City and Thameside streets where he did his research. His daughters Mary and Kate were born here. Not surprisingly, the house holds the world's most comprehensive Dickens library and is a place of pilgrimage for Dickens enthusiasts. The museum runs weekly two-hour walks (*Wed. at 11:00 a.m. & 5:00 p.m., separate fee: $$*) around

INSIDER TIP:

See who you can identify in the "Dickens's Dream" painting, depicting the author amid his characters.

—RACHAEL JACKSON
*Research manager,
National Geographic Channel*

Dickens's London that start at the house and end at St. Paul's Cathedral.

Saved from demolition in 1922 by the Dickens Fellowship, which now runs it, the house has been skillfully arranged to retain its atmosphere of literary output and its early Victorian interior decoration. Seeing the writer's desk and chair, marked-up copies of his readings, and other personal artifacts, it is easy to imagine him polishing off *The Pickwick Papers*, writing *Oliver Twist* and *Nicholas Nickleby*, or beginning *Barnaby Rudge*—feats all achieved here. The museum contains more than 100,000 artifacts.

In 2012 the museum completed a redevelopment that doubled its exhibition space and returned the interior rooms to a Victorian look. The house also has a small café and a charming walled back garden, and hosts a multitude of evening events. ■

Charles Dickens's house survives from the 19th century.

Theatrical architecture and two of the city's most glorious parks:
Regent's Park with its gardens and zoo, and Hampstead Heath

REGENCY LONDON & NORTH

Houseboats in Little Venice

REGENCY LONDON & NORTH

When the Prince Regent became King George IV he introduced a new order into London with the development of Regent Street and Regent's Park. Not since the great building projects of the Tudors of the sixteenth century had a royal exercised such influence on the shaping of London. The Prince Regent was the energy and inspiration behind the dream. John Nash, his planner and gifted architect, realized this dream with theatrical panache.

When Prince George came of age in 1783, he moved out of St. James's Palace into Carlton House, sited where the bottom of Regent Street is today, and for the next 30 years squandered a fortune having fun. It was during this period that he employed the architect John Nash.

The prince, influenced by the growing English Picturesque movement, which saw architecture as part of the environment, conceived a scheme that would make sweeping changes to the outer reaches of London. In 1811, when he and Nash were already making plans, three key events happened. The lease on 500 acres (200 ha) of Crown parkland, just north of smart Marylebone and Mayfair, expired; George III became so unwell that his son was made regent; and the tide turned in the Napoleonic Wars, firing London with optimism and jump-starting a building boom.

The idea was to create a garden city for aristocrats, a park dotted with villas, woods, a royal pleasure palace, a lake, and a canal. The plan also included a wide, mile-long street of suitable size for large carriages to link the park to his own home and thus to the Court and Parliament.

Most of the Prince Regent's dream was realized. Regent Street was built at the expense of hundreds of Soho houses, dividing Mayfair and Marylebone from all points east. Today, much rebuilt, it remains a stylish shopping street and happily links to James Adam's elegant Portland Place of 1776–1780. Carlton House was demolished when the prince moved to Buckingham Palace and the southern end of Regent Street closed with a staircase leading down to St. James's Park. At the north end, the great circus planned at the crossing with Marylebone Road was only half realized in Park Crescent, but even this is one of London's finest architectural set pieces.

Regent's Park may have fewer villas than planned, and no pleasure palace, but with its meandering lake, northern boundary canal, zoo, immaculate gardens, and gleaming terraces, it is one of London's most breathtaking royal parks.

At the southwest corner, Dorset Square's development in 1811 forced the famous Marylebone Cricket Club to move to Lord's in St. John's Wood (now the country's best known cricket ground). North of the park, as buildings covered the hills, Hampstead and, to a lesser extent, Highgate were brought into the London frame. ■

0
1 kilometer
0
1 mile

London

Area of map detail

Thames

FINCHLEY

NORTH CIRCULAR ROAD

FALLODEN WAY

EAST
FINCHLEY

East
Finchley

LYTTLETON RD.

AYLMER RD.

HAMPSTEAD
GARDEN
SUBURB

ARCHWAY ROAD

Highgate

HIGHGATE

Golders
Green

Kenwood House

HAMPSTEAD
HEATH

❻
WATERLOW
PARK

Archway

GOLDERS
HILL PARK

❺

HAMPSTEAD

Karl Marx
Tomb

HIGHGATE
CEMETERY

JUNCTION RD.

Fenton
House

Keats's
House

PARLIAMENT
HILL

FORTRESS RD.

Tufnell
Park

FINCHLEY ROAD

Hampstead

Belsize
Park

KENTISH
TOWN

Kentish
Town

KENTISH TOWN ROAD

❹

Finchley
Road

West
Hampstead

Swiss
Cottage

SWISS
COTTAGE

Chalk Farm

ABBEY ROAD

FINCHLEY ROAD

PRIMROSE
HILL

❼

CAMDEN
TOWN

❽

Camden Town

CAMDEN HIGH ST.

HAMPSTEAD RD.

ST. JOHN'S
WOOD

❾

Regent's Park
Terraces

ALBANY ST.

MAIDA
VALE

MAIDA VALE

St. John's
Wood

REGENT'S PARK

GROVE END RD.

❷
❸

ST. JOHN'S WOOD RD.

PARK ROAD

❿

Maida
Vale

Edgware
Road

Marylebone
Station

Regent's
Park

❶

Warwick
Ave.

EDGWARE ROAD

MARYLEBONE RD.

Baker
Street

Madame
Tussauds

All Souls Church,
Langham Place

A40

OXFORD STREET

Oxford
Circus

REGENT ST.

Carlton House
Terrace

Piccadilly
Circus

❶ Little Venice ❷ Abbey Road zebra cross-
ing ❸ Lord's Cricket Ground ❹ Freud
Museum ❺ Hill House ❻ Lauderdale
House ❼ Camden Lock ❽ Jewish Museum
❾ ZSL London Zoo ❿ Queen Mary's
Gardens ⓫ Institute of Contemporary Arts

REGENT STREET

Oxford Street may have more shops than any other street in Europe, but Regent Street has the edge for its mix of shops, style, and a drop of culture—all wrapped in architectural grandeur.

Regent Street
🗺 Map p. 145

Institute of Contemporary Arts
🗺 Map p. 145
✉ 12 Carlton House Terrace, The Mall, SW1
☎ 020 7930 0493
🕐 Closed Mon.
💲 $
🚇 Tube/Rail: Charing Cross

www.ica.art

At the southern end of Regent Street (and its extension, Waterloo Place), architect John Nash (see p. 148) tidied up the eastern side, creating Pall Mall East and planning ahead for Trafalgar Square. When the prince moved to Buckingham Palace, Nash replaced Carlton House with Carlton House Terrace (1827–1832). Today, No. 9 is home to the erudite Royal Society, whose presidents have included Wren, Newton, and Sloane. In the middle of the terrace stands Benjamin Wyatt's Duke of York's Column. Steps lead down to the **Institute of Contemporary Arts,** which shows state-of-the-art exhibitions and films.

Northward, **Piccadilly Circus** (see p. 118) marks the start of a change of Regent Street's direction and mood. Here is Austin Reed, Brooks Brothers, Anthropologie, and Burberry. Farther up is a huge Apple store as well as Liberty London, known for its quality exotic goods (and a basement barber; see sidebar below).

Oxford Circus marks Regent Street's intersection with bustling Oxford Street, one of the world's great shopping meccas. Stately **Selfridges** and **Marks & Spencer** both have their flagship stores here, as do a wide range of 70 clothing retailers. This famously crowded strip has been made a lot more inviting to visitors with wider sidewalks and an all-way pedestrian crossing at Oxford Circus.

North of Oxford Circus, the portico of **All Souls Church, Langham Place** has a bust of architect Nash looking down his street. ■

(see p. 148)

EXPERIENCE: Have Your Whiskers Trimmed

Combining the best of centuries-old ritual and 21st-century pampering, there are still a few spots in town where you can go for a traditional straight-edge wet shave, complete with scented hot towels, a hearty bristled brush, and thick lather.

Murdock London on the lower ground floor of Liberty London (*Regent St., W1, tel 020 7734 1234, liberty.co.uk, $$$$*) offers a full range of wet shaves, beard trimmings, and other grooming options.

Geo. F. Trumper (*trumpers.com, $$–$$$$*) has two locations in London—in Mayfair (*9 Curzon St., W1, tel 020 7499* 1850) and St. James's (*1 Duke of York St., SW1, tel 020 7734 1370*). You can further your education with a private shaving lesson at the Mayfair location.

Pall Mall Barbers (*27 Whitcomb St., WC2, tel 020 7930 7787, pallmallbarbers .com, $$–$$$$*) is an independent barber near Leicester Square with more than 25 years experience.

The Refinery (*18 Grosvenor Street W1, tel 020 7409 2001 and 5 Montpelier Street SW7, tel 020 7838 1117; the-refinery.com, $$$$*) offers massages, waxing, and manicures in addition to their shave service.

REGENT'S PARK

This is where John Nash left the French formality of Regent Street behind and returned to English Picturesque. Almost 500 acres (200 ha) of farmland had been appropriated by Henry VIII from the Abbey of Barking. These were sold by Cromwell, then reclaimed by Charles II and leased out. It was these leases that reverted to the crown in 1811. Of Nash's 56 planned villas, only 8 were built, but the terraces at the sides were completed.

Regent's Park offers boating on its lake and relaxing on its shores.

Regent's Park has great variety. In the southeast corner, the Victorian complexity and density of planting in Avenue Gardens, laid out in 1864, has been restored to full glory. Beside them the Broad Walk runs the length of the park, bordered by mature horse chestnuts. About 6,000 forest trees grow in the park.

Halfway up the Broad Walk, Inner Circle protects the park's most private and magical area, **Queen Mary's Gardens.** Laid out to celebrate the Jubilee of George V and Queen Mary in 1935, it includes formal and alpine gardens and a glorious rose garden. More than 30,000 plants and 400 varieties, both old and new, perfume the air with blooms throughout the summer. Rambling and climbing roses encircle beds of flowers, creating peaceful corners in the park.

The **Regent's Park Open-Air Theatre,** which offers Shakespeare and other eclectic productions during the summer months, is in Inner Circle, too. Regent's Park Lake, a sanctuary for waterbirds, meanders around Inner Circle; the bandstand's music floats over it, and boaters enjoy views of the Holme, a villa designed by Decimus Burton.

North across the lawns, the roaring of lions announces the 36 acres (15 ha) of **ZSL London Zoo,** opened in 1828. A bridge over Regent's Canal leads to Primrose Hill, with grand views across London. ∎

Regent's Park

- Map p. 145
- 0300 061 2000
- Closed at night
- Tube: Regent's Park, Baker Street, Great Portland Street, or Camden Town
  Train: London Marylebone

royalparks.org.uk

Regent's Park Open-Air Theatre

- Queen Mary's Garden, Regent's Park, NW1
- Tickets: 0333 400 3562
- May–Sep.
- $$$
- Tube: Baker Street

openairtheatre.com

ZSL London Zoo

- Map p. 145
- Outer Circle, Regent's Park, NW1
- 020 7449 6200
- $$$
- Tube: Camden Town, Regent's Park

zsl.org

REGENCY ARCHITECTURE

Architect John Nash's vision for London became the capital's chief expression of Regency architecture and town planning. Inspired by the Picturesque movement, this was a more adaptive style of architecture that reacted against the Enlightenment's classical severity.

The emphasis turned from quality of building and detail to overall effect; from a preoccupation with interior space to a desire for impressive facades; from a serious, formal approach to a more capricious, eclectic one that took inspiration from any period or culture.

Born in 1752, Nash produced his best work in his sixties and seventies when, as the Prince Regent's town planner, he brought freedom and imagination to the city's "metropolitan improvements," as the prince dubbed his project. Nash's gleaming stuccoed streets, terraces, and villas introduced a new theatricality and dignity to a city transforming itself from a port into the capital of a worldwide empire.

This Regency style is best displayed in Nash's imposing Regent's Park terraces, which surround the park: York, Cornwall, Clarence, Sussex, and Hanover, built in 1821–1823, were followed by Ulster, Cambridge, Chester, and Cumberland, and finally Gloucester in 1827.

York Terrace is strung along the south side of the park in two sections. In the middle, the stage-set design of York Gate cleverly frames Marylebone Church, built in 1813 with gilded caryatids supporting the tower's dome. The other early terraces are strung along the west side. York, Cornwall, and Clarence, ambitious conceptions by Nash, were built under his direction by James Burton and his son, Decimus. In Sussex Place, Nash drew on his Brighton Pavilion: The curved end wings, octagonal domes, and polygonal bay windows seem better suited to the seaside. Finally, Hanover Terrace returns to a classical simplicity.

Where the architecture lapses, however, the lighthearted theatrical effect does not. This is even more true of the terraces on the east side, which follow the south side's Ulster Terrace with its simple lines and bay windows at each end. Between the relatively modest Cambridge Terrace and the asymmetrical Gloucester Gate, Chester Terrace's 940-foot-long (287 m) facade is broken up by giant Corinthian columns; at either end, projecting wings are joined with thin triumphal arches. This is fun, but for architectural frolic Cumberland Terrace tops it. With its seven porticoes, courtyards, and arches, it makes one of the most impressive panoramas in London, a perfect backdrop to aristocratic partying.

Of the eight villas once sprinkled through the park, just three remain. Seen from across the lake, the Holme, designed by Decimus Burton for his father, looks just as it should: a suburban idyll of country houses surrounded by spacious grounds.

John Nash's architecture at Regent's Park

MADAME TUSSAUDS

Drawing some of the largest crowds in London, this waxwork temple to the famous, infamous, and sometimes unremarkable opened in 1835. Today it is especially popular with children and can make for a fun outing, even though it is of relatively minor importance in a city blessed with so many truly amazing museums for history, art, and science.

Madame Tussaud, whose real name was Marie Grosholtz, fled revolutionary Paris in 1802, toured England with her uncle's waxworks, then settled near here. Fans kept returning because she was always adding people in the news. Her sons moved the collection to this site, and today's owners keep the show up-to-date. Bring your camera; the photo ops come fast and furious.

The wide-ranging collection of personalities depicted includes Hollywood (and Bollywood) favorites such as Charlie Chaplin, George Clooney, Emma Watson, Brad Pitt, Angelina Jolie, and Shrek; Tiger Woods, Pele, Rafael Nadal, running star Mo Farah, and other sports figures; the Beatles, Freddie Mercury, and Michael Jackson from the world of music; and a selection of U.S. presidents, British prime ministers, members of the

■ War veteran Prince Harry stands proud in wax at Madame Tussauds.

British royal family, and other world leaders, both famous and infamous.

The "Scream" attraction pits you against live actors jumping out from the shadows to startle you. The old planetarium building continues the celebrity show, plus screens a changing selection of "4-D" features. ■

Madame Tussauds

🗺 Map p. 145

✉ Marylebone Rd., NW1

☎ 333 321 2001

🕐 Best to reserve tickets online in advance

💲 $$$$

🚇 Tube: Baker Street

madametussauds .com

Lord's Cricket Ground

Head north on Regent's Park Outer Circle—just behind Madame Tussauds—and at the northwest corner of the park you'll come to England's most famous cricket club. The Marylebone Cricket Club (MCC) lies behind high walls on St. John's Wood Road. The ground hosts club and Middlesex County matches and international test matches. Visitors may tour the buildings (one designed by Michael Hopkins) and museum *(tel 020 7616 8500, lords.org, closed on major match days).* **Cricket memorabilia include Donald Bradman's boots, the sparrow killed by Jehangir Khan's ball in 1936, and the tiny urn containing the Ashes. The Ashes—of the stumps burned after Australia's first victory over England in 1882—is a mock trophy given to the winner of a series of five test matches between the rival countries.**

REGENT'S CANAL, CAMDEN, & LITTLE VENICE

In the 18th century, England was crisscrossed by canals—water highways that transported much of the industrial revolution's new trading wealth. Regent's Canal, built as the park's north border, provided a vital link in the system. It ran from Paddington Basin, where the Grand Union Canal from the Midlands then ended, to the Port of London 8.5 miles (13.6 km) away, and quickly became England's busiest stretch of canal. Even after the railways were built, it was used for delivering expanding London's building materials.

Regent's Canal in Camden is a favored spot for relaxing on a summer day.

Jason's Trip

✉ Little Venice Opposite 42, Blomfield Road, W9; or Camden Lock 75 West Yard, NW1

🚇 Tube: Camden Town, Warwick Avenue

💲 $–$$

jasons.co.uk

Today, Regent's Canal is quiet. The towpath is a favorite spot to fish or take a leisurely stroll, and pleasure boats ferry passengers 45 minutes along the canal between Camden Lock and Little Venice. (Ferry options include Jason's Trip, the London Waterbus Company, and the *Jenny Wren.*)

The two destinations are quite different. Camden's modest, small-scale houses are now gentrified. Weekend life focuses in and around **Camden Lock,** whose ethnic market began in the 1970s and is now hugely popular. Thousands of bargain hunters flock to the markets (see p. 164) that have spread up Camden High Street

EXPERIENCE: Crossing Abbey Road

For visitors of a certain age, there's an almost inexorable draw to the famous crosswalk (generically called "zebra crossings" in the U.K. for their distinctive black-and-white stripes) that appears on the cover of the Beatles' 1969 album, *Abbey Road.*

To get there from Little Venice's pretty Blomfield Road (a 15- to 20-minute walk), follow Randolph Avenue and turn right onto Sutherland Road (which becomes Hall Road), then turn left onto Grove End Road. The crosswalk will be about 200 yards (182 m) in front of you. (Or take the short walk down Grove End Road from the St. John's Wood Tube stop.) You should be able to spot the crosswalk by the clusters of tourists loitering on either side of the street, waiting their turn to parade back and forth. Luckily, British law requires that drivers give pedestrians the right of way at zebra crossings (which, by and large, they do), but Abbey Road is a busy street, so don't dally too long trying to perfectly recapture the pose of the four Liverpudlians.

A few yards up Abbey Road, on the southwest side of the street, is **Abbey Road Studios,** where the Beatles recorded 90 percent of their music. You aren't able to visit, as it's still a working studio, so you'll have to make do with photos shot through the iron gates.

In 2010, both the zebra crossing and Abbey Road Studios were approved for listing by the Department for Culture, Media and Sport, affording them protected status.

INSIDER TIP:

In Little Venice, drop into Clifton Nurseries at Clifton Villas. It's London's oldest garden center and has a lovely café for breakfast, lunch, or tea.

—SIMON HORSFORD
Sunday Telegraph travel writer

and Chalk Farm Road. The **Camden Arts Centre** *(Arkwright Rd., NW3, tel 020 7472 5500, camdenartscentre.org, closed Mon.),* a free exhibition space for contemporary art, perfectly embodies Camden's alternative and artsy feel. Meanwhile, the **Jewish Museum** *(129–131 Albert St., NW1, tel 020 7284 7384, jewishmuseum.org.uk, closed Friday p.m. & Sat., $),* off the northeast corner of Regent's Park, displays particularly good collections of Jewish art and objects.

Little Venice, a couple of miles southwest, is, by contrast, a leafy and stylish haven. Painted barges are moored on the canal, including one that is a **puppet theater** *(opposite 35 Blomfield Rd., W9, tel 020 7249 6876, puppetbarge.com, moored in Richmond Aug.–Sept.).*

A walk here passes by the grand houses of the neighborhood of Maida Vale—the elegant ones on Blomfield Road border the canal—and a couple of notable pubs: the **Bridge House,** where upstairs the renowned Canal Café Theatre *(canalcafetheatre.com)* performs frequent comedy shows; and the perfectly preserved **Prince Alfred,** an old Victorian gin palace on Formosa Street behind the Warwick Avenue Tube stop. ∎

London Waterbus Company
- ✉ Camden Lock, Chalk Farm Road, NW1
- ☎ 07917 265114
- 🕐 Closed Oct. 8– Dec. 6 & Dec. 22–Jan. 4
- 💲 $$$
- 🚇 Tube: Camden

londonwaterbus.com

Jenny Wren
- ✉ 250 Camden High St., NW1
- ☎ 020 7485 4433
- 🕐 Closed Nov.–Feb.
- 💲 $$–$$$$

www.walkersquay.com

Clifton Nurseries
- ✉ 5A Clifton Villas, W9
- ☎ 020 7289 6851
- 🚇 Tube: Warwick Avenue

clifton.co.uk

HAMPSTEAD

Distanced from the central London developers, Hampstead watched the builders climb up the hill toward its doors but retained its distinct, hilltop village character. Healthy air and panoramic views across London to the Surrey hills attracted Tudor merchants to Hampstead. By the 18th century, its popularity ran parallel with Islington's, but its position farther from town made it a more select pleasure resort, and it has never lost its fashionable image.

Fenton House
- Map p. 145
- Hampstead Grove, NW3
- 020 7435 3471
- Closed Mon.–Tues.
- $$
- Tube: Hampstead

nationaltrust.org.uk

Burgh House & Hampstead Museum
- New End Square, NW3
- 020 7431 0144
- Closed Mon., Tues., Thur, & Sat.
- Tube: Hampstead

www.burghhouse.org.uk

The wealthy, artistic, and intellectual came to take the health-giving mineral waters at Hampstead's spa, and some stayed—statesman William Pitt and writers Lord Byron, Robert Louis Stevenson, and John Galsworthy all lived here. Despite the restaurants and shops that line High Street today, houses in Hampstead Square, Church Row, Flask Walk, Well Walk, and their surrounding streets still echo with Georgian holiday mood.

Notable Houses

Hampstead's contemporary intellectuals have saved several fine houses and gardens and made them museums. **Fenton House,** at the top of Holly Hill from the village, is perhaps the grandest. It is a William-and-Mary house of 1693, filled with fine ceramics and old musical instruments, and set in a delightful garden.

Burgh House & Hampstead Museum, located in the village center, a perfect Queen Anne house of 1703, was once owned by Hampstead physician Dr. William Gibbons.

Among the writers attracted to Hampstead was the poet John Keats, who lived in a modest Regency house (*10 Kests Grove, tel 020 7332 3868, keatshouse.org. uk, Mon.–Tues., $*) between 1818 and 1820. The house is now furnished with the poet's belongings.

The psychoanalyst Sigmund Freud lived at 20 Maresfield Gardens, today the **Freud Museum** (*tel 020 7435 2002, freud.org.uk, closed Mon.–Tues.*), where his analyst's chair is displayed.

Finally, the National Trust has opened **2 Willow Road** (*tel 020 7435 6166, nationaltrust.org.uk*), a modernist house with a severe exterior that belies its impressive art collection and intriguing interior design. The home was built by architect and furniture designer Erno Goldfinger in 1939. ■

Hampstead's handsome brick houses have long attracted writers and other intellectuals.

KENWOOD HOUSE &
HAMPSTEAD HEATH

Fine art in a spectacular setting is matched by panoramic views, rolling hills, and woodland, making this house and its surroundings one of the great joys of London.

Kenwood House

In 1754 the brilliant lawyer, the Earl of Mansfield bought the early 17th-century, hilltop Kenwood House with its fashionable "prospects" as a summer retreat from his city home in Lincoln's Inn Fields. Robert Adam, a fellow Scot, remodeled it in 1764–1769. Exhibiting his mastery of both exterior and interior design, Adam added another story to the long, classical garden front and balanced the older orangery with a sumptuous library, one of his best rooms anywhere. The ceiling is decorated with plasterwork by Joseph Rose and paintings by Antonio Zucchi.

After the Earl of Mansfield, the house languished until 1925, when Edward Guinness, Earl of Iveagh, bought it along with 80 acres (32 ha) of park and hung his pictures in Adam's suite of rooms. Guinness left the house and gardens to the nation, along with the paintings, which include Vermeer's "Guitar Player" (circa 1672), Rembrandt's "Portrait of the Artist" (circa 1665), and Turner's "Coast Scene with Fishermen" (1803).

From the front terrace, the lawns sweep down to a lake, now the setting for summer concerts; to the east, a path leads to the summit for breathtaking views of London.

■ **Parliament Hill in Hampstead Heath offers fine kite flying and sweeping views of London.**

Hampstead Heath

Walkers will itch to step out across Hampstead Heath, a tract of 789 acres (319 ha) fought for in the face of developers and accumulated piecemeal since 1829. Plunge down to the east to **Highgate Ponds,** then climb **Parliament Hill,** to the west, where Sunday kite flyers rule; continue west to the three bucolic freshwater swimming holes of **Hampstead Ponds.** ■

Kenwood House

🅐 Map p. 145

✉ Hampstead Lane, NW3

☎ 020 8348 1286

Ⓢ Charge for exhibitions

🚇 Tube: Hampstead, then walk 1 mile (1.6 km); or Golders Green or Archway and then 210 bus

www.english-heritage .org.uk

HIGHGATE

Living slightly in the shadow of Hampstead, Highgate's story has been a similar but quieter one. A hamlet grew up on land belonging to the bishops of London. By the end of the 16th century its waters and air were worth the journey from London, as were its open spaces for exercise and fun; wealthy merchants built their country mansions here. Today, Highgate is best known for its beautiful cemetery, where many famous Londoners lie.

Lauderdale House

- Map p. 145
- Highgate Hill, N6
- 020 8348 8716
- Tube: Highgate, Archway

lauderdalehouse
.co.uk

Highgate Cemetery

- Map p. 145
- Swain's Lane, N6
- 020 8340 1834
- East side: $ West side, guided tours only: $$
- Tube: Archway

highgate-cemetery
.org

One of the earliest mansions to be built here, **Lauderdale House** (1580) survives in part, with later additions. The large sloping garden, confusingly called Waterlow Park, has great beech, catalpa, and yew trees shading the heavily scented summer azalea blossoms.

INSIDER TIP:

Highgate's West Cemetery has more imposing monuments than the East Cemetery, but you must take a guided tour to see it.

—LARRY PORGES
*National Geographic
Travel Books editor*

The nucleus of Highgate, however, is farther up the hill, where the eccentric philanthropist William Blake built houses at Nos. 1–6 of The Grove in the 17th century. Nearby, delightful houses fill Pond Square, and more survive in South Grove: Old Hall at No. 17 (1690s), Moreton and Church Houses at Nos. 10 and 14, and the stuccoed Literary Institute (1839). Cromwell House, at 104 Highgate Hill, is a rare survivor: a London house of the 1630s.

The High Street has more 18th-century houses at Nos. 17–21, 23, and 42, and several attractive Georgian storefronts.

Highgate Cemetery, next to Waterlow Park, is the burial place of numerous interesting people, and well worth a visit. Opened in 1839, it was so popular for its ornate catacombs and fine views that an extension was opened in 1857, with an under-road tunnel to take the biers to the graves. In the eastern part today, obelisks and other elaborate monuments are shaded by mature trees.

Memorials in the cemetery include those to writer George Eliot (under the name Mary Anne Cross), who died in 1880, philosopher Herbert Spencer (1903), and Karl Marx, who died in 1883. Tours to the western side may pass memorials for the Rossetti family, the Dickens family (the author himself is buried in Westminster Abbey), and Charles Cruft, founder of Cruft's Dog Show. The most ostentatious mausoleums, though, are the Terrace Catacombs, supposedly the inspiration for Bram Stoker's *Dracula*. This sacred ground is closed during funerals; children under eight years of age are not allowed. ■

A family-friendly area with everything: a palace, gardens, parks, markets, and museums galore

KENSINGTON &
SOUTH KENSINGTON

■ A marker for the Princess of Wales memorial walk, which wends though Hyde Park and Kensington Gardens.

KENSINGTON & SOUTH KENSINGTON

In 1689 the asthmatic and bronchitic William III left dank Whitehall Palace with his wife, Mary II, for the fresh air of Kensington village, then well outside London. Thus began a royal association with the area that continues, for members of the royal family still live in Kensington Palace. The State Apartments are open to the public.

William and Mary invited Sir Christopher Wren and Nicholas Hawksmoor to remodel their house as Kensington Palace. They also fenced off some of Hyde Park to create the nucleus of Kensington Gardens. The palace still lies at the heart of Kensington. This was a favorite official palace of the 18th-century Hanoverian rulers until George III moved to Buckingham Palace in 1762. The proximity of royalty attracted the rich and wellborn: Even today, Kensington contains many of London's most fashionable residential streets.

London's grandest and most ostentatious street, Kensington Palace Gardens, was laid out in 1843 as a gated, tree-lined avenue. Edged with palatial mansions, it was soon nicknamed "millionaires' row." Today it is mostly devoted to foreign missions. Less ostentatious Kensington survives beyond, in the area bordered by

NOT TO BE MISSED:

two great shopping streets: Kensington Church Street, which curls up the hill to Notting Hill Gate and so to Portobello Road as a continuous parade of antiques shops; and Kensington High Street, which rose to prominence for more practical shopping after the Underground was built in 1868. The large estate of Holland Park was parceled off to become grand Holland Park houses at one end and a leafy idyll for artists such as the 19th-century painter Lord Leighton at the other.

A monument to Prince Albert stands across the road from the Royal Albert Hall, completed in 1871. Royal colleges for art and music are nearby, together with the Royal Geographical Society, the Imperial College of Science and Technology, and the Goethe Institute. The area is also the home to three of London's great museums: the Victoria and Albert, Science, and Natural History. ■

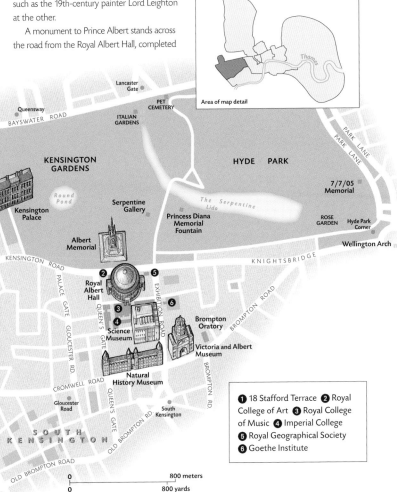

London

Area of map detail

1 18 Stafford Terrace 2 Royal College of Art 3 Royal College of Music 4 Imperial College 5 Royal Geographical Society 6 Goethe Institute

| 0 | 800 meters |
| 0 | 800 yards |

KENSINGTON PALACE

With its warm redbrick exterior and small, comfortable rooms, Kensington Palace instantly gives a feeling of informality that contrasts with the formal splendors of Hampton Court or Buckingham Palace. This family mood was created by William and Mary. In 1689 they bought their country mansion from Sir Heneage Finch, Duke of Nottingham. Sir Christopher Wren and Nicholas Hawksmoor made changes so the royal family could move in for Christmas.

■ Fronted by gardens, Kensington Palace displays its characteristic red brickwork.

Kensington Palace

- 🗺 Map p. 157
- ✉ Kensington Gardens, W8
- ☎ 020 3166 6000
- 💲 $$$
- 🚇 Tube: High Street Kensington

hrp.org.uk

The south and east facades, with their fine brickwork, are Wren's signature. The grounds feature statues of William III and Queen Victoria (by her daughter Louise) and a garden enclosed by pleached lime trees. On the right of the palace stands Hawksmoor's Orangery, built in 1704–1705 and now a café where customers can admire Grinling Gibbons's elaborate carved pine and pearwood festoons at either end. The back of the palace is home to some members of the royal family. After her separation from Prince Charles, Princess Diana lived here; and it was from Kensington Palace that her funeral procession left for Westminster Abbey. Diana's son, Prince William, along with Princess Kate and their growing

family, currently call the palace home. In 2012, Kensington Palace completed a major £12 million ($19 million) redesign that transformed the palace exterior as well as the visitor experience inside. The fences and trees that cordoned off the view from Kensington Gardens were removed, opening up the landscape and making the palace more accessible in look and feel.

Visiting the Palace

Past the ticket office, you'll find yourself in the central **Vestibule.** From here, it's decision time: You'll be able to follow any or all of the exhibition routes through the palace. (The first floor began hosting new exhibitions in May 2019).

The King's State Apartments: The public audience room, or Presence Chamber, marks the beginning of the high-ceilinged rooms designed by Colen Campbell for George I in 1718–1720. The rooms' gentle Palladian style is complemented by William Kent's ceiling decoration. The Privy Chamber's decor shows Mars and Minerva, symbolizing the king's military prowess and the queen's patronage of the arts and sciences. Wren and Kent together created the Cupola Room, where Victoria

INSIDER TIP:

Take afternoon tea at the Royal Garden Hotel's Park Terrace Lounge (just south of the palace, overlooking Kensington Gardens).

—JUSTIN KAVANAGH
*National Geographic
Travel Books editor*

was baptized in 1819, while the King's Drawing Room has yet another splendid Kent ceiling.

The King's Grand Staircase was designed by Wren, with ironwork by Jean Tijou. Kent's painting of the walls and ceiling is his most important decorative work: a Venetian-style view of a crowded gallery. Courtiers and visitors to Kensington Palace would have climbed this appropriately grand staircase to the King's Gallery, now rehung with George II's paintings as he had them.

The Queen's State Apartments:
Head up the original oak wooden staircase of William and Mary's renovated palace to reach the Queen's State Apartments, where selected art from the Queen's Royal Collection and period pieces fill the intimate suite of rooms. Her gallery has more Gibbons carvings on the overmantel mirror frames, while the Dining Room retains its original paneling. Mary's Drawing Room has a barometer made for the palace around 1695, while her Bedchamber

has original elm floorboards and a bed, complete with hangings, used by James II. All the rooms overlook Mary's garden.

Victoria Revealed: Queen Victoria's narrative tells the story of the queen's life in the very rooms in which she grew up. Quotations from her letters and diaries compliment and illuminate the jewelry, portraits, musical instruments, and dresses on show. Don't miss the young princess's oversize dollhouse and a display on the Great Exhibition of 1851 that highlights the important role that Victoria's husband, Prince Albert, had on her reign and the nation.

Modern Royals: This route leads you through temporary exhibitions that look at the lives and lifestyles of more recent royals. Since the 2012 renovation, the route has highlighted the royal fashion and wardrobe of the past few decades; an exhibition pays tribute to Princess Diana and her legacy. ■

Park Terrace Lounge, Royal Garden Hotel

✉ 2–24 Kensington High St., Kensington, W8

☎ 020 7937 8000

🕐 Open every day. Check the website for opening times

💲 $$$$$

Ⓜ Tube: High Street Kensington

royalgardenhotel.co.uk

Kensington Gardens

William and Mary's creation of a Dutch garden on the 26 acres (11 ha) they bought with Kensington Palace was the humble origin of the 275-acre (111 ha) Kensington Gardens. Queen Anne anglicized and enlarged those gardens and built the Orangery; she also laid out the promenade, Rotten Row. In 1728, George II's wife, Queen Caroline, and her gardener, Charles Bridgeman, fenced in more Hyde Park acres, dug the Round Pond, laid out the radiating avenues, and diverted a stream to make the Long Water. The gardens fully opened to the public in 1851.

A WALK THROUGH KENSINGTON GARDENS

A meander through Kensington Gardens is the prelude to a cornucopia of cultural feasts set in remarkable buildings.

Kensington Gardens (see sidebar p. 159), begun by William and Mary in the 17th century, were expanded by a succession of later rulers. From the Lancaster Gate Tube station, you enter the gardens at the **Italian Gardens,** added by Victoria and Albert in 1861. Follow the path beside the Long Water—perhaps spotting grebes and other waterfowl—to find George Frampton's 1912 statue of J. M. Barrie's fictional hero, **Peter Pan.** Through the trees to the right is George Frederick Watts's powerful 1904 bronze, "Physical Energy," and Queen Caroline's Round Pond. Back toward the Long Water, look for the Temple and the **Serpentine Gallery ❶** (tel 020 7402 6075, www. serpentinegallery.org), displaying contemporary art. Nearby, the **Princess Diana Memorial Fountain** was designed by American architect Kathryn Gustafson.

The **Flower Walk** leads to Sir George Gilbert Scott's **Albert Memorial ❷** (tel 020 7495 0916, guided tours), created between 1864 and 1876. John Foley's statue has the seated prince holding the catalog of his Great Exhibition and looking down his lasting legacy, the South Kensington cultural compound that dominates the hillside.

Kensington Cultural Institutions

This honeypot of institutions begins with the **Royal Albert Hall ❸** (Kensington Gore, SW7, tel 020 7589 8212, royalalberthall.com) in front of the memorial. Inspired by Roman amphitheaters, the great oval hall is encircled with a fine frieze made by the Ladies' Mosaic Class of the Victoria and Albert Museum. The frieze depicts the Triumph of Arts and Letters. Inside (guided tours are available via Door 12), the iron-and-glass dome is an engineering triumph. The Henry Wood

Promenade Concerts (bbc.co.uk/proms), an annual seven-week-long summer festival of nightly concerts known as the Proms, were transferred here in 1941, after being bombed out of Queen's Hall.

A cluster of small institutions surrounds the hall. Upon leaving it, turn left (west) to find the temporary exhibitions and art fairs of the **Royal College of Art** (Kensington Gore, SW7, 020 7590 4444, rca.ac.uk), founded in 1837, in H. T. Cadbury-Brown and Sir Hugh Casson's building (1962–1973). Go behind the Royal Albert Hall and down the Queen's Steps to Prince Consort Road. Ahead of you is the **Royal College of Music ❹** (tel 020 7591 4300, rcm.ac.uk), founded in 1882, whose instrument collection includes Haydn's clavichord. Students perform in Sir Hugh Casson's Britten Opera Theatre.

Walk east to the end of Prince Consort Road to find Exhibition Road. The energetic can divert uphill to the **Royal Geographical Society ❺** (1 Kensington Gore, SW7, tel 020 7591 3000, www.rgs.org, closed Sun.), founded in 1830 in Norman Shaw's Lowther Lodge (1873–1875), and the **Polish Institute** (20 Princes Gate, SW7, tel 020 7589 9249, pism .co.uk) and its Sikorski Museum. This is the major Polish museum outside Poland because, after the German invasion in 1939, the government-in-exile came to London.

The route downhill passes the **Goethe Institute ❻** (50 Prince's Gate, Exhibition Rd., SW7, tel 020 7596 4000, goethe.de/ins/gb/lon,

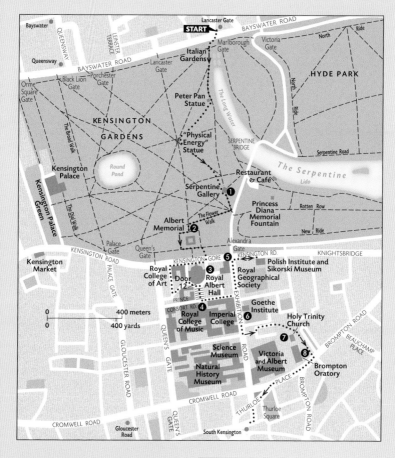

Map showing:

Bayswater, QUEENSWAY, LEINSTER TERRACE, Queensway, BAYSWATER ROAD, Black Lion Gate, Porchester Gate, Lancaster Gate, Orme Square Gate, START, Lancaster Gate, Marlborough Gate, Victoria Gate, BAYSWATER ROAD, North, Ride, Italian Gardens, HYDE PARK, The Long Water, North, Ride, The Broad Walk, KENSINGTON GARDENS, Peter Pan Statue, "Physical Energy" Statue, SERPENTINE BRIDGE, Serpentine Road, The Dial Walk, Round Pond, Kensington Palace, Kensington Palace Green, Restaurant & Café, Serpentine Gallery ❶, The Serpentine, Lido, The Flower Walk, Serpentine Road, Rotten Row, Princess Diana Memorial Fountain, Albert Memorial ❷, New Ride, Palace Gate, Queen's Gate, KENSINGTON ROAD, Alexandra Gate, KENSINGTON GORE, KENSINGTON RD., KNIGHTSBRIDGE, Kensington Market, PALACE GATE, Royal College of Art, Door 12, Royal Albert Hall ❸, ❺, Royal Geographical Society, Polish Institute and Sikorski Museum, PRINCE CONSORT RD., Royal College of Music ❹, Imperial College, EXHIBITION ROAD, Goethe Institute ❻, Holy Trinity Church ❼, BROMPTON ROAD, BEAUCHAMP PLACE, QUEEN'S GATE, GLOUCESTER ROAD, Science Museum, Natural History Museum, Victoria and Albert Museum, Brompton Oratory ❽, CROMWELL ROAD, THURLOE PLACE, BROMPTON ROAD, Thurloe Square, Gloucester Road, QUEEN'S GATE, South Kensington

0 400 meters
0 400 yards

opening times vary) on the left and expansive **Imperial College.** The **Science Museum** (see pp. 172–173) and the back entrance of the **Victoria and Albert Museum** (V&A; see pp. 169–171) are beyond. Turn left into Prince's Gate Mews; keep to the left, down past the mews cottages, and turn right into **Holy Trinity's garden ❼.** Go around the church and up the drive, then turn right to find the Oratory of St. Philip Neri. Known as the **Brompton Oratory ❽** (*Brompton Rd., SW7, tel 020 7808 0900, bromptonoratory.co.uk*), this branch of the oratory founded in Rome in 1575 was established by Father Faber in 1849.

Inside front cover A3
Lancaster Gate Tube station
2 hours
2.5 miles (4 km)
South Kensington Tube station

Inside the baroque church, Giuseppe Mazzuoli's exceptional "Twelve Apostles" from Siena Cathedral surround the huge nave.

Turn right out of the church along Brompton Road, past the V&A, then cross the road into Thurloe Place and Thurloe Square, built in the 1840s. The South Kensington Tube station is a couple of minutes away.

HYDE PARK

Stretching east of Kensington Gardens, Hyde Park is 350 acres (140 ha) of green and mostly open space, making it the perfect venue for lazy walks, jogs, pickup soccer games, concerts, and the occasional mass demonstration. Originally a hunting ground for Henry VIII, the park was first opened to the public in the early 17th century and contains a number of interesting sites.

■ Hyde Park contains a popular cycling route.

Hyde Park
🅰 Map p. 157

A clockwise circuit around the park takes in several highlights. Just off Bayswater Road, an old **Pet Cemetery** lies behind Victoria Gate Lodge. The cemetery began in the 1880s when a local dog met his end and was buried in the garden of the kindly gatekeeper. Eventually, more than 300 pets were buried here. The cemetery is closed to the public, so you'll have to content yourself with pictures of the tiny headstones taken through the bars.

Speakers' Corner stands at the northeast corner of Hyde Park. Busiest on Sunday mornings, this famous platform of free speech is a meeting point for anyone who wants to stand on a soapbox and speak his or her piece. The free speech goes both ways; sometimes the speakers end up in hearty debates with disagreeing crowd members.

Near the park, by the Speakers' Corner, is **Marble Arch,** an 1827 ceremonial arch designed by John Nash to honor British victories in the Napoleonic Wars. Originally situated on the Mall as an entrance to Buckingham Palace, it was moved to its present location in 1851. A few hundred yards down the east side of the park brings you to the simple and moving **7/7/05 Memorial** *(royal parks.org.uk),* commemorating the 52 lives lost in the London terrorist attacks of July 7, 2005.

Slightly farther south, near Hyde Park Corner, stands the impressive 18-foot-high (5.5 m) metal **statue of Achilles** atop the 1822 Wellington Monument that memorializes the great duke's campaigns against Napoleon.

Head west from Hyde Park Corner to reach a lovely **rose garden.** From here, continue west to the **Serpentine,** the large lake that bisects the park. Both rowboats and paddleboats are available for rent *(May–Sep., $ or more),* while sunbathers and swimmers should head to the small **lido** (waterfront) on the southern edge of the lake. Nearby is the popular **Princess Diana Memorial Fountain** (see p. 160) honoring the late Princess of Wales. ■

HOLLAND PARK & LEIGHTON HOUSE

Holland Park is, confusingly, the name for both the park surrounding Holland House and the two roads at the park's northwest corner, as well as for the whole area stretching from Kensington High Street to Holland Park Avenue.

First, the house: Holland House, now ruined, was built in 1606–1607 by Sir Walter Cope, minister to James I. It is the only Jacobean manor built to an E-shaped plan in London, and enough remains to enable us to imagine the grand life enjoyed by its owners. One was Henry Fox, created Baron Holland, who, using public funds for private speculation while paymaster-general in the government, bought it in 1768. The house became a center of Whig politics and literature, where Palmerston, Macaulay, Wordsworth, and Dickens made it a more significant court than the royal one. The picturesque ruins are now a backdrop for works of art. The **Orangery Gallery** holds periodic art exhibitions and has lovely terraced gardens.

The 54 green acres (22 ha) of Holland Park, opened to the public in 1950, begin with these terraces, shaded by magnificent horse chestnut trees. Modern additions include the Japanese **Kyoto Garden,** created in 1991, where resident peacocks strut their stuff. Cricket lawns to the south contrast with the wooded walks to the north. The rich woodland, with mature rhododendrons and azaleas, rose walks, and spring daffodils gives an idea of what first lured the nobility to Kensington.

All this is part of today's district of Holland Park. At the south end, a leafy residential enclave became home to wealthy artists and architects at the end of the 19th century, producing a crop of exotic houses. The most remarkable home in Holland Park is Frederick Lord Leighton's, designed by his friend George Aitchison in 1864–1866. It is London's first full expression of the aesthetic movement. The interior of **Leighton House** is a bachelor's indulgence typified by the lack of guest rooms. Red walls, ebonized wood, and gilt decorate the main rooms downstairs. Richly glazed tiles line the beautiful Arab Hall and staircase. ∎

18 Stafford Terrace

Behind its stuccoed, classical, Italianate facade in Kensington's Stafford Terrace, a perfect cameo of Edwardian London is lovingly preserved by the Victorian Society. The political cartoonist Linley Sambourne, born in 1844, moved into his newly built house in 1874, and by his death in 1910 he had filled it to capacity. Rooms are hung with Sambourne's own cartoons for *Punch* magazine. Decorative china lines the shelves and early photographs fill the bathroom walls. Do not miss Sambourne's illustrations to Charles Kingsley's famed novel, *The Water-Babies,* in the bedroom upstairs.

Leighton House
- Map p. 156
- 12 Holland Park Rd., W14
- 020 7602 3316
- Closed Tues.
- $
- Tube: High Street Kensington, Holland Park

rbkc.gov.uk

18 Stafford Terrace
- Map p. 156
- 118, Stafford Terrace, Kensington, W8
- 020 7602 3316
- Open Wed. & Sat.–Sun.
- $
- Tube: High Street Kensington

rbkc.gov.uk

LONDON'S MARKETS

London has more than 340 markets of all sizes and themes, from Sunday's huge Petticoat Lane to Berwick Street's weekday produce market in Soho.

Portobello Road market offers clothing, antiques, food, and more.

Food

All the big wholesale markets need to be visited early. Smithfield Meat Market (see p. 66), the last wholesale fresh market remaining in central London, sells its bloody carcasses in the early weekday hours. Billingsgate fish market left the City and is now at West India Dock on the Isle of Dogs, and New Covent Garden Market trades in fruit, flowers, and vegetables over the river on Nine Elms Lane in Vauxhall.

A destination recommended by many Londoners is the amazing array of food stalls at Borough Market (*boroughmarket.org.uk*), south of the Thames in the shadow of Southwark Cathedral. Hundreds of vendors sell (and offer free samples of) fruit, cheese, spices, vegetables, olives, sausages, fresh meat (including some exotic varieties such as boar, venison, and grouse), as well as prepared international foods for noshing such as Middle Eastern falafel, German wurst, and Greek fried halloumi cheese.

The market is open everyday, except Sunday (Limited Market, Mon.–Tues. 10 a.m.–5 p.m.; Full Market, Tues.–Thur. 10 a.m.–5 p.m., Fri. 10 a.m.–6 p.m., & Sat. 8 a.m.–5 p.m.). It is busiest on Saturdays; smart money arrives early to beat some of the crowds.

Clothes, Antiques, & Crafts

Other big markets specialize in clothing and antiques, such as Portobello Road on Saturdays (see p. 167). Camden Lock Market, by the canal, thrives on the weekends (be prepared to mingle with 150,000 other shoppers), but its hundreds of stalls selling gifts, jewelry, books, food, and crafts are open all week. Several other markets branch out on Camden's side streets; Camden Stables Market, for one, has more than 700 stalls selling vintage and alternative fashions. The souvenir, clothes, and antique markets that now fill Covent Garden's buildings daily make up one of London's newest markets, established in the 1970s. The weekend market at Greenwich, which has echoes of the great market that was closed down last century, is down by the Thames off of King William Walk and has an almost seaside feel to it. The whole atmosphere is fresh and lively, and stalls stocking clothes, antiques, books, and prints are complemented by the craft market in Bosun's Yard.

The best known large East London Sunday market is Petticoat Lane, where hundreds of stalls fill Middlesex and Wentworth Streets and the surrounding lanes to sell clothing of all kinds and London's best East End street salesmen-entertainers run through their patter to gullible crowds. Spitalfields Market, a short walk away, survives in its old building. Brick Lane, east across Commercial Street, teems with vendors and perfumes of Bengali and Indian food.

Local Markets

Dotted across London, little local markets vary their stock to suit their customers' tastes and traditions. Berwick Street's weekday market just north of Shaftesbury Avenue in Soho dates back to the 1840s when the area was an Italian and French quarter, and its quality vegetables, herbs, and flowers balance the supplies sold in nearby Italian food shops. Chapel Market in Islington has been lively for a century, serving the local population with no-nonsense food and basic household goods. Ridley Road market at Dalston is quite different: It has been thriving since the 1880s, but its injection of postwar Afro-Caribbean, Asian, and Turkish immigrants means such delicacies as live catfish are now on sale. Brixton Market is best for pure West Indian goods. Here, in the lanes around Brixton Underground station, you can find reggae and soul music shops, fish such as goat fish, smoked angera, and blue runner, Nasseri African fabrics, and calves' hooves.

Specialist Markets

For antiques, Camden Passage in Islington offers the traveler a fine array of shops and stalls, with plenty of good restaurants nearby. Portobello has a similar mix. Bermondsey Market, held in Bermondsey Square on Fridays, has the largest and best value stalls, but means a 5 a.m. to 6 a.m. start for bargains, which are inspected by flashlight. Prices vary, and only the most knowledgeable will be able to compete with the dealers and the clients, who would be as at home bidding in Sotheby's auction rooms. Safer to pick up a painting along Bayswater Road on Sunday, or a coin at the Collector's Fair on Villiers Street on Saturday. And there are markets in the courtyards of St. James's Piccadilly on Friday and Saturday, or St. Martin-in-the-Fields any day except Sunday.

EXPERIENCE: Learn to Cook Seafood

Poach, grill, and pan-fry your way to culinary excellence under the guidance of expert fishmongers and chefs at the **Billingsgate Seafood School** at Billingsgate Fish Market *(Trafalgar Way, E14, tel 020 7517 3548, seafoodtraining.org, $$$$).* The school, located amid the largest selection of seafood in the United Kingdom, teaches students how to select and prepare everything from trout to cuttlefish. Courses range from full-day affairs to two-hour evening classes and may also include a market tour, preparation of several types of seafood, and at least one meal. Students often leave with extra food, so if your accommodations don't include a kitchen, opt for the shorter classes.

NOTTING HILL &
PORTOBELLO ROAD

While Holland Park lured high society, the area to its north was developed with slightly lower aspirations to attract London's affluent Victorians. Farms and piggeries were soon mere memory as pretty villas and terraces spread north. Today, Notting Hill is best known for its Portobello Road antiques market and the annual Caribbean carnival.

The Travel Bookshop in Notting Hill was featured in the 1999 movie *Notting Hill.*

**Notting Hill &
Portobello Road**

Map p. 156

At the bottom of Notting Hill, Norlands Farm was transformed into the pretty, small-scale Norland Estate during the 1840s and '50s. Farther up, developer James Weller Ladbroke bought Notting Hill Farm, planning to create a utopian garden city of large villas with their own private gardens, which in turn opened onto communal gardens. When the estate was finished in 1870 it was London's most spacious, and its architecture was of unusually high quality. Handsome Lansdowne Road and Crescent, Stanley Crescent, and Ladbroke Square illustrate the achievement.

Portobello Road

Portobello Road slips northward down the side of, and in contrast to, the grandeur of Ladbroke Grove. It was once the farm track leading down to Porto Bello Farm. By the 1870s Gypsies were trading horses and herbs here and in the

Notting Hill Carnival

Every August Bank Holiday weekend, the streets of Notting Hill are one continuous Caribbean party. The Caribbean community grew here after World War II, when citizens of all newly independent British Empire countries were given British citizenship. The immigrants replaced Londoners who had left for a suburban life. They held the first African-Caribbean street festival in the 1960s, evoking the Trinidad Carnival that envelops the island for two days before Ash Wednesday. Today, it is Europe's largest street festival, drawing a million people and filling the areas between Chepstow Road and Ladbroke Grove. The action consists of music and the Children's Day parades on Saturday and Sunday, building up to Monday, when dozens of bands play reggae, soul, hip-hop, Latin jazz, funk, and calypso in Powis Square, or tour the streets playing in open-back trucks. Trinidadian influence is in the steel bands— whose use of steel oil pans evolved in response to the colonial ban on playing drums—and the costume parades. These parades are spectacular, up to 200 people in each, all in fantastic costumes following themes such as African warriors, butterflies, and flowers; central characters may have more colorful, elaborate costumes. The best music and costumes win cash prizes. (See *thenottinghillcarnival.com* for details.)

INSIDER TIP:

If you visit Portobello Road on a busy Saturday and want to find genuine bargains, go at 6 a.m., when the dealers are buying from each other.

—TIM JEPSON
National Geographic author

1890s Saturday-night markets were established. The antique dealers that now make the street famous began to arrive in 1948, when Caledonian Market near King's Cross closed.

Today, the **Portobello Road market** (*portobelloroad.co.uk*) is one of Britain's longest markets and, when augmented by its Saturday stallholders, provides a daylong party of guaranteed fascination, noise, and color—and possibly a bargain or two.

At the end of Notting Hill, the established antique shops and stalls between Chepstow Villas and Lonsdale Road have quality, often rare, collector's items. The sharp-eyed and informed may have a chance for some bargains. Good food shops between Lonsdale and Lancaster Roads can restore strength.

Beyond the Westway overpass, the imaginative hunter may find secondhand clothes and bric-a-brac to give individual character to an outfit or a room. Golborne Road has a fruit and vegetable market, and the shops between Aklam Road and Oxford Gardens sell the latest street fashion, worn by stylish Londoners sitting in the neighborhood bars. Beyond that, find vendors with secondhand bicycles, new clothes, and household goods. ∎

PRINCE ALBERT'S DREAM

South Kensington is the living legacy of one man, Prince Albert of Saxe-Coburg-Gotha. From the day of his marriage to Queen Victoria in 1840, he was her closest adviser and worked ceaselessly for his adopted country.

■ **Prince Albert, Queen Victoria's consort, has a gilded memorial in Kensington Gardens.**

Albert's crowning achievement was the Great Exhibition of the World of Industry of All Nations, held in Hyde Park in 1851. It was a celebration of Victorian dynamism. Sir Joseph Paxton, once gardener to the Duke of Devonshire, designed a great cast-iron-and-glass building, nicknamed the Crystal Palace. In it, 100,000 exhibits were shown by 13,937 exhibitors, half of whom were from Britain and its empire. Conceived as a platform for and celebration of industrial enterprise worldwide, the exhibition ran from May to October and was visited by six million people, a third of Britain's population.

The exhibition's success, and its substantial profits, inspired Albert to an even more ambitious dream: a cultural campus that would provide free learning for all people. The plan was to have an avenue of colleges for the arts and sciences leading to a huge national gallery, with museums and learned societies, concert halls, and a garden beyond.

Albert's devotion to his project, soon known as "Albertopolis," was unstinting. Tragically, he died of typhoid in 1861. While the queen withdrew into seclusion, Prime Minister Benjamin Disraeli told a stunned public: "This German Prince has governed England for twenty-one years with a wisdom and energy such as none of our Kings have ever shown."

Nothing stopped Albert's dream, the biggest development for public use that London had yet seen. When the National Gallery refused to move, the Royal Albert Hall took its place in the scheme, and music and art colleges surrounded it. The Victoria and Albert

INSIDER TIP:

The Albert Memorial is stunning at night, when its bronze statue and marble figures seem to glow against the sky.

—LARRY PORGES
National Geographic Travel Books editor

Museum, which Albert hoped would be of practical help to students, grew so fast that its art college became the separate Royal College of Art, and its science collections became the Science Museum. Meanwhile, the British Museum's natural history departments overflowed and were given space; the Geological Museum arrived from St. James's in 1935 and was later absorbed by the Natural History Museum.

VICTORIA AND ALBERT MUSEUM (V&A)

The world's largest museum of decorative arts and design is encyclopedic. In fact, it is several museums in one. Primarily the national museum of art and design, it also includes the national collections of sculpture, watercolors, portrait miniatures, art photography, wallpaper, and posters, as well as the National Art Library. It has the best set of Italian sculpture outside Italy and the finest Indian decorative arts collection in the world.

The V&A began as a collection of plaster casts, engravings, and a few objects from the Great Exhibition. It was Prince Albert who, with art patron Henry Cole, conceived the idea of a museum of objects "representing the application of Fine Art to manufacture," to inspire British people. Cole, the first director, wanted a museum about design and craft in a commercial context, not craft for craft's sake. This is still the museum's philosophy today.

The humble museum with big ideas was first housed in wooden sheds, then in an engineer's iron-and-glass building known as the Brompton Boilers. It grew fast. While the keeper amassed quality objects for his students, gifts began to arrive: Sheepshanks's British paintings, the Bandinel Collection of pottery and porcelain, the Gherardini Collection of models for sculpture, and many more. Rooms were built piecemeal to form the central quadrangle and the eastern courts, and Sir Aston Webb's slab of galleries was added to the front in 1899–1909. Whole departments later left to find space as V&A outposts or as independent museums, such as the Science

Museum (see pp. 172–173) and V&A Museum of Childhood in Bethnal Green (see p. 211).

The best of past and contemporary design was bought by, or given to, the museum. Some pieces are tiny, such as the Canning Jewel; others are vast—the Raphael Cartoons (magnificent 16th-century designs for tapestries for the Vatican's Sistine Chapel),

EXPERIENCE:
Explore the V&A's Learning Programs

If the holdings in the V&A's extensive collection leave you wanting to know more, you can immerse yourself in the world of British design through the museum's wide variety of special programs, classes, and lectures. The eclectic series includes designers, writers, photographers, and other artists discussing their work; live presentations of music, poetry, and fashion; practical workshops on everything from embroidering souvenir napkins to the art of creating digital portraits with your tablet; and seminars on important people and movements in the history of design, style, and art that range in length from an afternoon to a full year.

Some programs are free, but many have a fee *($–$$$$)*. Check out *vam.ac.uk* for complete information.

The Future at the V&A

The V&A is in the midst of an extensive renovation program to provide new exhibition spaces and facilities for visitors as well as to restore original architectural elements to historic galleries. Funded almost completely by private donations, Future-Plan work has so far raised £166 million ($267 million) and seen more than 45 capital projects realized.

Projects completed include the lovely John Madejski Garden at the rear of Level One, as well as a new museum café behind it; the renovated Cast Courts (containing plaster copies of monumental sculptures);

the V&A's collection of more than 3,000 gems in the jewelry collection (Rooms 91–93); the new exhibition space for 14th- to 16th-century European stained glass and sculpture in Rooms 16a and 25–27; a furniture gallery, featuring British and international pieces from the 15th century onward; a new center for textiles and fashions; and the Photography Centre (to be expanded in 2020). In 2017, the "V&A Exhibition Road Quarter" project was completed and the museum entrance is now facing Exhibition Road. The new Sainsbury Gallery was also added.

Victoria and Albert Museum

🅐 Map p. 157

✉ Cromwell Rd., SW7

☎ 020 7942 2000

🕐 Check website for schedule during construction

💲 Charge for some exhibitions

🚇 Tube: South Kensington

vam.ac.uk

for instance—and whole rooms, including the Duke of Norfolk's Music Room. Today, most of the 2,000 or so annual acquisitions for the design, prints, and drawings departments are contemporary, and the museum regularly commissions silver, furniture, and other pieces. In addition, galleries are constantly being added; recent ones include ceramics, glass, photography, fashion, and furniture.

Just some of the museum's 4.5 million objects are exhibited in more than 170 galleries arranged on seven levels around four courts and organized by five main themes: Europe, Asia, Materials and Techniques, Modern, and Exhibition. Look out also for temporary exhibits that complement the permanent galleries.

Basically, there are two types of rooms: art and design galleries, such as the recently opened Europe 1600–1800, where objects of a type are exhibited in their cultural context; and materials and techniques galleries, such as

silver, jewelry, and ceramics., where objects of one material or type are displayed to show their form, function, and technique.

For those who know what they want to see, a combination of the map, the list of galleries, and a sense of direction will be enough—though the museum also offers free daily guided gallery tours. For those who feel overwhelmed before they start, here are some interesting stops on an easy route (with room numbers indicated, as marked on the museum maps available at the information desk).

The Trail

The museum is undergoing a multiyear refurbishment (see sidebar above), so temporary closures may affect this trail.

From the entrance hall, turn right and go through Rooms 50a and 50b, part of the museum's impressive **Medieval and Renaissance** collection. Then turn left from Room 50b (through the Korean gallery), into Rooms 46 and 46b, crowded with Victorian plaster cast reproduction, where the casts of Trajan's Column and Michelangelo's "David" have inspired generations of students.

Backtrack through Chinese art in Rooms 47e and 47f and turn right into another extensive **gallery of Chinese art** in Room 44. Adjoining is the **Japanese gallery** in Room 45. The V&A's collection of Japanese art and design is one of the largest in Britain.

Down the steps at the end of the Japanese gallery, turn left for the Hintze sculpture collection in Rooms 24–21a before turning left again to Room 41, the **Nehru Gallery of Indian Art,** where a tiny fraction of the Indian collection is on show, usually including some exquisite miniature paintings and some fine textiles. Go through the gallery to corridor rooms 47a and 47b, filled with Southeast Asian objects; these lead to the extensive **hall of fashion,** Room 40, a feast of European costumes from the permanent collection as well as temporary exhibits from the 16th century to today.

Bypass the temporary closed areas and cross the corridor to see the medieval European religious sculptures to the right (east) of the John Madejski Garden.

Upstairs: Three more stops complete this introduction. The first is a wander through the stunning, renovated **British Galleries** upstairs, feasting your eyes on a jewel Francis Drake gave Elizabeth I, Huguenot silver, the Great Bed of Ware, King James II's wedding suit, and

whole rooms saved from Jacobean and Georgian houses. The second is to find the dazzling national collection of English and international silver on the third floor. The third is the new **Photography Centre** (Rooms 99–101), home to a collection that traces back the history of photography from the 19th century to the present, with works by famous authors, instruments, and early experiments. ∎

▪ Two Victorian rooms in the V&A display plaster casts of famous sculptures, such as Michelangelo's "David."

SCIENCE MUSEUM

Even the most unscientific person will be excited by the Science Museum, where learning often demands more active participation than merely reading labels. In 1909 this museum became fully independent of the V&A, and in 1928 completed its move into Richard Allison's new building. His department-store format, with big windows and large, simple spaces, has been ideal. As the collection has grown, there is flexibility to display the full thrill of scientific discoveries through the ages, and it is easy to find one's way around.

The Science Museum presents the world in a surprising and captivating way.

Science Museum

- Map p. 157
- Exhibition Rd., SW7
- 0333 241 4000 or 020 7942 4000
- Charge for special sections
- Tube: South Kensington

sciencemuseum .org.uk

Today, some of the more than 300,000 items are displayed in 70 galleries on 5 floors, telling compelling stories of inventions and discoveries that have affected our lives, from the plastic bag and the telephone to the offshore oil rig and the airplane. And yet the arrangement is straightforward: Lower galleries are geared to young people and are often more crowded; upper ones are dedicated to a more sophisticated level of interest. This trail explores every floor, seeking out one or two highlights on each.

The Trail

At the main entrance, there is information on the day's events and demonstrations. Here, too, is the Dana Centre schedule for debate on scientific issues.

The ground floor's **Energy Hall** includes James Watt's steam engines and models of early locomotives. **Exploring Space** provides a history of rockets from tenth-century China until today. **Making the Modern World**—a family favorite—explains landmark modern inventions from the Ford Model T to the brain scanner and the Apollo 10 command capsule. **The Secret Life of the Home** exhibition in the basement presents a surprisingly fascinating look at the history of home appliances.

Now go to the **Wellcome Wing,** where state-of-the-art galleries include the **IMAX 3-D cinema** and **Pattern Pod,** an educational play area for children under eight, to develop their scientific abilities in a captivating, multisensory area.

Upstairs: On the first floor, agriculture, meteorology, time measurement, and the cosmos are tackled at the back.

Challenge of Materials explores the world of materials using installations and audiovisual displays. At the other end of the floor, in the Wellcome Wing, the **Who Am I?** exhibition challenges young visitors to think about their own personalities, use of language, and the other workings of their brains through artwork, quizzes, and interactive displays.

Up on the second floor, **Information Age** explores the six networks (e.g., the electric telegraph, the telephone exchange, mobile communications, etc.), that led to today's uber-interconnected world. Among the 800 artifacts on display is the original Marconi transmitter that launched the radio age in 1922.

The new **Mathematics Gallery** is also located on the second floor (see sidebar above). New exhibitions on this floor include: **Atmosphere,** an interactive

---

The Science Museum's "Masterplan"

The Science Museum has undergone a massive redevelopment, completed in 2019, that has transformed nearly two thirds of the museum space.

Highlights of the "Masterplan" renovation include several new permanent exhibits: the Mathematics Gallery, illustrating the history of math and its integral role influencing human progress; the impressive Interactive Gallery, which utilizes hands-on exhibits to engage minds young and old in the principles of science and math; and, finally, the new Medical Gallery, incorporating artifacts and exhibits from the museum's impressive medical collection, which will soon be opened to visitors.

---

journey through climate change; and **The Clockmakers' Museum,** that explores the evolution of clocks from the 1600s to the present day.

Steps lead up to the third floor. This is all about taking to the air: **Flight** has hands-on exhibits for testing the principles of flight, while a hangar full of aircraft includes Amy Johnson's *Jason,* in which she flew to Australia in 1930. A walk down the hallway leads to the museum's flight simulators, basically motion rides, for which a fee is charged.

The other end of this floor includes **Wonderlab,** an exciting interactive gallery about the wonders of science, and the **Engineer Your Future** gallery, which tests problem-solving and engineering thinking skills.

Roaming the exhibit are live "Explainers" to answer visitors' questions. ∎

NATURAL HISTORY MUSEUM

Both the collection—consisting of 80 million specimens, including one million books and manuscripts—and the magnificent building could be daunting. But this museum has made its exhibits and knowledge highly accessible and exciting for the general public without sacrificing the prime job of informing and educating. The famous dinosaur exhibition explains what we can learn from these ancient bones about the evolution of modern animals.

■ Visitors to the Natural History Museum's Hintze Hall swirl around the reproduction of a *Diplodocus* skeleton.

The Building

The building is as remarkable as its contents. When in 1881 the natural history collection of the British Museum (see pp. 134–138), including pieces from Sir Hans Sloane's collection, came to the burgeoning South Kensington cultural campus, it needed a suitable home. This was realized in the cathedral-like proportions of Alfred Waterhouse's Romanesque building, whose towers, spires, arches, and columns look to the churches of the Rhineland. The iron-and-steel framework is covered with cream, blue, and honey-colored terracotta, which introduced color into dirty Victorian London.

The Layout

The museum has recently been reorganized into four distinct color-coded zones.

The **Green Zone** includes the impressive main central Hintze Hall, accessed from the Cromwell Road entrance, dominated by the 85-foot-long (26 m) replica skeleton of a *Diplodocus*. Spreading east from Hintze Hall, the rest of the Green Zone highlights fossils, minerals, primates, ecology, insects, and birds, including a model of the extinct Dodo, and the place of humans in evolution.

At the end of the 20th century, the Natural History Museum formally amalgamated with the Geological Museum next door. The geological collection, now called the **Red Zone,** tells the story of the Earth itself and the natural forces that shape it, from a delicate 330-million-year-old fern fossil to the reenactment of an earthquake in Japan in 1995. The Red Zone connects to the eastern end of the Green Zone and can also be entered directly from Exhibition Road.

West of Hintze Hall lies the **Blue Zone,** which gets a lot of foot traffic from its galleries featuring dinosaurs; fishes, amphibians, and reptiles; marine invertebrates; and mammals, including a 75-year-old model of a massive blue whale, which at the time was one of the mystery creatures of the deep.

Head west from the Blue Zone to reach the **Orange Zone** and its **Darwin Centre,** which opened in 2002 and houses the museum's research facilities and specimen collection. The best way to see the Darwin Centre's zoological specimens (in the delightfully Victorian-named Zoology Spirit Building, after the industrial alcohol used to preserve the creatures) is to sign up for a guided tour. Lasting about 30 minutes, visitors get a closer look at some of the museum's vast store of animal specimens, including some kept in tanks, see the laboratories, and talk to scientists.

In 2009, the center expanded and the **Cocoon** opened; here you can take a self-guided tour of some of the 30 million insect and plant specimens in the museum's extensive collection.

The Trail

In recent years there have been, or are planned, interventions in the layout of the galleries, so be sure to pick up the free museum map when you arrive.

Start in the vast **Hintze Hall,** where Waterhouse's painted ceiling and zoo of terra-cotta animals, birds, flowers, and reptiles running up the columns and hiding in the arches is the setting for the famous *Diplodocus* skeleton.

INSIDER TIP:

Check out the exhibits on the balconies around Hintze Hall. You'll find specimens from diamonds to a slice of a Sequoia tree.

—TOM O'NEILL
*National Geographic
magazine writer*

Turn left, westward, and follow **Dinosaur Way** to the dinosaurs in the Blue Zone. Here are bones from creatures that roamed the Earth for 160 million years until their extinction 65 million years ago. They come in all varieties, and from these skeletons we can understand their lives—whether they lived alone, fought by charging like a ram, or hunted in packs.

Across Dinosaur Way, the **Human Biology** gallery takes a closer look at a recent development, human beings. Models

Natural History Museum

🗺 Map p. 157

✉ Cromwell Rd., SW7

☎ 020 7942 5000

🕐 10 a.m.–5:50 p.m.; closed Dec. 24–26

💲 Charge for some exhibitions

🚇 Tube: South Kensington

nhm.ac.uk

show how the memory works and the development of a baby from a single cell; optical illusions explain the relation between sight and knowledge.

Now cross Hintze Hall to **Fossil Way,** which is lined on either side with fossils of marine reptiles, from tiny ammonites found in Jurassic rocks in Dorset to sea dragons. To the left is a kid-popular gallery devoted to **Creepy Crawlies:** insects, spiders, crustaceans, and centipedes, whose highly adaptable nature, sophisticated social systems, and defense mechanisms have helped them survive the eons.

INSIDER TIP:

Be sure to attend a free Nature Live talk in the Attenborough Studio, where you'll get to meet the scientists.

—PETER GWIN
National Geographic magazine writer

The **Birds** gallery seems untouched by time, with several specimens (and specimen cases) dating back to the 1880s.

Return to Hintze Hall. From here, stairs lead up to the first floor, where the **Treasures** gallery (Cadogan Gallery) hosts 22 of the most significant and valuable items selected from the museum's collection, ranging from a rare first edition of Darwin's *On the Origin of Species* to the first dinosaur tooth ever found.

Nearby are galleries devoted to minerals, meteorites, and plants around the world. This area offers great views down onto Hintze Hall and its decoration.

Earth Hall, in the Red Zone, is the big introduction to the Earth galleries, focusing on the planet itself. Displays of specimens line the gallery, including a piece of the moon and another of soft graphite, which is chemically identical to hard diamonds. The most intact fossilized Stegosaurus skeleton ever found, 10 feet (3 m) tall and almost 20 feet (6 m) long, will welcome you here.

Then take the escalator on a journey through a vast iron, zinc, and copper globe. Upstairs, **Volcanoes and Earthquakes** chronicles the restless surface of the Earth. You'll hear the very affecting stories of what it's like to survive one of the world's most destructive earthquakes, such as the San Francisco earthquake of 1906 or, more recently, the 2004 Indian Ocean tsunami. You'll also delve deep into the scientific foundations of a volcano as you look inside Mount Vesuvius, Italy—which famously destroyed the Roman cities of Pompeii and Herculaneum—and Mount Tambora in Indonesia, which caused one of the most powerful eruptions in history. A free earthquake simulator brings these awesome experiences to life.

On the ground floor, the **Human Evolution** gallery leads visitors on a journey of seven million years, from the first hominids to the last surviving human species. ∎

Four London neighborhoods and two favorite institutions: Harrods in Knightsbridge and Tate Britain in Pimlico

CHELSEA, BELGRAVIA, & KNIGHTSBRIDGE

A statue of a Chelsea Pensioner in his red uniform sits outside the Royal Hospital Chelsea.

CHELSEA, BELGRAVIA, & KNIGHTSBRIDGE

It was when the trendsetting Prince Regent became George IV in 1820 and began to remodel Buckingham Palace that developers recognized the promise of this area. Open fields and marshy but drainable land lay right next to the Palace. Soon bargeloads of building materials were being unloaded along this stretch of the Thames. So began Belgravia. This, together with the Great Exhibition of 1851 and the development of South Kensington's museums and upmarket housing, stimulated the creation of Knightsbridge.

Chelsea

The most interesting area is Chelsea, which had been a favorite aristocratic country retreat from London since Tudor times, when manor houses set in spacious orchards grew up around a fishing village. Charles II chose Chelsea for the Royal Hospital in the 1680s, and Sir Hans Sloane bought Chelsea Manor in 1712 and made it the repository for his collection, later the foundation for the British Museum (see pp. 134–138).

Later, 19th-century Chelsea attracted writers and artists, from Thomas Carlyle to Oscar Wilde. Architects returned to a more vernacular Queen Anne style using red brick. First adopted for houses along the Embankment, this style was chosen by the Cadogan family when, in the 1870s, they laid out Cado-gan Square and its sur-roundings. King's Road, running through the hearts of Chelsea and Fulham, was reborn in the 1960s as a catwalk for the mod/avant-garde, while the terraces off it, built as mass-produced housing for artisans, became the immaculate, if cramped, homes of successful City businesspeople.

Belgravia

Belgravia's story is shorter, but spectacular. With Mayfair and St. James's overflowing, this was the last London project to be developed by the rich (in this case, the Grosvenors) for the rich. Begun in 1824, the scheme centered on Belgrave Square, where the Regency style was taken to new heights. It was here that architect Thomas Cubitt brought success and quality to a wobbling project—such success

NOT TO BE MISSED:

Christopher Wren's magnificent Royal Hospital Chelsea 180–181

Taking a meditative stroll among the herbs and rare plants at Chelsea Physic Garden 181

Pimlico and Belgravia's Regency squares and majestic building facades 182–183

Browsing the over 860,000 square feet (80,000 sq m) of retail space at Harrods 184–185

Exploring more than 500 years of British art at Tate Britain 186–188

that the Grosvenors themselves have left Mayfair for Belgravia, and Belgrave Square accommodates a clutch of foreign missions.

Knightsbridge

Knightsbridge, meanwhile, was boosted by the Great Exhibition and the building of Belgravia. The first village on the road that led west out of London from Mayfair was transformed from fields into a densely packed area whose heartbeat was, and is, retail commerce. Today, the heart of Knightsbridge is Harrods, whose international shoppers are content to feel they have visited London only if they have shopped there. ■

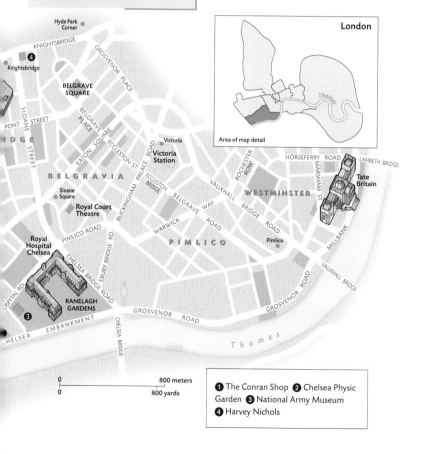

London

Area of map detail

Hyde Park Corner

KNIGHTSBRIDGE

④ Knightsbridge

GROSVENOR PLACE

BELGRAVE SQUARE

SLOANE STREET

PONT STREET

IDGE

BELGRAVE PLACE

EATON SQUARE

ECCLESTON ST.

ECCLESTON ST.

BUCKINGHAM PALACE ROAD

Victoria

Victoria Station

BELGRAVIA

Sloane Square

Royal Court Theatre

BELGRAVE BRIDGE

BELGRAVE WAY

VAUXHALL BRIDGE ROAD

ROCHESTER ROW

HORSEFERRY ROAD

LAMBETH BRIDGE

WESTMINSTER

MARSHAM ST.

Tate Britain

Royal Hospital Chelsea

PIMLICO ROAD

EBURY BRIDGE RD.

WARWICK WAY

PIMLICO

Pimlico

MILLBANK

③

RANELAGH GARDENS

HELSEA EMBANKMENT

SPITAL RD.

CHELSEA BRIDGE ROAD

CHELSEA BRIDGE

GROSVENOR ROAD

GROSVENOR ROAD

VAUXHALL BRIDGE

Thames

0 | 800 meters
0 | 800 yards

❶ The Conran Shop ❷ Chelsea Physic Garden ❸ National Army Museum ❹ Harvey Nichols

CHELSEA

When the Scottish historian and philosopher Thomas Carlyle (1795–1881) chose to live in Chelsea in 1834, the lanes that are now so sought after were considered unfashionable.

▪ The statue of King Charles II in the Figure Court of the Hospital was cast in copper alloy.

Royal Hospital Chelsea

- 🗺 Map p. 179
- ✉ Royal Hospital Rd., SW3
- ☎ 020 7881 5200
- 🕐 Open 8:30 a.m.–8:30 p.m. in Summer & 8:30 a.m.–4:30 p.m. in Winter
- 💲 Donation
- 🚇 Tube: Sloane Square. Train: Victoria Station

chelsea-pensioners.co.uk

Chelsea Flower Show

- ☎ 0845 260 5000
- 💲 $$$–$$$$$, reservations required
- 🚇 Tube: Sloane Square. Train: Victoria Station

rhs.org.uk

Sloane Square

Sloane Square resides at the juncture of Chelsea, Belgravia, and Knightsbridge, at the start of King's Road (Chelsea's main artery and one of the epicenters of London's Swinging Sixties). Along with the myriad bistros and shops, two sites well worth visiting are the **Saatchi Gallery** (*King's Rd., saatchigallery.com*), with (free) contemporary art by young artists, and the dozens of artisanal producers offering up snacks at the **Saturday food market** next door in Duke of York Square (*tel 020 7823 5577, dukeofyorksquare.com*).

Royal Hospital Chelsea

A block south of the Saatchi

Gallery is the Royal Hospital. The best views of the hospital are from a leafless, wintertime Royal Avenue off King's Road, or from a boat on the river, looking up the lawns to the main river-facing facade. The building was designed by Sir Christopher Wren for Charles II to house almost 500 army veterans and is still home to red-coated Chelsea Pensioners (residents) today.

Wren broke new ground with this, his first large-scale civil work. Inspired by Louis XIV's Les Invalides in Paris, it became a blueprint for institutional buildings in Europe and America: a central hall and chapel flanked by two side courts for the dormitories. The stables were added in 1814 by Sir John Soane, while he was Clerk of Works to the hospital.

On the garden facade, benches in Figure Court overlook Grinling Gibbons's bronze of Charles II and the formal gardens that once ended at the water. The more informal gardens to the left were, from 1742 to 1803, the infamous Ranelagh pleasure gardens.

Inside the hospital are three magnificent rooms. In the paneled Great Hall, today's pensioners dine beneath Verrio's painting of Charles II. In the chapel, they pray in box pews amid the decoration that includes Sebastiano Ricci's "Resurrection" altarpiece.

National Army Museum

Next to the western flank of the Royal Hospital Chelsea stands the National Army Museum *(Royal Hospital Rd., SW3, tel 020 7730 0717, nam.ac.uk)*. The galleries explore the army's role in British history and also display works from the museum's impressive art collection.

Since 2014 the museum has undergone a massive renovation and reopened in 2017.

Carlyle's House

Despite its then unfashionable location, Carlyle relished his "old-fashioned" street and his "most massive, roomy, sufficient old house" at 24 Cheyne Row.

Today, like so many housemuseums, the personality of its owner still pervades it. Carlyle would wander the house and quiet back garden in his dressing gown, smoking hat, and pipe. Here the intellectual, famous after his account of the French Revolution was published, and his witty wife would receive John Stuart Mill in the drawing room, Dickens and Browning in the parlor, and Darwin or Thackeray in the back dining room. Carlyle lived here for 47 years, and his ghost seems to haunt the garden and its vines.

Carlyle's House

- Map p. 178
- 24 Cheyne Row, SW3
- 020 7352 7087
- Open Wed.–Sun. 11 a.m.–5 p.m. March–Oct.
- $
- Tube: Sloane Square. Train: Victoria Station, then bus 170

nationaltrust.org.uk

EXPERIENCE:
Chelsea Flower Show

Immerse yourself in all things botanical at the Royal Horticultural Society's (RHS) annual spectacle, held in and around huge marquees erected in the Royal Hospital's gardens. For five days in late May, Chelsea's streets are crowded with plant-minded people. Nurseries and plantsmen, garden designers, and manufacturers of gardening equipment exhibit their triumphs, from a new rose to a repellent for slugs. Visitors can get tips or just enjoy the show's profusion of perfect blooms. Check the RHS website *(rhs.org.uk/shows-events)* for the public access days.

Chelsea Physic Garden

Carlyle undoubtedly visited this walled garden located a mere two minutes' walk from his house. Founded in 1673 by the Society of Apothecaries to grow plants for medical study, the 4-acre (1.6 ha) garden was stocked with specimens cultivated for the first time in England. With its herbs and exotic trees, the garden remains a place of serious study as well as a peaceful haunt for visitors. ∎

Chelsea Physic Garden

- Map p. 179
- 66 Royal Hospital Rd., SW3; entrance on Swan Walk
- 020 7352 5646
- Closed Jan., Sat.–Sun. Nov.–Dec. & Feb.–Mar.
- $$$
- Tube: Sloane Square

chelseaphysicgarden .co.uk

BELGRAVIA & PIMLICO

With Britain enjoying an economic boom and George IV rebuilding Buckingham Palace, the 2nd Earl of Grosvenor focused on his 400 undeveloped acres (161 ha) south of Hyde Park. Over this marshy scrubland, notorious for highwaymen and duels, he created a 200-acre (81 ha) estate that stole the limelight from his 100-acre (41 ha) Mayfair estate. Georgian brick, simplicity, and modest scale gave way to high Regency stucco. Thus Belgravia was born, a suburb for the very grand. Soon society moved west to take up residence there, Knightsbridge and South Kensington moved upscale to meet it, and Chelsea was linked to the continuous London sprawl.

■ The elegant stucco facades of Belgravia are exemplified in the buildings of Cadogan Place.

Belgravia

The master plan had a traditional square (Belgrave) surrounded by a network of streets, Georgian in concept but Regency in scale. Three big developers took on the site. Two went bankrupt; the third, Thomas Cubitt (see sidebar opposite), made a fortune. Work began in 1824 and continued for 30 years. Cubitt, backed by three Swiss bankers, took the lease on Belgrave Square and employed George Basevi as architect. The square was an instant social success: Dukes and duchesses moved into the palatial mansions and held glittering parties in their ballrooms. Soon Cubitt had added Upper Belgrave Street, Chester Square, and Eaton Place (where he had his offices).

A Belgravia Stroll: To appreciate Belgravia's magnificence, take a walk around these awe-inspiring streets and squares. From Sloane Street, walk east on Pont Street past Cadogan Place's stucco to Chesham Place. Turn left into Belgrave Mews West, once the stables for the grand houses in the square in front and now converted into attractive (and pricey) little houses,

Thomas Cubitt

London's most successful developer in the early 19th century was Thomas Cubitt. He revolutionized the building industry and, with a mixture of commercial acuteness and bold imagination, oversaw a series of large construction projects across the breadth of London.

As a young man, he worked as a ship's joiner on a voyage to India, making enough money to start his own business on his return. By 1815, the 25-year-old Cubitt had recognized that contracting each building trade as needed was not the most efficient way to work. So at his Gray's Inn Road workshops he employed a full set of laborers and craftsmen on a permanent wage, creating London's first modern building firm. The need to keep these workers busy helped encourage his hugely successful career as a speculative builder.

Cubitt's London work took off in Bloomsbury, where he laid out Gordon Square, Endsleigh Place, and Tavistock Square. When the Grosvenor family developed Belgravia, he moved into the big time. He crowned his career with Pimlico, a daring piece of speculation. In Belgravia, Pimlico, and the government project that created Battersea Park, Cubitt raised the low-lying land and firmed up the clay by using the earth that was being excavated from the great docks in the East End, in which he was heavily involved. Meanwhile, he baked his bricks on-site. This rags-to-riches builder also fought for the improvement of London's drainage system and the creation of open spaces for public use.

to find Halkin Place leading into the grandeur of Belgrave Square to the right.

Turn left onto Wilton Terrace, which runs into Wilton Crescent. Walk the sweep of Wilton Crescent, which will bring you back to Belgrave Square. On the opposite side of the square, Upper Belgrave Street leads to magnificent, colonnaded Eaton Square.

Today, foreign embassies and high-flying international entrepreneurs fill Belgravia houses and streets, along with a sprinkling of old British aristocrats.

Pimlico

The dry, formal atmosphere of Belgravia is quite different from Pimlico's, where Londoners step out of less opulent houses to join their lively community in Tachbrook Street's market *(Mon.–Sat.)* and Wilton Road's

INSIDER TIP:

Check out the retail enclave, Pimlico Green, best known for the food emporium and café Daylesford Organic *[44b Pimlico Rd.]*.

—TIM JEPSON
National Geographic author

many restaurants. Pimlico was Thomas Cubitt's own project. After years of negotiation, Cubitt finally persuaded the Grosvenors to lease him the land south of the canal, today cut off by Victoria Station. In this area, he laid out two squares, Eccleston and Warwick, set on terraced streets of houses. ■

Belgravia

⚠ Map p. 179

Pimlico

⚠ Map p. 179

HARRODS & THE KNIGHTSBRIDGE SHOPS

The most devoted shopper can no more "do" Harrods than the most curious art lover can "do" the British Museum. The world's most famous store is enormous. Its 300 departments on seven floors spread over 20 acres (8 ha). Every day, 4,000 staff serve 35,000 customers and take in around £1.5 million ($2.4 million).

■ **The vast, landmark department store Harrods is lit by thousands of bulbs at night.**

Harrods

- Map p. 178
- 87–135 Brompton Rd., SW1
- 020 7730 1234
- Tube: Knightsbridge

harrods.com

It all started when Charles Henry Harrod, a tea merchant, opened a grocery shop in the hamlet of Knightsbridge in 1849, bringing in about £20 ($32) a week. Two years later, the Great Exhibition brought plenty of trade and, as Knightsbridge began to expand and move up the social scale, business boomed. Charles's son, another Charles, took over in 1861, rebuilt, and soon quintupled his takings. After a devastating fire in 1883, he simply informed his customers that their deliveries would be delayed "a day or two." Harrods's reputation for service was established. When Richard Burbidge took over the shop in 1894, he created the slogan "Harrods serves the world." In addition, he installed London's first escalator in 1898.

Burbidge also rebuilt. The pink, domed Edwardian building we know today was designed by Stephens and Munt and built between 1901 and 1905. Louis de Blanc added the back extension in the 1920s. The Food Halls were decorated with W. J. Neatby's mosaic friezes and tiles. Burbidge's store has always been a royal favorite: George V made him a baron for his service.

The Shopping Experience

Many visitors to London feel their trip is incomplete without a session at Harrods, and most are not content merely to window-shop at the 80 displays or gaze at the thousands of light bulbs illuminating the building; 40 percent of all sales go abroad, packed in the now famous moss green bags. Londoners may say they can do without Harrods, but many go there for something—perhaps the patient children's hairdresser, or the health juice bar, or the massive greeting card department, and almost always their route will go via the Food Halls to pick up some perfectly ripened cheeses, fine patisserie, freshly made sandwiches, or delicious terrines.

To go inside Harrods is truly to enter the ultimate self-contained retail city. It has everything a dedicated shopper needs to survive the day, or several days. Most entrances have an information desk, which supplies events information and the essential free map of the store. Bars and restaurants are scattered throughout the store. Departments range from beauty parlor, pet shop, and bridal gowns to London's best toy department, Harrods own brand shop, a sweet-smelling Perfume Hall, a ticket agency that can get tickets for almost anything officially sold out, a choice of more than 150 whiskeys, and of course the irresistible Food Halls.

Harvey Nichols & Other Nearby Shops

Naturally, other retailers hoping to benefit from foot traffic at Harrods set up shop nearby. Using profits from the Great Exhibition's visitors, Benjamin Harvey's daughter brought an experienced silk buyer, Colonel Nichols, to the family drapery business. The long-term result, Harvey Nichols, is a paradise for women: floors of designer clothes and accessories topped by the Fifth Floor, with a stylish food hall, bar, and restaurants.

The Harvey Nichols store stands a few hundred yards east of Harrods at the corner of Sloane Street, the site of a solid string of international designer clothing stores that rivals New and Old Bond Streets. Other recent designer shop arrivals fill Brompton Road. A honeypot of home furnishing and fashion shops surround **The Conran Shop** in the decorated Michelin building at Brompton Cross, where Brompton Road meets Walton Street and Fulham Road. ■

Harvey Nichols
- Map p. 179
- 109–125 Knightsbridge, SW1X
- 020 7235 5000
- Tube: Knightsbridge

harveynichols.com

The Conran Shop
- Map p. 178
- Michelin House, 81 Fulham Rd., SW3
- 034 4848 4000
- Tube: South Kensington

conranshop.co.uk

Harrods Trivia

Harrods has an unparalleled shopping legacy, with a storied retail history going back more than 160 years. As a savvy customer, you might indeed know that the store contains a wine shop, a men's grooming center, and more than two dozen fine restaurants. But here are some facts about Harrods that you might not know:

• Harrods sells airplanes through its Harrods Aviation subsidiary. The store first began selling airplanes (and accompanying flying lessons) in 1919.

• More than 11,000 lights illuminate the store each night. This practice began in 1959 when Harrods started dressing itself up for Christmas.

• In the early 1900s, Harrods had its own Ladies Club where female customers could write letters, leave messages for each other, or simply relax in luxury.

• Harrods once had its own embalming and funeral service. Established in 1900, some of its "clients" included psychologist Sigmund Freud (d. 1939) and British prime minister Clement Attlee (d. 1967).

• The store offers safety deposit boxes on the lower ground floor for customers to stash their cash and jewelry. The service started in 1896 and is still available today.

• A memorial to the staff members who were killed in World War I stands near Door 3 (leading to Basil Street).

TATE BRITAIN

A century after it opened in 1897, the Tate split in two. Its superb national collection of British art from 1500 to the present day—the foremost collection of its kind—fills the renovated and expanded buildings here on the north bank of the Thames. Its modern international collection is now housed in the separate Tate Modern at Bankside in Southwark on the south bank (see pp. 104–105). Tate Boat water taxis ply between the two. The Tate has two outposts: one in Liverpool and the other in St. Ives, Cornwall.

Art in Tate Britain ranges from the 16th through the 21st century.

Tate Britain

- Map p. 179
- Millbank, SW1; secondary entrance on Atterbury St.
- 020 7887 8888
- Charge for temporary exhibitions
- Tube: Pimlico

tate.org.uk

The Site & the Building

The story of the Tate begins with controversy. Henry Tate, an 18th-century sugar millionaire, led a public movement demanding a showcase for British art. Tate himself offered the nation his collection of Victorian paintings and some money to pay for housing it. The government dithered before grudgingly accepting Tate's offer. There was then a wide debate on its location: South Kensington, Blackfriars, or Millbank, whose land became

available first. Tate's money paid for Sidney Smith's building. The new gallery replaced the octagonal Millbank Prison, built between 1812 and 1821.

Smith's neoclassical facade, entrance hall, and rotunda were completed for the opening. Many additions followed. The most significant were nine galleries added in 1899 and the central cupola and sculpture galleries given by the art dealer Joseph Duveen and his son in 1937. One small but delightful addition in 1983 was the Whistler Restaurant, where Rex Whistler's landscape mural called "Expedition in Pursuit of Rare Meats" (1926–1927) keeps art and food in harmony.

Stirling and Wilford's Clore Gallery opened in 1987 to house the Turner Bequest. The artist left some 300 paintings, 20,000 drawings, and nearly 300 sketchbooks to the nation. Top-lit galleries admit natural light without damaging Turner's fragile watercolors. The Centenary Development increased gallery space by a third and renewed Henry Tate's vision of a showcase for British art. The foundation collection had grown quickly since 1916, when the Tate was given the additional responsibility of forming the national collection of international modern art (which is now at Bankside).

The Collection

Tate Britain holds nearly 3,500 paintings, plus prints—including those belonging to the Turner Bequest—and sculptures. Visitors can walk through a half-millennium of art in the numerous galleries along the outer perimeter of the museum, view works from the 16th to the 19th century in the central gallery space, and explore other galleries and temporary exhibitions.

Although re-hangs are frequent to ensure as wide a cross section of the collection is displayed as possible, following are some stars that may be on view.

The earliest work on display is John Bettes's "A Man in a Black Cap" (1545). The artist is said to have spent several years doing decorative work for Henry VIII's court in the 1530s.

Later, the 18th century saw British painters responding to the Enlightenment. Look for George Stubbs's "Reapers" (1785) and "Haymakers" (1785), Sir Joshua Reynolds's "Self-Portrait as a Deaf Man" (circa 1775), and

INSIDER TIP:

Explore art after hours on select Fridays every month, when Tate Britain remains open until 10 p.m. for Late at Tate.

—JUSTIN KAVANAGH
National Geographic Travel Books editor

several Thomas Gainsborough works, including the delightful "Rev. John Chafy Playing the Violoncello in a Landscape" (1750–1752). Also check out William Hogarth's "The Painter and his Pug" (1745). The artist, England's first great native-born painter, is said to have included his dog, called Trump, to represent his own pugnacious personality.

Nineteenth-century British painting developed in several directions, and the Tate has examples of each. Several paintings by John Constable include the well-loved "Flatford Mill" (1816–1817). Pre-Raphaelite paintings include many of the best known: John Millais's

"Ophelia" (1851–1852), William Frith's "The Derby Day" (1856–1858), and William Holman Hunt's "The Awakening Conscience" (1853). Look for John William Waterhouse's "The Lady of Shalott" (1888), inspired by the Alfred Tennyson poem.

This diversity and originality continued into the 20th century. Stanley Spencer's mystical paintings include "The Woolshop" (1939). Works by Francis Bacon are equally powerful.

More recently, the Tate's remit to buy contemporary British art has generated controversy, inevitably, given the nature of some such work (bricks, sliced-up animals, and so on). Much of the gallery's art was questioned when the gallery acquired it. Looking at works by Anthony Caro, Richard Hamilton, and David Hockney, now classics, it is hard to understand the fuss. The same is true of Eduardo Paolozzi, Frank Auerbach, Lucian Freud, and Richard Long, as well as Bridget Riley's black-and-white geometry. Future visitors must judge purchases of the still-controversial Damien Hirst.

In addition to modern art, the Tate's collection of works on paper ranges from 18th-century watercolors to postwar prints. There are also good examples of Britain's preeminent achievement in sculpture in the 20th century, notably by Henry Moore (in his dedicated central gallery) and Barbara Hepworth.

Tate Britain runs and exhibits the annual Turner Prize (see p. 41). The Tate also dedicates some of its gallery space to pieces not usually displayed to the public, to new acquisitions, and to work conducted by specialists. ∎

■ Gillian Ayres's "Phaethon" (1990) is among Tate Britain's many modern works.

Elegant houses and their parks, Kew botanic gardens, and Hampton Court Palace, as seductive now as they were centuries ago

WEST LONDON

▦ Fuchsias at Kew Gardens

WEST LONDON

From Tudor times until the 20th century, the Thames was the principal highway for escaping the city. Kings, queens, aristocrats, and merchants wound their way up the river to reach their country estates. More modest Londoners boarded pleasure boats for day trips upstream to the taverns strung along the waterside at Chiswick, Kew, and Richmond. Most of the splendid buildings were built alongside the Thames, or within easy reach of it. Even today, the most pleasant way to reach them is by boat (see pp. 52–54).

Though now surrounded by urban sprawl, these one-time rural estates have preserved pockets of green space for Londoners.

As the Thames begins to turn southward (see map p. 48), large patches of parkland, some wild, some tamed, lie on either bank. Inside the curve, there are the wide-open spaces of Barnes Common and the adjoining Putney Lower Common. Together, Wimbledon Common and Putney Heath make up London's largest common, 1,060 protected acres (429 ha) of rough grassland, with heather and gorse bushes, oak and birch woodland, wildflowers, and many bird species. Farther upstream, the 2,358 acres (954 ha) of Richmond Park make it the largest of London's royal parks and one of southern England's important nature reserves. Its mixture of grass, woods, lakes, marsh, and managed forest includes more than 200,000 trees, many of them descendants of the ancient oak, elm, and lime forest once surrounding London. Highlights here include the herds of dappled fallow and red deer, Isabella Plantation's azaleas and rhododendrons, and magical views through the trees over the Thames.

Beside the river lie the intricately planted Royal Botanic Gardens at Kew, with their remarkable glasshouses and renovated royal palace, and the evocative 17th-century Ham House at Twickenham, whose garden has been partially reconstructed. Enjoy the square lawns, hornbeam hedges, and cherry garden.

Outside the Thames's curve, the grounds surrounding Chiswick House, Osterley Park, Syon House, and Marble Hill House were all tamed in the 18th century. Richmond's royal connections made this a favorite spot, as did the fashionable prospects from Richmond Hill.

Royal gardener Charles Bridgeman and poet Alexander Pope designed Marble Hill's garden, and both they and William Kent worked with Lord Burlington at Chiswick. For Syon House, the Northumberland family brought in Capability Brown, who created lakes and a formal rose garden, and planted specimen trees such as swamp cypresses and oaks. At Osterley, banker Francis Child improved his flat, viewless estate with garden follies and trees. The lake now attracts great crested grebes, corn buntings, kestrels, kingfishers, and other birds.

The river twists back northwest again at Kingston. The whole bowl contained within is filled with Hampton Court Palace, whose gardens include the restored Privy Garden, the deer park, and the deliciously wild Bushy Park. ∎

NOT TO BE MISSED:

The stunning glasshouses and beautifully maintained grounds of Kew Gardens 192–193

Taking in a chukka or two at a Sunday summer polo match in the Ham Polo Club 195

The 17th-century Ham House in its beautiful Thameside setting 196

Getting lost in Hampton Court Palace's romantic halls, gardens, and, naturally, its famous hedge maze 197–200

0   2 kilometers
0   1 mile

OSTERLEY PARK
Osterley Park
Osterley
GREAT WEST ROAD
M4
M4
Kew Bridge
KEW BRIDGE RD
Chiswick House
Chiswick
GREAT CHERTSEY ROAD
Thames
BRENTFORD
SYON PARK
Syon House
Royal Botanic Gardens, Kew
OLD DEER PARK
KEW
KEW ROAD
MORTLAKE RD
Kew Gardens
CHISWICK BRIDGE
DUKE'S MEADOWS
BARNES
MORTLAKE
Hounslow East
ISLEWORTH
TWICKENHAM BRIDGE
TWICKENHAM RD.
Richmond
RICHMOND ROAD WEST
EAST SHEEN
ROEHAMPTON LANE
RICHMOND
GREAT CHERTSEY ROAD
Twickenham
RICHMOND BRIDGE
MARBLE HILL PARK
Marble Hill House
TWICKENHAM
PETERSHAM
ROEHAMPTON
RICHMOND PARK
Ham House
HAM COMMON
HAM
ROEHAMPTON VALE
WIMBLEDON COMMON
ROBIN HOOD WAY
TEDDINGTON
HAMPTON HILL
BUSHY PARK
HAMPTON WICK
KINGSTON BRIDGE
HOME PARK
KINGSTON UPON THAMES
HAMPTON COURT RD
HAMPTON COURT BRIDGE
Hampton Court
Hampton Court Palace
Thames

1 Orleans House
2 Hogarth's House

London
Thames
Area of map detail

ROYAL BOTANIC GARDENS, KEW

This is London's living museum of plants, landscapes, buildings, and statuary. Visitors to the 300-acre (121 ha) garden gasp at some of the 50,000 species of plants and explore glasshouses (greenhouses) full of lilies and orchids. Meanwhile, behind the scenes, for more than a century this has been a center for the identification and distribution of plants from around the world.

Kew's giant South American water lilies can support weights up to 100 pounds (45 kg).

You need no botanical knowledge to revel in the sheer beauty of the gardens. They began as two very different estates. The part on the west, bordering the river, belonged to George II and Queen Caroline's country house, White Lodge on the Richmond Estate. Capability Brown created the original lake and the dell, now planted with rhododendrons. The eastern part was the 9-acre (3.6 ha) Kew estate, where Prince Frederick's widow, Princess Augusta, lived in Kew Palace. Now exquisitely refurbished, it was built in 1631 by a London merchant of Dutch descent (hence the Dutch gables).

In 1759 the princess took up gardening. In 1761 her builder Sir William Chambers designed the Orangery, now the Tea House, and the Pagoda, Kew's ten-story landmark. George III, who came to the throne in 1760, inherited both estates from his mother, Princess Augusta, and his grandfather, George II. George III stayed in tiny Kew Palace and soon employed Sir Joseph Banks to enlarge and replant both gardens, now joined. Banks had collected specimens on his travels with Captain Cook, and he sent gardeners off to find additional plants.

More acres were added, and in 1841 the gardens were given to the state, with Sir William Hooker as director. It was Hooker who founded the Department of Economic Botany, the museums, the herbarium, and the library. And in 1844 the first of Kew's custom-designed glasshouses was built (see sidebar below). Later, W. A. Nesfield, who also worked at Regent's Park, laid out the four great vistas—Pagoda Vista, Broad Walk, Holly Walk, and Cedar Vista. He also designed the lake and pond. His son, W. E. Nesfield, designed the delightful Temperate House Lodge in 1866–1867, one of London's first Queen Anne Revival buildings. Note the detailing of the central chimneys.

Visiting the Gardens

Whatever the season, Kew has something glorious to see. Kew Palace or the Orangery are good places to start. There, the magic of a perfect garden is yours to explore. In spring, there are the daffodils, crocuses, tulips, and bluebells, especially around Queen Charlotte's Cottage. Early summer brings a blaze of azaleas, magnolias, rhododendrons, and flowering cherries—there is a fine view across to Syon House from the end of the azalea walk. After the autumn color, there are winter-flowering prunus, the Heath Garden by the pagoda, and the glasshouses. At all times, Nesfield's vistas are impressive, as are the groves of tree collections including willow, beech, and birch. Each tree is identified by its country of origin. ∎

Royal Botanic Gardens, Kew

🅰 Map p. 191

✉ Kew, Richmond, Surrey, TW9

☎ 020 8332 5655 Information: 131 552 7171

🕐 Open 10 a.m.–5 p.m. Check occasional area closures on the website. Queen Charlotte's Cottage closed in Winter (it reopens in April).

💲 $$

🚇 Tube/Rail: Kew Gardens, then walk Riverboat: See pp. 52–54.

kew.org

Kew Glasshouses

Kew's glasshouses possibly look for inspiration to Syon's huge Great Conservatory (see p. 195), built in the 1820s by Charles Fowler. The gardens' first glasshouse was the Aroid House (Nash Conservatory), designed by Nash in 1836 as a garden pavilion for Buckingham Palace. The Palm House, though, was specially designed in 1844–1848 by Decimus Burton and Richard Turner. Its slender cast-ironwork makes it the finest glass-and-iron structure in England. The Palm House predates Paxton's Crystal Palace by three years. The Waterlily House (1852) was followed by Burton's Temperate House, built between 1860 and 1898 as the world's largest glasshouse. More recently, the Princess of Wales Conservatory, completed in 1987, contains ten climatic zones and replaces 26 old glasshouses.

EIGHTEENTH-CENTURY COUNTRY RETREATS

With a new appreciation for the picturesque sweeping the country, and in particular for fine prospects, the pretty stretch of the riverside that included Chiswick, Richmond, and Twickenham villages became the favorite choice for aristocratic country houses. It also had royal associations and was accessible by the river, the preferred method of travel.

Marble Hill House
- Map p. 191
- Richmond Rd., Twickenham, TW1
- 020 8892 5115
- Open Sat.–Sun., guided tours only. Closed Nov.–Mar.
- $$
- Tube: Richmond, then cross the bridge

www.english-heritage.org.uk

Twickenham

Several 18th-century country idylls survive, with settings that evoke the elegance of their period. **Marble Hill House** is an early one, built between 1723 and 1729 for George II's mistress, Henrietta Howard, Countess of Suffolk. This white Palladian villa overlooks the Thames between Twickenham and Richmond. Both

Elegant details abound in Syon House's anteroom.

house and park were inspired by the classical idea of an earthly Elysium, as revived in the 16th-century villas of the Italian Veneto. Nature was tamed to produce good views down to the river and, just as important, up from the river for arriving guests.

Just off the northwest corner of the park, Montpelier Row, dating from about 1720, is one of Twickenham's gracious early terraces. Follow the riverside path through the woods to James Gibbs's octagonal 1720 **Orleans House** and art gallery (*Riverside, tel 020 8831 6000, richmond.gov.uk, closed Mon.*); just enough survives to hint at its former grandeur. Bell, Water, and Church Lanes have more old houses, and the ferry to **Ham House** runs from here.

Chiswick

Downriver from Twickenham, Richard Boyle, 3rd Earl of Burlington and a connoisseur of great refinement, built his perfect Palladian temple to the arts, **Chiswick House,** in 1725–1729. Burlington's town house, the inner part of what is today the Royal Academy, had already broken with Wren's English baroque for Palladio's light, Italian style. Here, at Chiswick, the earl went further. Inspired by Palladio's Villa Capra

EXPERIENCE: See a Polo Match

Players on horseback still gallop between goalposts at the **Ham Polo Club** (Petersham Rd., Richmond, Surrey, TW10, tel 020 8334 0000, hampoloclub.com, $), the only surviving polo club in London's metropolitan area. Pack a picnic and catch Sunday games in the summer, but dress sharp—no shorts allowed at this establishment, which was founded in 1926 beside Ham House (see p. 196) and across the Thames from Marble Hill House. To reach it, take the train or Tube to Richmond, then bus no. 65 or 371, or enjoy the pretty 20-minute Thameside walk. The more adventurous can saddle up and learn ($$$$) how players whack a 3-inch (8 cm) ball while riding a horse.

The game is divided into "chukkas," or seven-minute segments, and you may notice something different about the horses—their manes are shaved so loose hair doesn't affect the game. But don't call them horses. In polo parlance, regular-size horses are "ponies," a term dating from a 19th-century rule that the animals be less than five feet (1.5 m) tall.

near Vicenza, he built an exquisite Palladian villa and garden in which to display his art and entertain his friends, rather than a house to live in. William Kent added ideas on decoration and greatly influenced the design of the garden, one of London's most interesting.

Like the house, the garden breaks away from the geometric designs of English baroque. Its design moves toward the freer curves of Capability Brown, which evolved into later English landscape garden concepts. The layout is given informality through the use of statuary, garden buildings, and unevenly planted trees.

The property reopened some years ago after a two-year, £12 million ($19 million) restoration project that returned the gardens to their original 18th-century look: 1,600 new trees were planted, and others removed, to restore historic sight lines and views.

Syon & Osterley

The mansions of Syon and Osterley are grand indeed. Sumptuous

and magnificent **Syon House** is a 16th-century stone building, totally remodeled in 1761 by Robert Adam for Sir Hugh Smithson, 1st Duke of Northumberland. Adam controlled the whole project, from the building and fine plasterwork to the gilding, carpets, and even the doorknobs. Most of it survives in perfection: the Matthew Boulton fireplaces, the Wedgwood pottery, the Spitalfields silks. Later, in 1827, Charles Fowler's magnificent **Great Conservatory** was added, linking the house to its gardens, landscaped by Capability Brown in 1767–1773.

Adam created another masterpiece nearby, **Osterley Park** (tel 020 8232 5050, nationaltrust .org.uk, closed Mon.–Tues.). Again, he took a 16th-century house—this one of red brick—and transformed it into a Palladian mansion suitable for City bankers Francis and Robert Child. Today, Adam's great portico leads to a string of state rooms furnished with Gobelin tapestries. ∎

Chiswick House

- Map p. 191
- Burlington Lane, Chiswick, W4
- 020 3141 3350
- House closed Nov.–Mar. (closed Tues. in Apr.–Oct.); gardens open year-round
- House: $
- Tube: Turnham Green, then walk south Rail: Chiswick, then walk along Burlington Lane

chgt.org.uk

Syon House

- Map p. 191
- Brentford, Middlesex, TW8
- 020 8560 0882
- Closed Mon.–Tues. & Fri.–Sat.; and Nov.–mid-Mar.
- $$ Gardens only: $
- Tube: Gunnersbury Rail: Kew Bridge, then bus 237 or 267

syonpark.co.uk

HAM HOUSE

This is one of London's earliest and loveliest grand houses. Scrupulously run by the National Trust since 1949, it is furnished with pieces lent by the V&A. Built in 1610 for Sir Thomas Vavasour, Knight Marshal to James I, it was dramatically remodeled in 1673–1675 by William Samwell for Elizabeth, Countess of Dysart, and her second husband, John Maitland, Duke of Lauderdale, who was the virtual ruler of Scotland for some time after the Restoration. Together they created a flamboyantly palatial baroque home.

Ham House

- Map p. 191
- Richmond, Surrey, TW10
- 020 8940 1950
- House 12 p.m.–4 p.m. Gardens 10 a.m.–5 p.m.
- $$
- Tube/Rail: Richmond, then bus 65 or 371

nationaltrust.org.uk

Using house records and original plans, the Trust has fully restored both house and gardens, so that it gives a more accurate and extensive idea of grand domestic 17th-century life than any other house in England.

Start by looking at the facade of the house: three simple stories of brick with stone dressings. The busts in the oval niches, however, give a taste of what is to come once you enter the house.

INSIDER TIP:

A short walk through the meadows that front Ham House brings you to the quiet banks of the Thames. The pathway here leads you a very pleasant 1.5 miles [2.4 km] to Richmond.

—LARRY PORGES
National Geographic Travel Books editor

Inside, the two-story, galleried Great Hall has a pre-refurbishment ceiling by Joseph Kinsman dating from 1637–1638. Here, too, are 18th- and 19th-century paintings of the Dysart family by artists such as Sir Joshua Reynolds and John Constable. Up the great staircase, the North Drawing Room is hung with English tapestries depicting the months of the year, probably woven in Soho around 1700. The Long Gallery, decorated in 1639, has a remarkable set of 17th-century portraits in contemporary gilded frames. The Cabinet of Miniatures, also known as the Green Closet, has exquisite works by Hilliard and Cooper.

The rooms of the Queen's Apartment, added in the 1670s, are at the other end of the Long Gallery. The Queen's Closet, the richest room of all, has a Verrio ceiling, marbled flat surfaces, early examples of scagliola decoration around the fireplace, and full baroque carving on the wainscoting.

Return through the State Rooms and head back downstairs: Several ground-floor rooms have ceilings painted by Neapolitan artist Antonio Verrio; the Dining Room has leather wall hangings; and the Duchess's Private Closet has its original japanned furniture. Outside, the 18 acres (7 ha) of formal gardens should not be missed. ∎

HAMPTON COURT PALACE

Of all London's royal palaces, Hampton Court has the most to offer the visitor, including two sets of regal rooms (intimate Tudor and grand Wren), numerous gardens (Tudor, Dutch, the Maze, and more), and two great parks (Home and Bushy). In all, more than 500 years of enlightened royal patronage is now proof of the ancient splendor of the court.

Henry VIII appropriated the magnificent Hampton Court Palace from disgraced Cardinal Wolsey.

Choices will have to be made, and the first is whether to whisk out there by train to enjoy the rooms relatively empty in the morning, possibly returning to London by riverboat; or to glide up by riverboat, find more crowded rooms, and spend a summer's afternoon and in the gardens and parks.

History

The palace began as a 12th-century moated estate office. By 1514, it became a courtyard house. That year, Thomas, Cardinal Wolsey, Henry VIII's chief minister, leased it as his country house. Wolsey built grandly. He added most of the Tudor buildings that stand today: 44 lodgings for his guests in Base Court; three stories of rooms

expressly to honor Henry VIII's visit in 1525; a long gallery; and a magnificent chapel.

When Wolsey fell from favor in 1528, Henry VIII took over this ready-made palace. He immediately extended the kitchens, and in 1532–1535 added the Great Hall. His daughter Elizabeth laid out Italian gardens. Of the Tudor sovereigns' 60 residences, Hampton Court was one of the few capable of housing the entire 1,000-strong court. Yet it was not the service rooms that impressed visitors so much as the royal apartments; most are gone now, and only the Great Watching Chamber, the chapel, and Wolsey Closet remain.

William and Mary, after their accession in 1689, made dramatic

Hampton Court Palace

- 🅰 Map p. 191
- ✉ East Molesey, Surrey, KT8
- ☎ 020 3166 6000
- 💲 Palace & gardens: $$$. Parks: free
- 🚉 Rail: Hampton Court, then walk over bridge. Riverboats from Westminster pier in summer (see p. 53).

hrp.org.uk

NOTE: The palace offers an extensive program of tours, talks, and special events.

Rooms at the palace range from grand to intimate.

work was completed in 1700 and William moved in, but died two years later.

Queen Anne redecorated the chapel and the Queen's Drawing Room, employing the Neapolitan artist Antonio Verrio. Georges I and II resided in Hampton Court. After the death of Queen Caroline (George II's wife), the court ceased to stay here. Gradually, the rooms became "grace and favor" apartments for retired servants of the crown, though the royals continued to care for Hampton Court. Queen Victoria added the Great Hall's stained glass, "improved" the palace's Tudor style by adding most of the tall, brick chimneys, and, in 1838, opened it to the public. The railway station opened in 1849, making the palace easily accessible.

changes. They brought in Sir Christopher Wren to create a new baroque palace. Wren began by replacing Henry's royal apartments. The queen's suite of rooms overlooked Charles II's garden and his Long Water. The king's overlooked his Privy Garden and the Thames. After Mary died in 1694, building stopped for four years. The

Hampton Court Palace

Great Gatehouse

Hampton Court Routes

Because the palace is so vast, its curators have devised several routes, each exploring a theme. Guides can be booked for routes, and maps are available for self-guidance. Here are two approaches, one Tudor, the other William and Mary.

Trail 1—The Tudors: Henry VIII's **State Apartments** are found through Wolsey's Great Gatehouse at the far end of Base Court. From the passage leading to Clock Court, head upstairs: The **Great Hall** (1532–1535) is hung with Henry's 1540s Flemish tapestries. Through the **Great Watching Chamber,** the Processional Gallery leads to the **Chapel Royal** and its sumptuous Tudor ceiling. Next to Chapel Royal is the quiet **Chapel Court Garden,** a former burial ground for the Order of the Knights of St. John.

From here, visit **Henry VIII's kitchens,** entered from Base Court. They occupied 50 rooms, and 200 staff fed Henry's 1,000-strong court. Ten rooms are open, including the Beer Cellar, Roasting Kitchen, and

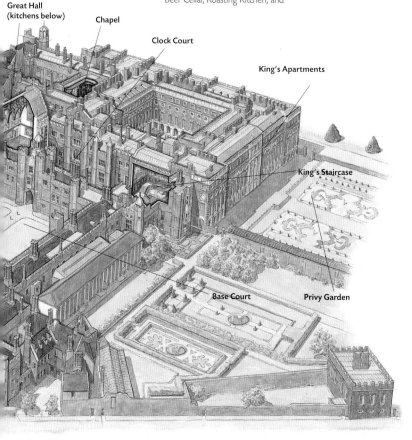

Great Hall (kitchens below)

Chapel

Clock Court

King's Apartments

King's Staircase

Base Court

Privy Garden

INSIDER TIP:

Look closely at the steps at the bottom of the King's Staircase to see 18th-century graffiti etched into the stone by soldiers stationed at the palace.

—TOM O'NEILL
National Geographic magazine writer

Wine Cellar—where some of the 600,000 gallons of ale drunk annually were stored.

From Clock Court go upstairs to find the **"Young Henry VIII"** exhibit. Here are Tudor paintings and exhibits that tell the story of the famous king's formative years. The art collection includes the "Field of the Cloth of Gold," recording Henry VIII's meeting with Francis I of France in 1520.

Trail 2—William and Mary:
Return to Clock Court to visit William III's Apartments. Up the monumental **King's Staircase,** decorated with Verrio's allegory of William's good government, find the **King's Guard Chamber,** which displays some of the room's original 3,000 weapons. The **Presence Chamber** has its original throne to which courtiers would bow, even if empty; Sir Godfrey Kneller's equestrian portrait of the king; and tapestries made for Whitehall Palace. Ahead is the King's Eating Room, Privy Chamber, Withdrawing Room, Great Bedchamber, Little Bedchamber, and Closet. The king's private apartments continue downstairs, with views of the formal **Privy Garden** (see sidebar below).

The **Cumberland Art Gallery** opened to the public in 2014 in renovated rooms once occupied by George II's son, the Duke of Cumberland. Here, rotating masterworks from the Royal Collection—think Rembrandt, Canaletto, and Holbein—focus on art from the peak of Hampton Court's royal era, the Tudor period to the mid-18th century. ■

Hampton Court Gardens

The Tudor, baroque, and Victorian gardens are minutely tended. Of Henry VIII's grand layout, little survives. The secluded Knot and Pond Gardens give a flavor—Henry's Pond Garden (1536) was stocked with edible fish for the kitchens. The Great Vine is grown from a cutting taken in 1768 from the original. In the nearby Mantegna Gallery, the painter's stage designs "Triumphs of Caesar" (circa 1486–1494) are on display. William's 3-acre (1.2 ha) Privy Garden is now restored to its 1702 state, complete with authentic flowers, shrubs, and 33,000 box plants. Wren designed the riverside Banqueting House; other parts to enjoy include the Maze, first planted in 1690, and the Wilderness, with a million bulbs. Beyond the Long Water, Home Park's 300 fallow deer are descended from Henry VIII's herd. This is where the annual Royal Horticultural Society Hampton Court Palace Garden Festival, the largest of its kind in Europe, is held in July.

The Tower of London, jolly East End markets, the reborn Docklands, and maritime Greenwich

EAST LONDON

Tower Bridge is a gateway to East London.

EAST LONDON

Here is the flip side to stuccoed Belgravia and the art dealers of St. James's. The medieval Tower of London still slams its doors shut against the London mob each night. Downstream, the palatial splendors of Royal Greenwich Palace and Park are matched by its maritime museum and ships. In between, the East End throbs once more with a vitality that first exploded into life when the enclosed docks were built following the 18th-century industrial revolution.

The romance of the overcrowded, poor, but spirited East End—of Cockney rhyming slang, pearly kings, and music halls—was born in the 19th century. Older areas, such as Spitalfields and Whitechapel, and the East End villages of Hackney and Limehouse, were swallowed into the giant Victorian sprawl of housing for British workers from rural areas and migrants from other countries. Men and women worked on the docks and in their related trades—shipbuilding, engineering, furniture-making, and, at the Whitechapel Bell Foundry, making bells for London's many Victorian churches. They brewed beer, ran the street markets, and entertained great crowds in the music halls. Here Charlie Chaplin made his stage debut at the Royal Cambridge music hall. Meanwhile, the government created a "green lung," Victoria Park, and well-wishers and missionaries started such charitable institutions as the Ragged School.

Today, having slumped after the docks were closed, the heart of the East End beats again. The map is once again dotted with interesting places to visit.

Spitalfields, focused on Christ Church, mixes new gentility with the rag trade, restaurants, and the mosques of the Bangladeshis. Whitechapel Art Gallery is the heart of a large community of artists, who live in the surrounding neighborhoods. Jazz has replaced the music hall, and one set of almshouses in Bethnal Green is home to the Geffrye Museum (closed for renovation until summer 2020). Farther north, the Hackney Empire variety theater entertains full houses, while just around the corner the National Trust tends Sutton House, a rare surviving 16th-century merchant's home. Most surprising of all, a few streets southwest of Victoria Park the V&A has its easternmost outpost: the Museum of Childhood (undergoing a huge renovation project).

Down by the Thames, the revival of the 11-mile (17 km) strip of once disused docks began in 1981 with huge government help. It is now well established, as evident in the success of London City Airport and the soaring beauty of the towers of Canary Wharf.

Docklands building continues on this massive chunk of London. The Isle of Dogs now has the Museum of London Docklands and a host of restaurants at West India Docks. Farther east, Royal Victoria Docks has Excel, the London International Exhibition Centre. Still farther east, Royal Albert Dock has the Royal Albert Dock Regatta Centre.

At Greenwich, the *Cutty Sark* is restored, while the O_2 Arena, where the new millennium officially began, is the world's largest dome. But the biggest boost to the whole East End came in recent years: The 2012 Olympic Games were staged in the Lower Lea Valley, an area now being revitalized. ■

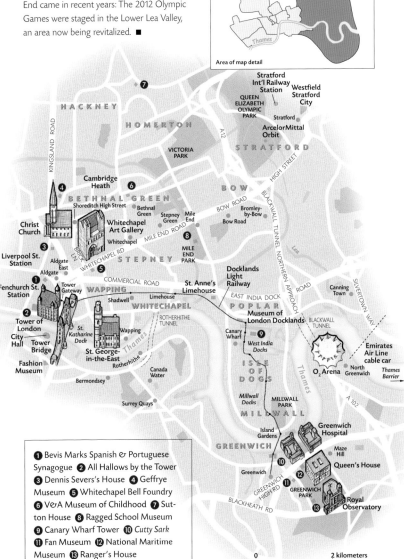

London

Thames

Area of map detail

① Bevis Marks Spanish & Portuguese Synagogue ② All Hallows by the Tower ③ Dennis Severs's House ④ Geffrye Museum ⑤ Whitechapel Bell Foundry ⑥ V&A Museum of Childhood ⑦ Sutton House ⑧ Ragged School Museum ⑨ Canary Wharf Tower ⑩ Cutty Sark ⑪ Fan Museum ⑫ National Maritime Museum ⑬ Ranger's House

0   2 kilometers
0   1 mile

TOWER OF LONDON

Britain's most perfect surviving medieval fort is tucked behind the sleek City towers, forgotten by most Londoners but ever popular with visitors. In fact, the tower is not just a fort; it contains a palace, prisons, an execution site, chapels, and museums. Since William the Conqueror began building it soon after his 1066 conquest, it has served the sovereign. Today, covering 18 acres (7.3 ha), it is London's smallest village, with a population of 36 families.

The story of the tower is as much about people as about buildings. Following its story is a good way of familiarizing yourself with the kings of England.

The Tower of London began as a temporary fort, constructed by William to keep watch on untrustworthy City merchants. He built it between their Saxon walls and the high surviving Roman ones. Later, he built what is now the central White Tower, completed by William II and Henry I. Constructed of stone from Caen in France, this keep had walls 90 feet (27 m) high and 15 feet (4.6 m) thick, with room inside for three wells, a banqueting hall, a council chamber, and even the tiny St. John's Chapel, plus a prison and dungeon. Henry I also built the tower's second church, St. Peter ad Vincula. The last Norman king, Stephen, was the first to live in the tower.

The Plantagenet kings used the tower well. Henry II added kitchens, a bakery, and a jail. William of Longchamp, loyal servant of Richard II, added more wall, the Bell Tower, Wardrobe Towers, and the ditch while the king was at the Crusades—to no avail, however. Prince John besieged it, became king, and further strengthened the walls. Henry III began the inner wall, the moat, his own water gate, and the royal palace. He whitewashed the White Tower and began a zoo—the King of Norway gave him a polar bear that went fishing in the Thames on a leash. Edward I completed the western Inner Wall and the Outer Wall including Byward Tower and

■ The medieval Tower of London was a fort, a prison, a palace, and a jewel house.

Traitors' Gate. He moved the mint and crown jewels here from Westminster.

Since then, the tower has changed little. Such extras as the

INSIDER TIP:

Check out the exhibition of Henry VIII's armor in the White Tower: It ranges from slim (young Henry) to XXL (old Henry).

—PATRICIA DANIELS
National Geographic contributor

tower's 14th-century cupolas, Henry VIII's half-timbered houses and two circular bastions on Tower Green, and the barracks of 1840 are minor additions.

The Tower witnessed both great joys and great horrors. Henry IV initiated the Ceremony of the Bath here in 1399. Under Henry VI, the Duke of Exeter introduced the rack for torture and Edmund Campion, the English Jesuit martyr (1540–1581), was stretched on it three times. The Yorkist Edward IV picnicked and played on the tower lawns. But when Richard III went off to be crowned in 1483, his two prince nephews were murdered in the Bloody Tower. Then came the Tudors: Henry VIII may have built houses on Tower Green, but he also had two of his wives executed there: Anne Boleyn and Catherine Howard. In fact, they were comparatively lucky; Thomas Cromwell, Archbishop Laud, and others ending with Lord Lovat in 1747,

provided public spectacle when they were beheaded up on Tower Hill. Princess Elizabeth first arrived as a prisoner through Traitors' Gate, but later began her coronation procession in a golden chariot from here. Then the Stuarts: James I, the last king to live in the tower, watched his lions and bears fighting from the Lion Tower. Charles I sent six Members of Parliament to the tower for insulting his favorite, the Duke of Buckingham. Charles II held the tower's last pageant in 1661, extravagant spring festivities that included an entire new set of crown jewels, as Cromwell's men had destroyed most of the previous ones.

Visiting the Tower

The tower is very popular. There is much to see; reentry tickets allow for a lunch break on Tower Wharf or at St. Katharine Dock. If the lines are long, consider visiting the church of All Hallows by the Tower, Tower Bridge (see p. 208), and St. Katharine Dock, or taking the ferry from Tower Pier to H.M.S. *Belfast* (see sidebar p. 106); then return to the tower later.

The Trail

Arrival by river (see pp. 52–54) means going under London Bridge, where prisoners such as Princess Elizabeth would have gazed up at the heads of previous inmates, exhibited on spikes. Arrival on foot from the City allows a visit to All Hallows and a first view of the tower, with the Victorian Tower Bridge beyond.

You enter the Tower of London through the Byward Tower, at

Tower of London

🅰 Map p. 203
☎ 0844 482 7777
💲 $$$
🚇 Tube: Tower Hill; or Monument, then walk to it through the City Overground: Fenchurch Street

hrp.org.uk

NOTE: It's worth reserving online in advance.

All Hallows by the Tower

🅰 Map. p. 203
✉ Byward St., EC3
☎ 020 7481 2928
💲 Donation
🚇 Tube: Tower Hill

www.allhallowsby
thetower.org.uk

the southwest corner, not far from Tower Pier. You can walk around on your own or join a free tour led every half hour by one of the Yeoman Warders, or Beefeaters, who have guarded the tower since 1485.

The Crown Jewels: It is best to visit the crown jewels, housed in the Waterloo Barracks, first. To get there, go straight ahead and find Traitors' Gate on the right; turn left, go up the stairs past Tower Green and straight on to the Waterloo Barracks. There are plenty of sparkling, egg-size diamonds to note: the First Star of Africa (530 carats) in Charles II's scepter; the 2,800 diamonds in the Imperial State Crown worn for the State Opening of Parliament; and the Koh-I-Noor diamond from India, in the Queen Consort's crown. Also exhibited are the ampulla and spoon for anointing the sovereign, made in 1399, and the beautifully ornate baroque plate made for Charles II.

Other Tower Highlights:
The Brick Tower, just behind Waterloo Barracks, features an exhibit on the historic menagerie that the tower housed for many centuries, starting with several lions and leopards received as royal gifts in the 13th century.

From here return to Tower Green to see the Chapel Royal of

Waterloo Barracks
(crown jewels)

Inner Ward

Royal Chapel
of St. Peter ad
Vincula

Outer
Ward

Execution
site

Middle Tower
(main entrance)

Byward Tower

Tower Green

Tower of London

Queen's House

St. Peter ad Vincula, the execution site, and, in Bloody Tower, the rooms where Elizabeth I's favorite, explorer Sir Walter Raleigh, spent 13 years as a prisoner. Then proceed to the original keep, the White Tower, whose most magical wardrobe tower) leads down to the home of the six tower ravens, who have their own Raven Master.

Alternatively, Martin Tower in the northeast marks the starting point of the Wall Walk through Henry III's towers and walls, down to Salt Tower. To finish, see some of the tower's best rooms, in the medieval palace. Strung along the south side, overlooking the

rick Tower

Martin Tower

St. John's Chapel

Salt Tower

Moat

White Tower

Wakefield Tower

Traitors' Gate

St. Thomas's Tower

THAMES RIVER

Bloody Tower

room is the tiny St. John's Chapel on the second floor. Beside this, a chunk of Roman wall (adjacent to the ruins of the 12th-century river, they include St. Thomas's and Wakefield Towers, sensitively restored to give an idea of their structure, possible decoration, and probable use during the reign of Edward I. ∎

TOWER BRIDGE

This is the capital's only bridge downriver of London Bridge and, begun in 1886, it is also one of its newest. It was designed to relieve congestion on the other City bridges, while still enabling large vessels to enter the Upper Pool of London's port.

The lower span of Tower Bridge opens to allow tall ships to pass through.

Tower Bridge

- Map p. 203
- Tower Bridge Road, SE1
- 020 7403 3761
- $$
- Tube: Tower Hill Tube/Rail: London Bridge

towerbridge.org.uk

A special Act of Parliament in 1885 authorized the construction of a double drawbridge. It stipulated a Gothic-style bridge to sympathize with the neighboring Tower of London and an opening span width of 200 feet (61 m) and 135 feet (41 m) of headroom.

The Prince of Wales opened the now iconic bridge in 1894. It was 800 feet long (244 m) and cost the huge sum, for the time, of £800,000 ($1.3 million). At the top, the **Tower Bridge Experience** offers changing exhibitions, and the 2014 opening of a new glass walkway provides bird's-eye views of Tower Bridge Road and the Thames from a height of 138 feet (42 m). ■

Tower Bridge Mechanics

Despite its Gothic design, Tower Bridge was extremely modern for its day. The bridge's two towers have a steel frame covered in stone to house the hydraulic machinery and to support the 1,000-ton (1,016 tonne) weight of each bascule; they also contain the elevators to the footbridge. The two side spans are on the suspension principle, the decks being hung from curved girders.

It takes just 90 seconds to raise the bridge. In its heyday, it was opened up to 50 times a day. Today, with the wharves closed, the bridge opens about 500 times a year (up to 15 times a day in summer). Sometimes the openings are for ceremonial occasions, such as the arrival of the royal yacht *Britannia* for the 50th anniversary celebrations of the end of World War II.

THE EAST END

A day spent in this up-and-coming area, though still slightly rough around the edges, is rewarding for its local flavor and relative lack of tourists. Plan your schedule carefully to be sure the places that interest you are open.

Whitechapel & Aldgate

A ten-minute walk north of the Tower of London brings you to Whitechapel, an area long associated with poverty and Jack the Ripper, but which today contains a variety of fascinating stops. **Whitechapel Art Gallery** was founded as a permanent showcase for the visual arts in the East End. C. H. Townsend's art nouveau building of 1897–1899 is still that, and local artists can be found through the gallery. The museum reopened in 2009 after an expansion that doubled the size of its exhibition space.

Wending its way north from Whitechapel Road (via Osborn Street) is **Brick Lane,** center of the East End's Bangladeshi community (and subject of Monica Ali's 2003 novel of the same name) and home to a bustling Sunday market. The area has a long history of attracting immigrants: Huguenots settled the area in the 17th century and Jews migrated en masse in the late 19th century, as did Bengalis a century later. As a result of the latter, the street is famous for its many curry houses serving tasty South Asian cuisine and for its distinct Bengali Muslim atmosphere. Meanwhile, Jack the Ripper buffs will be interested to know that several of the notorious 19th-century murders occurred nearby.

Back on Whitechapel Road is an unusual stop—the **Whitechapel Bell Foundry** (*32–34 Whitechapel Rd., E1, tel 020 7247 2599, whitechapelbellfoundry.co.uk*), where descendants of the men who made Big Ben still practice their skills. Farther west, Aldgate has the sumptuous **Bevis Marks Spanish**

Spitalfields Market has operated since the 19th century.

and Portuguese Synagogue, built in 1701 by a Quaker, Joseph Avis, for Jewish refugees.

Spitalfields

Spitalfields, east of Liverpool Street station, has several interesting sites. On Commercial Street, the covered **Spitalfields Market,** dating from 1893, is liveliest on Sundays. Across from the market's eastern exits, Nicholas Hawksmoor's painstakingly

Whitechapel Art Gallery

- 🅼 Map p. 203
- ✉ 77–82 Whitechapel High St., E1
- ☎ 020 7522 7888
- 🕐 Closed Mon.
- 🚇 Tube: Aldgate East

whitechapelgallery.org

Bevis Marks Spanish and Portuguese Synagogue

- 🅼 Map p. 203
- ✉ Entrance on Bevis Marks, EC3
- ☎ 020 7626 1274
- 🕐 Closed Sat.
- 💲 $
- 🚇 Tube: Aldgate, Liverpool Street

sephardi.org.uk/bevis-marks

Christ Church

- Map p. 203
- Commercial St., E1
- 020 7377 2440
- Closed Sat.
- Tube: Aldgate East Tube/Rail: Liverpool Street Overground: Shoreditch High Street

ccspitalfields.org

Geffrye Museum

- Map p. 203
- 136 Kingsland Rd., E2
- 020 7739 9893
- Closed until summer 2020. Front Gardens open for events (closed Sun.)
- Donation
- Tube/Rail: Liverpool Street or Old Street, then bus or taxi Overground: Hoxton

geffrye-museum .org.uk

restored **Christ Church** (1720) should not be missed. A few blocks south, the market on

---

INSIDER TIP:

Many of the shops and cafés around Columbia Road are open only during the limited time the Sunday flower market is in full swing—plan accordingly!

—JUSTIN KAVANAGH
National Geographic Travel Books editor

Petticoat Lane (actually named Middlesex Street) offers clothes, shoes, handbags, jewelry, and bric-a-brac of non-designer quality. The market teems with life on Sundays, when more than 1,000 vendors hawk their wares on Middlesex and neighboring

streets; the action is confined to perpendicular Wentworth Street from Monday to Friday.

Spitalfields also is home to a rare concentration of fine houses. By the end of the 18th century, 12,000 silk looms built by immigrant French Huguenots thundered in the Georgian lanes. Many houses have been restored, including **Dennis Severs's House** (see sidebar below).

Just north of Spitalfields lies **Hoxton,** one of London's hippest neighborhoods. The scene is constantly in flux, but the streets around Hoxton Square and Old Street host a variety of trendy bars, clubs, restaurants, and art galleries.

A few minutes' walk east of Hoxton brings you to **Columbia Road,** a riot of color and scents during its weekly flower market *(Sun. only, 8 a.m.–3 p.m.).* The dozens of stalls—selling herbs, plants, and bulbs as well as fresh flowers—and the antique shops, art galleries, and cafés nearby have

---

Dennis Severs's House—A House Tour Like No Other

A glimpse of the unassuming three-story house just off Bishopsgate *(18 Folgate St., E1, tel 020 7247 4013, dennissevershouse .co.uk, $$$)* reveals few clues about the unusual experience that awaits inside. The Georgian home has been turned into a living work of art, a three-dimensional canvas that was the brainchild of artist Dennis Severs, who ran the house from the 1970s until his death in 1999.

Each of the ten period rooms is packed with dozens of subtle details to evoke the daily lives of the elusive (and fictitious) Jervis family who theoretically lived in the house from the 18th to the 20th century.

As you stroll from room to room and absorb the atmosphere, a sense of place and time slowly emerges. It's all in the details: a toppled glass; crumbs from a half-eaten muffin; a live pet cat meandering about; the haunting sound of distant footsteps on creaking wooden steps; ticket stubs and other personal keepsakes tucked into a mirror edge; the warmth of a glowing fire; the muffled voices of what purports to be our just-out-of-sight family. The tours are conducted in total silence and soft light to help evoke the mood.

The house's motto is, "You either see it or you don't."

■ The Emirates Air Line cable car crosses the river from Greenwich Peninsula to the Royal Docks.

been officially discovered, so arrive early or close to closing time if you want to beat the crowds.

East End Museums

The East End is home to several excellent small museums.

Geffrye Museum: This elegant museum, currently undergoing a major renovation (reopening scheduled in the summer of 2020), has for a century presented the history of the English home since 1600: Furniture, textiles, and woodwork are arranged in the 1715 building, surrounded by four period gardens. The Front Gardens and the 18th-century almshouse (now home to exhibitions) remain open to visitors.

V&A Museum of Childhood: About a mile (1.6 km) east of the Geffrye Museum, the Victoria and Albert Museum's oversize dollhouses, teddy bears, marionettes, model circus, and much more fill the V&A Museum of Childhood.

Here, the history of children's toys—complete with play areas, rideable rocking horses, and craftmaking stations—draws an enthusiastic under-12 audience as well as nostalgic adults. The museum is currently undergoing a reorganization project.

Ragged School Museum: On the canalside site of the largest Victorian "ragged" (free) school, set up by Thomas Barnardo in 1877, the museum explores the social history of the East End during the darkest days of Industrial Revolution inequity. Try to visit on a Sunday afternoon, when an actor leads a live Victorian classroom lesson.

Sutton House: A couple of miles north of the Ragged School Museum, **Sutton House** *(2–4 Homerton High St., E9, tel 020 8986 2264, nationaltrust.org .uk, $, closed Mon.–Fri.)* is a red-brick Tudor merchant's home. You can tour the historic rooms and bask in the quiet courtyard; there's also a café and art gallery.

V&A Museum of Childhood

🗺 Map p. 203
✉ Cambridge Heath Rd., E2
☎ 020 8983 5200
🚇 Tube: Bethnal Green

www.vam.ac.uk/moc

Ragged School Museum

🗺 Map p. 203
✉ 46–50 Copperfield Rd., E3
☎ 020 8980 6405
🕐 Open Wed.– Thurs. & Sun. p.m.
🚇 Tube: Mile End

raggedschool museum.org.uk

The 2012 Olympic Legacy

According to the mandate of the London Olympic organizing committee, the 2012 games would bring lasting benefits to the previously neglected district around Stratford and the Lee Valley with the structures created for the games. The London Legacy Development Corporation oversaw the urban requalification process of Olympic Park and the surrounding areas. The largest venue, Olympic Stadium, is now home to the East London soccer team, West Ham United, and will host other major sporting and musical events.

Queen Elizabeth II Olympic Park has a number of residential complexes, including the East Village public residential community, which was once lodgings for athletes and now has a school and health center, and the neighborhood of Cobham Manor. Some of the permanent structures from the Olympic Games are open to the public: the VeloPark, where cycling events were held during the games, the Lee Valley Hockey and Tennis Center with numerous public courts, and the London Aquatics Center with public swimming and diving pools.

Theatre Royal Stratford East

- ✉ Gerry Raffles Square, E15
- ☎ 020 8534 0310
- 💲 $$ or more
- 🚇 Tube/Rail: Stratford

stratfordeast.com

Emirates Air Line

- 🗺 Map p. 203
- ✉ Emirates Cable Car Terminal, Edmund Halley Way, S10 (Greenwich side) 27 Western Gateway, E16 (Royal Docks side)
- ☎ 0343 222 1000
- 💲 $
- 🚇 Tube: North Greenwich (Greenwich side) DLR: Royal Victoria Docks (Royal Docks side)

emiratesairline.co.uk

Stratford

Farther east still lies Stratford and the Lee Valley, which were transformed into the epicenter of London's 2012 Olympic and Paralympic Games.

Stratford Town Center:

The revitalization of the area, an ongoing endeavor, has brought formerly impoverished Stratford into the fore. **Westfield Stratford City** shopping center, a high-end mall, connects directly to Stratford's tube/rail/DLR station. A more local mall, the **Stratford Centre,** lies across Meridian Square. Pass its 99p stores and the hallway fruit vendors to reach two fine performance theatres: **Theatre Royal Stratford East** and the **Stratford Circus** (Theatre Square, E15, stratford-circus.com).

Queen Elizabeth Olympic Park:

Stratford's Queen Elizabeth Olympic Park is still in the process of reworking itself into a fully functional post-Olympic community space (see sidebar this page). Though walking trails abound and major rock concerts pop up regularly on the park grounds, the park's biggest and most striking element is the **ArcelorMittal Orbit,** Britain's tallest steel sculpture and an observation tower that dominates the skyline. The elevator, or over 400 stairs, brings you up some 375 feet (114 m) to an airy observation deck that affords sweeping views of cityscapes up to 20 miles (36 km) away, including many of London's most iconic buildings.

Emirates Air Line

South by (and over) the Thames is one of London's newest modes of transportation, the Emirates Air Line cable car. Soaring nearly 300 feet (91 m) over the river, the ten-minute trip offers great views of the capital and connects North Greenwich (near the O₂ Arena but not the town's main tourist sites) with the East End's Royal Docks. ∎

DOCKLANDS

The saving grace of this forthright example of free-market inner-city redevelopment is its setting. For this was a renovation scheme that both flew in the face of the great conservation movement and passed up the opportunity to create something that would be a British 20th-century city of architectural significance. Use the Docklands Light Railway (DLR) to enjoy a spectacular overview of one section, from the Tower of London down to Island Gardens.

Canary Wharf contains some of London's tallest buildings.

The DLR has numerous lines— the route described below terminates at Lewisham and its trains are so marked.

Board your DLR train at either the Bank or Tower Gateway DLR station. (Tower Gateway is a short walk to **St. Katharine Docks,** just east of the Tower of London, an oasis of dockside pubs and restaurants.) The first stop east from both Bank and Tower Gateway is Shadwell, the station to alight for Hawksmoor's handsome church of **St. George-in-the-East** (1714–1729). Next comes Limehouse station, near another magnificent Hawksmoor church, **St. Anne's** (1714–1730), and Narrow Street's pretty houses and historic pub, **The Grapes** (76 Narrow St., tel 020 7897 4396, thegrapes.co.uk), a local favorite since 1583.

The dock views begin just before the line turns southward after Westferry station. Look left to see Greenwich Peninsula's **O₂ Arena,** formerly called the Millennium Dome. West India Quay is the station for the excellent **Museum of London Docklands** (see p. 214), Canary Wharf for the three soaring **Canary Wharf** towers and its associated shopping malls. Heron Quays hovers between two strips of dock, while Island Gardens has the best views of Greenwich—reach it by a

Docklands

- Map p. 203

St. George-in-the-East

- Map p. 203
- Cannon Street Rd., E1
- 020 7481 1345
- DLR: Shadwell

stgite.org.uk

St. Anne's Limehouse

- Map p. 203
- Three Colt Street, E14
- 020 7987 1502
- DLR: Limehouse

stanneslimehouse.org

Museum of London Docklands

⬜ Map p. 203

✉ No. 1 Warehouse, West India Quay, E14

☎ 020 7001 9844

🚇 Tube: Canary Wharf
DLR: West India Quay

museumoflondon .org.uk

long, narrow pedestrian tunnel under the Thames.

Museum of London Docklands

Housed in a Georgian warehouse across the waters from Canary Wharf's gleaming high-rises, this is the ideal spot to explore the turbulent story of London's great port. The museum itself is an object: a handsome, three-story brick building that once stored exotic spices, rum, and cotton.

Starting on the top floor, the chronological arrangement of galleries presents 2,000 action-packed years, from Roman times to the river's heyday as the entrepôt for a world-circling empire, from wartime years to its revival as a modern landscape for living and working.

After an intriguing display on the early Londons—Londinium, Lundenwic, and Lundenburh, each in a slightly different

location—the medieval high-lights include large models of Old London Bridge covered in houses. Later, to illustrate the Tudor period, when explorers searched for riches overseas, there is a splendid interactive story of a voyage on an East Indiaman.

INSIDER TIP:

Don't miss the rare British and German archival footage at the museum's "Black Saturday" film on the 1940s Blitz.

—LARRY PORGES
*National Geographic
Travel Books editor*

As London's wealth grew, so did its quays, and by 1794 some 3,663 laden ships arrived and departed annually. Hence the enclosed docks that surround the museum. Their complexity and atmosphere are captured in the full-scale models of ship's chandlers, alleys, taverns, and shops. Goods of all kinds arrived, from tobacco and sugar to rum and timber; some 14 million tons (12 billion kg) of tea alone were being unloaded annually in the 1930s.

The museum also holds a gallery of boats, an extensive exhibit on the slave trade, and the full story of the 1889 Great Dock Strike. The final chapter, "New Port, New City," looks at the Docklands today, after which you long to go out and explore them. ∎

▪ The warehouses that now host the Museum of London Docklands were originally sugar depots.

GREENWICH

The elegant buildings and excellent museums in and around the expansive Greenwich Park and the delightful town of Greenwich are a peaceful refuge from the resurging Docklands and Greenwich Peninsula, its neighbors.

Greenwich's National Maritime Museum stands out against the skyscrapers of Canary Wharf.

The view of Greenwich from the riverside is one of London's finest. The fabulous setting was created piecemeal in the 17th and 18th centuries, yet Greenwich's true heyday was during the 16th century, during the reign of the Tudors.

Henry V's brother, the Duke of Gloucester, built the riverside Bella Court in 1427, and six years later enclosed 200 acres (80 ha) to make Greenwich Park. Tudor king Henry VII remodeled it in 1500, then Henry VIII, born at Greenwich, adopted it as his favorite palace. His daughters, Mary and Elizabeth I, were born here, as was his son, Edward VI.

Little remains of this period. Anne of Denmark, James I's queen, introduced a new style of architecture from the Continent. Sweeping away some of the vernacular timber palace buildings, she employed Inigo Jones to start building the Queen's House in 1616. This Palladian villa was England's first Renaissance building and Jones's earliest surviving English work. Another queen, Charles I's Henrietta Maria, completed and decorated it, and Jones's son-in-law, John Webb, then enlarged it, building bridges to overcome the problem of the main London–Dover road running through the grounds. During the

Greenwich

Map p. 203

Cutty Sark

- Map p. 203
- King William Walk, SE10
- 020 8858 2698
- $$
- DLR: Cutty Sark DLR/Rail: Greenwich

rmg.co.uk/cutty-sark

Commonwealth, Cromwell's men turned the Queen's House into a biscuit factory.

Then Charles II, who spent his exile in France and dreamed of creating an English Versailles here, returned and began by building a riverside wing in 1664. He also brought in Louis XIV's Versailles gardener, André Le Nôtre, to design a plan for the park, with avenues spreading out from the Queen's House up the hill. When

EXPERIENCE:
Stroll Under the Thames

A little-known way to cross the Thames is to walk underneath it—the **Greenwich Foot Tunnel** opened in 1902 as a means for South Londoners to make it to their jobs at the docks on the Isle of Dogs. More than 1.2 million London commuters take this time-honored route to and from downtown Greenwich each year.

Refurbished in 2012, the 1,217-foot (371 m) pedestrian-only tunnel—running 50 feet (15 m) under the Thames and open 24 hours a day—has the inside wall covered with white glazed tiles. The North access tower has 87 steps, the South one has 100.

William and Mary came to the throne, their extensive building projects also included Greenwich. They invited Sir Christopher Wren to create a hospital for retired sailors, following the success of Royal Hospital Chelsea, his hospital for soldiers (see pp. 180–181). Between 1696 and 1702, he created the breathtaking sight we see today. Demolishing the last of the Tudor buildings, he added a mirror wing to Charles's, with a

great staircase between them. The two U-shaped buildings face each other, with the Queen's House the main focus.

Getting Oriented

Greenwich's many sights and museums, spread out over hundreds of acres, call out for orientation. Start at the Tourist Information Centre, across King WIlliam Walk from *Cutty Sark*, to pick up maps and get your day planned.

Cutty Sark

Toward the foot tunnel opening (see sidebar this page), *Cutty Sark* tea-clipper, built at Clydeside in Scotland in 1869, is the only survivor from a brief period when the fastest ships then available raced between the Far East and London with their high-value cargoes. *Cutty Sark* sailed from China to England in 99 days and then, as a wool carrier, zipped from Australia to London in just 72. The ship recently reopened to the public after a devastating 2007 fire.

Greenwich Town

Now is a good moment to take in a little bit of Greenwich town. Behind elegant Nelson Road and College Approach, the Victorian covered market *(Wed.–Sun., shopgreenwich.co.uk)* survives near Hawksmoor's much restored **St. Alfege Church** (1714). Walk up Stockwell Street, which turns into Croom's Hill at the **Fan Museum** *(tel 020 8305 1441, thefanmuseum.org.uk)*, where the social history and craft of the fan (and the museum's 4,000-piece collection) is laid out in two Georgian town houses.

Painted Hall & Chapel

To visit the grand public rooms of Wren's baroque hospital, once home to 2,710 sailors, find the West Gate entrance on King William Walk. The gateposts are topped with symbolic celestial and terrestrial domes. Walk down College Way. The hospital, now composed of buildings of the **University of Greenwich,** is mostly closed to visitors, but the Painted Hall and Chapel can be visited. The Painted Hall was designed as the sailors' dining room but rarely used. Wren's design, Hawksmoor's architectural decoration, and Sir James Thornhill's paintwork make this England's grandest secular interior of the period. Thornhill's ceiling, painted between 1707 and 1726, shows William and Mary handing down Peace and Liberty to Europe, and a crushed Louis XIV holding a broken sword below them.

Stop and admire the view between the Painted Hall and the Chapel. To the north stands the skyscrapers of Dockland's Canary Wharf; to the south, the lovely Queen's House and the Royal Observatory up the hill.

When the chapel burned down in 1779, James Stuart designed its coolly classical replacement. Stuart's assistant, William Newton, controlled the refined decoration, some of London's finest. See especially the doorway between the chapel and the vestibule.

■ Renovations at the National Maritime Museum include a covered courtyard.

National Maritime Museum

Off Romney Road, the National Maritime Museum—the world's largest nautical museum—traces the history of Britain and the sea. It is also one of the most beautiful museum complexes in Britain. The extensive collection ranges from porcelain and glass to royal barges and clocks.

The museum was founded in 1934. Its 2007 renovation adds a stunning glass-roofed courtyard, themed galleries with plenty of visitor participation, and the Sammy Ofer Wing's café and temporary exhibits .

The collection looks at Britain's navy, merchants, explorers, and their related trades. It considers explorations to the Arctic, mapping the British Empire, and the great migration to North America. There are especially fine collections of ship models, paintings, medals, uniforms, and navigational instruments. Highlights include the gilded state barge designed by

Painted Hall & Chapel

✉ Old Royal Naval College, King William Walk, SE10

☎ 020 8269 4747

🚇 DLR: Cutty Sark DLR/Rail: Greenwich

venuehire.ornc.org

National Maritime Museum

🗺 Map p. 203

✉ Romney Rd., SE10

☎ 020 8858 4422

💲 $$ or more

🚇 DLR: Cutty Sark DLR/Rail: Greenwich

rmg.co.uk/national-maritime-museum

Royal Observatory

- Map p. 203
- Blackheath Ave., SE10
- 020 8858 4422
- $$$
- DLR: Cutty Sark DLR/Rail: Greenwich

rmg.co.uk/royal-observatory

Ranger's House

- Map p. 203
- Chesterfield Walk, SE10
- 0370 333 1181
- Closed Fri.–Sat. & Nov.–Mar.
- $
- DLR/Rail: Greenwich Rail: Blackheath

english-heritage.org.uk

William Kent for Frederick, Prince of Wales, in 1732; Captain Cook's reindeer-hide sleeping bag; and the huge collection devoted to Admiral Lord Nelson, including his silver, swords, uniform, and the last letter he wrote to his daughter before he famously met his death at Trafalgar in 1805.

The Queen's House

Do not miss the interior of the Queen's House. The hall is a perfect 40-foot (12-meter) cube and has Nicholas Stone's black-and-white floor laid in 1638, a Tulip Staircase, and a boldly cantilevered balcony. The building now houses the Maritime Museum's fine-art collection.

Royal Observatory

Up in the 200-acre (80 ha) park, the Royal Observatory consists of several buildings housing the museum's astronomical collection. **Flamsteed House** was built by Wren in 1675 for John Flamsteed, the first Astronomer Royal, and used by his successors until 1948. Timekeepers tick-tock in the rooms, and since 1833 the Time Ball on the eastern turret drops at 1 p.m., so passing sailors can check their clocks.

In 1884 an international convention agreed that Greenwich would mark zero degrees longitude. The Greenwich Meridian passes through the courtyard, dividing the western and eastern hemispheres. This fountainhead of practical science opened a planetarium and horology center in 2007.

Greenwich Park & Ranger's House

Greenwich Park has many fine trees dating back to Le Nôtre's landscaping for Charles II. Along the regular avenues, there are gnarled sweet chestnut, old cypress, paper birch, and prickly castor-oil trees, as well as Indian bean and tulip.

From just below the Pavilion Tea House, the panoramic view of the East End and the City is truly spectacular—one of the best vistas anywhere in London. The refurnished, pretty, 18th-century redbrick Ranger's House is the setting for the eclectic but high-quality collection amassed by Julius Wernher. The German-born millionaire enjoyed spending his money on everything from Italian majolica to medieval ivories and Memling paintings. ∎

Greenwich's Historic Riverside Pubs

For centuries, people have downed pints and dined at Greenwich's riverside pubs. Charles Dickens used to patronize the **Trafalgar Tavern** (Park Row, tel 020 3887 9886, trafalgartavern.co.uk), which still serves cask ales and whitebait, a dish of tiny fried fish, as it did in Dickens's day. The 1837 building has views of the Thames from its bay windows and ample outdoor seating. A couple of hundred yards downriver is another history-steeped alehouse: the **Cutty Sark** (4–6 Ballast Quay, tel 020 8858 3146, cuttysarktavern.co.uk). While Londoners have been making merry at the site since at least 1743, when it was known as the Green Man, the current building dates from 1810. The pub anchored itself to its current identity in the 1950s, when the clipper ship Cutty Sark permanently docked in Greenwich.

Easy escapes from London by train to the comparative calm of Windsor Castle, Oxford, the Cotswolds, Brighton, or York Minster

EXCURSIONS

Swans on the Thames at Windsor

EXCURSIONS

London can sometimes be simply too stimulating, too overwhelmingly urban and noisy, and relentlessly busy. It is comforting to know that this is a very easy city to leave. Yet the story of London until the 20th century was one of people arriving rather than leaving. England's great 19th-century railway system was built to bring people, trade, and supplies into London.

Today, while the congested roads discourage some potential travelers, the railway system has become a vital tool for escaping the city. London's grand Victorian stations invite you to dip into the clean air of England's lush countryside. Travel by train is easy and bargain ticket deals abound *(National Rail inquiries, tel 03457 48 49 50, nationalrail.co.uk).*

For ideas on where to go, the British Tourist Authority *(visitbritain.com)* has details on monuments, historic houses, gardens, music festivals, and accommodations. The National Trust owns and cares for a large number of properties; the National Trust Handbook lists and explains the houses and gardens under its care. Membership brings unlimited free entry to their properties *(tel 0344 800 1895, national trust.org.uk).* English Heritage membership

also offers free entry to their properties *(tel 0870 333 1181, www.english-heritage.org.uk).* For garden enthusiasts, the National Gardens Scheme's annual list of gardens open in England is essential *(ngs.org.uk),* as is the National Trust's guide to 200 gardens.

A 40-minute train ride westward from Waterloo station brings you to Windsor, a delightful outing. In addition to the castle, there are the twin towns of Windsor and Eton to explore, the Great Park, boat trips on the Thames, and Legoland. Trains from Waterloo go southwest to Salisbury, with its magnificent cathedral and close. The ancient monumental stones of Stonehenge stand a few miles to the north on Salisbury Plain, while Inigo Jones's Wilton House and the classic landscape gardens of Stourhead are to the west.

Eurostar trains run from St. Pancras Station to central Paris in less than 2.5 hours, a real day trip or weekend opportunity. Lille (1.5 hours) and Brussels (2 hours) are even closer *(Eurostar inquiries, tel 03432 186 186, eurostar.com).*

From Paddington station, trains snake out westward to Oxford's dreamy college spires. The unashamedly grandiose Blenheim Palace is at nearby Woodstock. Beyond them lies the central Cotswold market town of Cirencester, surrounded by rolling, sheep-dotted hills and picturesque villages. Another train line from Paddington leads to the birthplace of Shakespeare, Stratford-upon-Avon, and to the well-known towns of Broadway and Moreton-in-Marsh, charming but best avoided in the crowded summer months. A third Paddington rail service brings you to the elegant Georgian crescents of Bath.

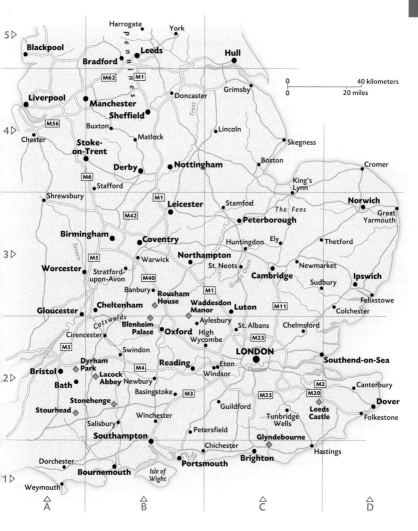

Trains leaving from Charing Cross, Victoria, and Waterloo stations go to England's southeast. Here Canterbury's magnificent cathedral dominates the city, while romantic Leeds Castle, bought by Queen Eleanor in 1278, is near Maidstone. Trains from Victoria also speed down to Lewes for summer opera at Glyndebourne and to coastal Brighton for seaside promenading, antique shops, and the Prince Regent's Pavilion.

Trains from Liverpool Street and King's Cross head north to Cambridge's colleges and cloisters, with Ely's and Peterborough's magical cathedrals nearby.

Farther afield, but perfectly manageable on a long day trip or for a weekend, are York and Leeds. York has its fine Minster, Jorvik Viking Centre, and ancient city walls to explore, while handsome Leeds sits amid the rolling Yorkshire hills so vividly brought to life in the Brontë novels, with the North Yorkshire Moors National Park nearby. ■

WINDSOR

Set beside the Thames 20 miles (32 km) west of central London, Windsor is quick and easy to reach. The castle is magnificent, and is complemented by other things to see and do. A string of annual events includes the Royal Windsor Horse Show in May; the Windsor Carnival in June; the Royal Windsor Rose Show and polo matches in July; and the Windsor Festival in September. All are very jolly, friendly occasions.

▪ The richly decorated surfaces of the King's Dining Room at Windsor Castle

Windsor

🗺 221 C2

Visitor Information

✉ The Old Booking Hall, Windsor Royal Shopping, Thames St.

☎ 01753 743 900
Accommodations: 01753 743907

windsor.gov.uk

Windsor Castle stands on a hill in the town center, its fairy-tale towers silhouetted against the sky. It was William the Conqueror who, in about 1080, threw up this defense as part of his ring of fortifications around London. The Norman castle was converted into a Gothic palace by Edward II. He founded the College of St. George in the Lower Ward and rebuilt the Upper Ward, while Edward IV

built **St. George's Chapel** and Henry VIII added the grand gate in the Lower Ward. For King Charles II, who wanted to make Windsor his principal palace outside London, architect Hugh May created England's grandest suite of baroque **State Apartments,** decorated by wood-carver Grinling Gibbons. Later, George III brought in James Wyatt to enhance the castle's romantic character; but it was George IV

INSIDER TIP:

At Windsor Castle you can enjoy all the pomp and pageantry of the Changing of the Guard without battling large crowds.

—LARRY PORGES
National Geographic
Travel Books editor

who employed Jeffrey Wyatville to raise Henry II's famous **Round Tower** to its present height of 215 feet (66 m) and improve the castle's medieval silhouette with extra towers. Wyatville also refurbished the State Rooms and completed the park's **Long Walk,** begun by Charles II.

Queen Victoria made Windsor her principal palace, so it was natural that when her consort, Prince Albert, died in the castle in 1861 she chose to create his memorial chapel here.

After a devastating fire on November 20, 1992 (see sidebar right), the Grand Reception Room, State Dining Room, Crimson Drawing Room, and other casualties were meticulously restored in a modern Gothic style. This style can be seen especially in the **Lantern Lobby.**

The State Apartments, embellished with art from the queen's unmatched collection, may be the central showpiece of the castle, but do not miss other special things. There is the exquisite **Queen Mary's Dolls' House,** designed by Sir Edwin Lutyens for

the queen in 1924 to a scale of 1:12; the **China Museum,** whose display cabinets contain Sèvres, Worcester, Meissen, and more; **St. George's Chapel,** built 1475–1528; and the **Albert Memorial Chapel,** created by Sir George Gilbert Scott.

At the foot of Windsor town, past the **Theatre Royal** *(Thames St., tel 01753 853888, theatre royalwindsor.co.uk)* and the house where Sir Christopher Wren lived, lies the Thames. Towpath walks hereabout are beautiful, and riverboats journey up- and downriver. Over the bridge lies **Eton,** whose college buildings were the haunt of such schoolboys as the Duke of Wellington. The town is bounded in the south and east by **Windsor Great Park,** whose 4,800 acres (1,942 ha) contain trees more than 500 years old. Just to the south, **Legoland** lives up to expectations. ∎

Windsor Castle

☎ 020 7766 7304

🕐 Open daily except during state occasions & official engagements. St. George's Chapel is closed to visitors on Sunday unless attending services.

💲 $$$$ Tour of the castle: $$$

royalcollection .org.uk

Legoland

☎ 0871 222 2001

🕐 Closed Nov. 2–Mar. 8

💲 $$$$$

legoland.co.uk

The Windsor Fire

On November 20, 1992, fire spread through Windsor Castle after a spotlight ignited a curtain in the queen's private chapel. The flames consumed nine main rooms and about 100 smaller rooms in the 900-year-old royal fortress. Afterward, the fire sparked a national debate over who should pay for repairs: Queen Elizabeth II or the taxpayer-funded government, which owns the castle. Ultimately, the queen assumed most of the £37 million ($60 million) bill and, to help cover the costs, opened the State Rooms of Buckingham Palace for summer tours. The castle reopened in 1997. A new stained-glass window in the chapel depicts a fireman spraying water onto a burning castle.

OXFORD

Lying between the Rivers Cherwell and Thames (called the Isis here), the honey-colored walls and spires of Oxford's ancient university buildings give the center of this busy city a timeless tranquility. By joining a guided walk, visitors can see colleges that are little changed in their layout and traditions since their medieval or Tudor foundation.

 Looking over the Radcliffe Camera and All Souls College at Oxford University

Oxford

🏛 221 B2

🚂 Train takes
1 hour from
Paddington
station;
National Express
(08717 818181,
nationalexpress
.com) coach
about 1 hour
and 45 minutes
from Victoria
Coach station

Visitor Information

✉ Broad St.

☎ 01865 252 200

oxfordcity.co.uk

Among the oldest colleges is **Merton** (Merton St., tel 01865 276310), founded in 1264. Its 14th-century Mob Quad contains the oldest library in England still in use. **Balliol** (Oxford, OX1, tel 01865 277 777) has nurtured more politicians than any other college. Poet Percy Bysshe Shelley was "rusticated" (sent away for a term) for writing subversive pamphlets from **University College** on High Street, called The High (tel 01865 276602). **Magdalen** (pronounced "Maudlin"; Oxford, OX1, tel 01865 276000) was built at the end of the 15th century and

has a lovely deer park behind it. The largest college, **Christ Church** (St. Aldate's, tel 01865 276150), was founded by Cardinal Wolsey in 1525. Its chapel is also Britain's smallest cathedral, built in the 12th century as a priory church. In summer, a towpath stroll might go across **Christ Church Meadow** to Britain's oldest **Botanic Gardens** (tel 01865 286 690, www.botanic-garden.ox.ac.uk, $), whose most exotic plants are kept in riverside greenhouses.

To join undergraduates in a traditional Oxford pastime, test your skills by renting a punt on the Cherwell (pronounced "Char-well") from beside Magdalen Bridge or on the Isis from Folly Bridge near Christ Church, where boat trips depart. Summer events include the Summer Eights rowing competitions at the end of May or in June.

Out at Garsington village, operas are staged at **Garsington Manor** (tel 01865 361 234) in June, when the audience picnics in the gardens in fine clothes to create a *fête champêtre* atmosphere.

Oxford's impressive museums are open all year. The **Ashmolean** (*Beaumont St., tel 01865 278000, ashmolean.org, closed Mon.*), founded in 1683 and Britain's

---

INSIDER TIP:

The small, atmospheric Turf Tavern [4–5 Bath Place], popular with students and dons, is a great place to get a pint.

—PATRICIA DANIELS
National Geographic contributor

---

oldest public museum, houses Egyptian, classical, Oriental, and European art, plus silver and ceramics. The city's own story is told in the **Museum of Oxford** (*St. Aldate's, tel 01865 249 811, oxford.gov.uk/museumofoxford*), and that of the universe is explored in the glorious building of the **Oxford University Museum of Natural History** (*Parks Rd., tel 01865 272950, www.oum.ox.ac.uk*), complete with dodo remains. The **Pitt Rivers Museum** (*Parks Rd., tel*

01865 613 000, www.prm.ox.ac.uk) is devoted to archaeology and anthropology. Other Oxford buildings to seek out include the **Bodleian Library,** founded in 1598, and the round **Sheldonian Theatre,** both on Broad Street; the domed **Radcliffe Camera,** part of the Bodleian Library, is next to the Sheldonian.

Around Oxford

There are three interesting country houses to visit in the vicinity of Oxford, each with a fine garden.

The Duke of Marlborough's 18th-century **Blenheim Palace** stands outside the charming village of Woodstock, 8 miles (13 km) northwest of Oxford on the A44. John Vanbrugh's huge Italianate palace is surrounded by a very English park. Tapestries, paintings, and fine furniture fill the gilded State Rooms and Long Library. The rolling acres of park include a narrow-gauge railway, a lake, and the Marlborough Maze.

Another grand house near Oxford is **Waddesdon Manor,** a French Renaissance château built by Baron Ferdinand de Rothschild between 1874 and 1889. Approximately 20 miles (32 km) northeast of Oxford, the house now belongs to the National Trust. French furniture gleams in the gilded salons, and the French-influenced gardens are clipped to perfection. Less grand **Rousham House,** 12 miles (19 km) north of Oxford on the A4260, is a 17th-century house standing in a garden little changed since it was landscaped by William Kent in the 18th century. ■

Blenheim Palace
- 🗺 221 B2
- ✉ Woodstock, Oxfordshire
- ☎ 01993 810530
- 🕐 Daily
- 💲 Palace, park, & gardens: $$$ Park & gardens: $$

blenheimpalace.com

Waddesdon Manor
- 🗺 221 B2–B3
- ✉ Waddesdon, Buckinghamshire
- ☎ 01296 820 414
- 🕐 Opening times may vary: check the website before your visit
- 💲 $$$$ Grounds: $$

waddesdon.org.uk

Rousham House
- 🗺 221 B3
- ✉ Rousham, Oxfordshire
- ☎ 01869 347110
- 🕐 House open only by appt. Gardens open all year. No children under 15
- 💲 $$

rousham.org

SALISBURY & STONEHENGE

South Wiltshire is best known for two truly magnificent sites: the soaring elegance of Salisbury Cathedral, set in its magnificent close, and Stonehenge's standing stones on the open grasslands of Salisbury Plain. This is ideal country for walking, horseback riding, cycling, and exploring unspoiled villages.

■ Horizontal lintels still crown some of the upright sarsen stones in Stonehenge's outer circle.

Salisbury

⚐ 221 B2

Visitor Information

✉ Fish Row

☎ 01722 342860

visitwiltshire.co.uk/ salisbury

Salisbury Cathedral

✉ The Close, Salisbury

☎ 01722 555120

🕐 Open daily. Evensong Sun., 4:30 p.m.

$ Donation. Various tours: $$

salisburycathedral .co.uk

Salisbury

The Avon, Wylye, and Bourne Rivers twist their way through the chalk valleys to meet at New Sarum, or Salisbury. A good place to start exploring this city, however, is at **Old Sarum,** just north of the city. Here mounds, ditches, and walls tell the silent story of an Iron Age fort, a Roman settlement, a fortified Saxon town, and a Norman castle *(Castle Rd., tel 01722 335398)* and **cathedral.**

It was Bishop Richard Poore who moved Old Sarum's cathedral to its present site. In 1220 he began the only medieval cathedral in England to be built in a single, unified style throughout. Completed in 1258, its 400-foot-tall (122 m) spire was added a

generation later. While the exterior is rich in traceried windows and ornate friezes, the interior's simple symmetry is emphasized by a lack of furnishings and by stained glass. There are some grand tombs, however, such as that of Bishop Giles de Bridport (1260). The Chapter House, in the cloisters, exhibits one of the four surviving copies of the Magna Carta.

Salisbury's **Cathedral Close** is the finest and largest of its kind in the country. Once the precinct of the ecclesiastical community serving the cathedral, it is now a peaceful square overlooked by elegant houses. Pierced by three strong gateways, its walls were built around 1330. The gates are still locked each night.

Several buildings in the close can be visited. **Mompesson House** *(The Close, tel 01722 335 659, closed Thurs.–Fri. & Nov.–Mar., $, nationaltrust.org.uk),* run by the National Trust, was built for Charles Mompesson in 1701 and later decorated by Charles Longueville with fine plasterwork and a carved oak staircase. The Wardrobe *(tel 01722 419419, thewardrobe.org.uk)* dates from 1254, when it was built to store the bishop's clothing; today it houses the **Rifles Berkshire and Wiltshire Museum**'s thousands of military items from the Infantry Regiments of Berkshire and Wiltshire's collection. Sit beneath the magnificent roof of the **Medieval Hall** (tel 01722 324 732) to see a 40-minute show recounting Salisbury's history. For information on Stonehenge and related sites, visit the **Salisbury Museum** (The King's House, The Close, tel 01722 332151, $, salisburymuseum.org.uk).

Around Salisbury

Another elegant building, just west of the city, is **Wilton House,** home of the Herbert family since 1544. Its magnificent rooms are matched by a romantic park. For garden lovers, **Heale Garden** (Middle Woodford, tel 01722 782504) is a pretty 5-mile (8 km) drive north through the Wiltshire countryside, and **Houghton Lodge Gardens & Hydroponicum** (near Stockbridge,

tel 01264 810502) are 16 miles (26 km) east, beside the river Test in Hampshire.

Stonehenge

One of the most significant prehistoric sites stands on the rolling chalklands of Salisbury Plain. This mystical, enigmatic, and surely symbolic circle of giant standing stones may have marked the center of an ancient administrative, cultural, and social territory that was important as long ago as 3000 B.C. It stands near the sites of five prehistoric communities, marked by the remains of ceremonial and domestic structures, including burial mounds and the markings of Celtic farms and fields.

The original function of the stone circle has been discussed endlessly: Perhaps it was the center for a religious celebration of the winter and summer solstices, aligned to moon and sun; perhaps a gigantic astronomical stone calendar. At a later date, a 2-mile-long (3.2 km) avenue to the Avon River was added to mark the line of Midsummer's Day sunrise, and about 80 blue stones, some weighing 2 tons (1.8 tonnes), were transported 240 miles (386 km) from the Preseli Hills of South Wales. Later still, trilithons were added at the heart of the complex.

Stonehenge is a center for revived Druid ceremonies; several thousand people attend the summer solstice. To protect the stones from wear and vandalism, visitors are no longer allowed into the circle itself, but may walk around the circle close to the stones. ■

Wilton House
- ⊠ Wilton, Salisbury
- ☎ 01722 746729
- ⊕ Open Sun.–Thurs. Closed Sep.–May
- ⑤ $$

wiltonhouse.com

Stonehenge
- △ 221 B2
- ⊠ Near Amesbury, Wiltshire, SP4
- ☎ 08073 331181
- ⑤ $$$ (includes excellent audio guide)

www.english
-heritage.org.uk

Visiting Beyond the Henge

Stonehenge's famous circle is not the only local reminder of the lives once lived by ancient British peoples. The Stonehenge World Heritage site encompasses 6,500 acres (2,600 ha) of protected land containing the Cursus (a long rectangular earthwork), other henge monuments such as Woodhenge and Durrington Walls, neolithic and Bronze Age barrows (burial mounds), and an Iron Age hill fort.

BATH

Straddling the Avon River in a great bowl of softly curving hills, Bath was the Roman spa Aquae Sulis, popular from the first to the fifth century. The mineral-rich waters and natural hot spring have ensured the city's prosperity through the ages.

Bath

221 A2

Visitor Information

✉ Bath Visitor Information Centre, Bridgwater House, 2 Terrace Walk, Bath, BA1

☎ 1225 614 420

visitbath.co.uk

After speeding along high above the Avon Valley, the train from London slows down for a magnificent panorama of the city, with **Bath Abbey's** *(Bath, BA1 1LT, tel 01225 422462)* pinnacled tower rising above Georgian terraces and crescents. The abbey is a good place to start a visit. It is the last complete monastic church to be built before the 16th-century Dissolution of the Monasteries.

Nearby, the **Roman Baths** complex, with temple, baths, and a museum of sculptures, coins,

and other remains, constitutes one of Europe's best Roman sites. Adjoining them, the Pump Room was the social center of 18th-century Bath, whose fashionable visitors included the Prince of Wales, later George IV. Architect Nicholas Grimshaw has incorporated some of the complex into Britain's only natural thermal spa.

It was during the 18th century that much of Bath was built, the mellow, local stone creating an elegant Georgian town that is lovingly preserved. Great Pulteney Street is particularly fine, reached across Robert Adam's Pulteney Bridge, built in 1770. Other remarkable buildings worth seeking out include **Guildhall** *(bath venues.co.uk)*, on the High Street next to the old covered market, the beautiful **Theatre Royal** *(tel 01225 448844)*, on Milsom Street, and the **Octagon** building lying off it. The **Circus** and **Royal Crescent** are two superb buildings created by Bath's chief architects, John Wood the Elder and his son, John Wood the Younger. **No. 1 Royal Crescent** has been meticulously restored and furnished and is open to the public. It is worth comparing with the home of astronomer **William Herschel** *(19 New King St., tel. 01225 446865)*.

Bath abounds in museums, many celebrating its history. The **Building of Bath Museum**

■ Bath's ancient baths are part of a Roman complex.

EXPERIENCE: Taking the Waters in Bath

Make like a Roman and experience the natural, hot waters that have drawn people to Bath for centuries. The original **Roman Baths** (Pump Room, Stall St., tel 01225 477785, romanbaths.co.uk, $$$) are now a museum and historic site. The bath's Pump Room restaurant offers free tastes of the water (with paid admission), bursting with 43 minerals; in the 17th century, drinking the spa waters replaced the soaking bath as the vogue method of absorbing the curative minerals.

The nearby **Thermae Bath Spa** (Hot Bath St., tel 01225 33 1234, thermaebath spa.com) still offers hot baths and treatments for today's visitors (including a "Watsu" flotation stretch and massage in the city's famous waters).

(The Vineyards, tel 01225 333895) tells of Georgian Bath, while the **Georgian Garden** at No. 4, The Circus, perfectly re-creates an 18th-century town garden. The **Book Museum** celebrates the craft of bookbinding and Bath's place in English literature; the story of one small Bath firm is told at the **Museum of Bath at Work** (Julian Rd., tel 01225 318348). **Bath Postal Museum** (27 Northgate St., tel 01225 460333, www.bath postalmuseum.org) reminds visitors that the world's first stamp was posted from Bath on May 2, 1840. The **Bath Boating Station** (Forrester Rd., tel 01225 312900, bath boating.co.uk) is a living museum of skiffs, punts, and canoes for rent.

Another museum worth visiting is the **Holburne Museum and Crafts Study Centre** (Great Pulteney St. tel. 01225 388569, holburne.org), Sir William Holburne's collection of silver, porcelain, paintings, and more, housed in the 18th-century Sydney Hotel. In the basement of the grand 18th-century Assembly Rooms, the **Fashion Museum** (Bennett St., tel 01225 477789, fashionmuseum.co.uk) has an excellent collection covering Tudor times to the present.

Around Bath

On the southeastern outskirts of the city, the **American Museum in Britain** displays its collection in 18 re-created period rooms of the 17th to 19th century. **Bradford-on-Avon** is a delightful riverside town about 8 miles (13 km) southeast of Bath. Farther afield, but still easily reached, the National Trust runs three superb sites: **Dyrham Park,** 8 miles (13 km) north on the A46, an early 18th-century house with deer park; **Lacock Abbey** (Lacock, tel 01249 730459, abbey closed Tues. & Nov.–Feb., $$), 12 miles (19 km) east of Bath, just off the A350, a country house founded as an abbey in the 13th century and now home to a museum commemorating Henry Fox Talbot, father of photography; and **Stourhead** (near Mere, Wiltshire, BA12, tel 01747 841152, nationaltrust.org.uk/stourhead, $$$), 20 miles (32 km) south of Bath off the B3092, a beautiful 18th-century English landscape garden. ■

American Museum in Britain

- ✉ Claverton Manor, Bath
- ☎ 01225 460503
- 🕐 Closed Mon. & Nov.–mid-Mar.
- 💲 $$$

americanmuseum.org

Bradford-on-Avon

Visitor Information
- ✉ 50 St. Margaret's St.
- ☎ 01225 865797

bradfordonavon.co.uk

Dyrham Park

- 🅰 221 A2
- ✉ Dyrham, near Bath, Gloucestershire
- ☎ 01179 372501
- 🕐 Check website for opening hours
- 💲 $$

nationaltrust.org.uk/dyrham-park

STRATFORD & THE COTSWOLDS

The town where the poet, actor, and playwright William Shakespeare was born is now so bound up with its renowned citizen that avoiding crowds of fellow visitors is a challenge. The same applies to the surrounding countryside and the Cotswolds that stretch southward from here. Try the off-season; and always reserve tickets in advance for the Royal Shakespeare Theatre *(tel 1789 403493)*.

■ Shakespeare's birthplace is furnished as it might have appeared in the 16th century.

Stratford-upon-Avon

🗺 221 B3

Visitor Information

✉ Bridgefoot

☎ 01789 868191

stratford-upon-avon .co.uk

Gloucestershire

🗺 221 A2–B3

Visitor Information

✉ Corinium Museum, Park St., Cirencester

☎ 01285 654180

cotswolds.com

✉ 77 Promenade, Cheltenham

☎ 01242 522 878

visitcheltenham.com

For Shakespeare pilgrims, there are five key sites to see. In Stratford, **Shakespeare's Birthplace** *(tel 01789 204016, shakespeare .org.uk)* on Henley Street; **Nash's House and New Place** *(tel 01789 292325)* on Chapel Street, home of Shakespeare's granddaughter and site of his retirement house, where an Elizabethan knot garden has been planted; and the Tudor **Hall's Croft** *(tel 01789 204016)*, where his daughter and son-in-law, Dr. John Hall, lived, furnished in period style. Outside the town, you can visit his wife **Anne Hathaway's Cottage** *(tel 01789 292100)*, a thatched Tudor farmhouse at Shottery; and his mother Mary Arden's half-timbered house at **Wilmcote.**

Ten miles (16 km) north of Stratford on the A46, **Warwick Castle** *(tel 08712 652 000, warwick-castle.com)* is one of England's finest, having grown from a wooden motte and bailey built by William the Conqueror in 1068 into a huge complex. A few miles north again, the ruins of **Kenilworth Castle** *(tel 01926 852078)* include a Norman keep, Great Hall, and gardens. **Ragley Hall** *(8 miles/13 km west of Stratford, tel 01789 762090, ragley.co.uk)* and its 400-acre (162 ha) park is matched by some smaller estates in the area, including **Snowshill Manor** *(tel 01386 852410)* and **Hidcote Manor Gardens** *(tel 01386 438333).*

The Cotswolds

South of Stratford, sheep grazing the rolling hills of the Cotswolds brought prosperity that can be seen today in handsome stone-built market towns. **Cirencester** is the grandest, **Burford** has an impressive main street, and **Charlbury** is set in the timeless Evenlode Valley. **Tetbury** and **Chipping Norton** both testify to wool wealth. However, there may be too many visitors to enjoy the beauty of such towns as Bourton-on-the-Water, Moreton-in-Marsh, and Stow-on-the-Wold. ■

CANTERBURY & LEEDS CASTLE

Canterbury Cathedral, founded in A.D. 597, is the Mother Church of the Anglican Communion and the Seat of the Archbishop of Canterbury. As such, it is not only full of interest inside; it also dominates the city's history. To explore the streets and sights, you can walk alone or take a guided tour, gaze at the city from a punt, or ride through in a horse and carriage.

The present **Cathedral** building *(tel 01227 762862, canterbury -cathedral.org),* started in 1070, displays more than four centuries of architectural progress from the Norman choir and crypt to the high Gothic nave. The landmark Bell Harry Tower rises 235 feet (72 m) high and was built in 1495, in the Gothic style. Archbishop Thomas Becket was murdered in the northwest transept in 1170 by Henry II's knights because he had dared to criticize the king. The shrine to the saint became a major medieval pilgrimage site. (Geoffrey Chaucer's fictional pilgrims in *The Canterbury Tales* were typical.) The shrine itself was pillaged by Henry VIII, but candles still burn on the site in Trinity Chapel at the cathedral's east end.

In the town, walk through the streets of half-timbered medieval buildings from the cathedral to **St. Augustine's Abbey** *(Longport, tel 1227 767 345),* the **Roman Museum** *(Longmarket, tel 01227 785575),* and **The Canterbury Tales** *(St. Margaret's St., tel 01227 696 002)* where Chaucer's pilgrims' tales are reenacted.

Just east of Maidstone, **Leeds Castle** was one of Henry VIII's palaces. Built in the middle of a lake and surrounded by 500 acres (202 ha) of parkland, this is the epitome of the romantic castle. ∎

Canterbury

◭ 221 D2

Visitor Information

✉ 18 High St.

☎ 01227 862162

canterbury.co.uk

Leeds Castle

◭ 221 C2

✉ Broomfield, Maidstone

☎ 01622 765400

⑤ $$$

leeds-castle.com

▪ Canterbury Cathedral's soaring Gothic nave

BRIGHTON & HOVE

The Prince Regent put Brighton on the map when he built his Royal Pavilion, an India-inspired palace. Ever since, Brighton has welcomed visitors and offered them entertainment.

Brighton

📍 221 C1

Visitor Information

✉ King's Rd.

☎ 01273 290337

visitbrighton.com

Glyndebourne

📍 221 C1

Festival Opera

✉ Glyndebourne, Lewes, East Sussex

☎ 01273 818321

💲 $$ or more

🕐 Performances late May–end Aug.

glyndebourne.com

Visit the **Royal Pavilion** *(tel 03000 290900)* to catch a glimpse of Regency high life. Nearby, you can get lost in the maze of lanes crammed with antiques shops, while a walk along the seafront passes Regency terraces and Palace Pier. Brighton also has an excellent **Museum & Art Gallery** *(Church St., tel 03000 290900)*, haunting Victorian memorials in **Lewes Road Cemeteries** *(tel 01273 604020)*, the **Booth Museum of Natural History** *(194 Dyke Rd., tel 03000 290900)*, and the **Brighton Fishing Museum** *(201 King's Rd., tel 01273 723064)*, as well as a delightful theater and a calendar of arts festivals and fairs. North of the city center, there is Edwardian **Preston Manor** *(tel 03000 290 900)*. In neighboring **Hove,** the **Regency Town House** *(13 Brunswick Square, tel 01273 206306)* has been restored and is open to the public, while on the outskirts **Foredown Tower** *(Foredown Rd., Portslade, tel 01273 415625)*, a converted Edwardian water tower, gives fine views over the Sussex Downs.

Walks on the downs can be combined with visits to pretty Alfriston or Firle, villages within a few miles of each other. They lie about 15 miles (24 km) east of Brighton, near **Charleston Farm House** *(tel 01323 811265)*, associated with the Bloomsbury Group. Opera enthusiasts can enjoy world-class opera in Michael Hopkins's theater at **Glyndebourne,** taking picnic supper on the lawns in their formal evening dress during the interval. ■

EXPERIENCE: Going Local in Brighton

From antique motorcycles to paper unicorns, you never know just what you might find on Madeira Drive, Brighton's beachfront corridor and home to more than a dozen annual events (see *brighton run.co.uk*).

In December the road practically ignites as residents parade with glowing, handmade paper lanterns in shapes ranging from whimsical clocks to unicorns and suns. Dubbed **"Burning the Clocks"** and held on the winter solstice, the celebration culminates when marchers toss the lanterns into a beach bonfire.

Madeira Drive also hosts a number of motorcycle events, including the **Pioneer Bike Run,** which invites owners of motorcycles built before 1915 to ride from London to Brighton. Some entrants are little more than bicycles with motors, and roadside repairs are common, but more than 300 vehicles sputter through the run every March.

In September (usually on the second Saturday) the **National Speed Trials** (brightonandhovemotorclub.co.uk) zip in for quarter-mile (0.4 km) car and motorcycle sprints that date back to 1905.

CAMBRIDGE

Set in a loop of the Cam River in flat countryside, Cambridge is an idyllic, tranquil university city, quite different from bustling, hectic Oxford.

The oldest college is **Peterhouse** *(tel 01223 338200)*, founded in 1284. Each one that followed was a superb example of its architectural period. The most beautiful is **King's College** *(tel 01223 331100)*, best seen from a boat on the Cam River or from the secluded walks of the "Backs," meadows across the river from the colleges. King's College Chapel is probably Britain's finest example of Perpendicular Gothic architecture.

Queens' *(tel 01223 335 500)* has wonderful Tudor courts and the Mathematical Bridge built in 1749 without nails or bolts (but subsequent repair work has added them). **Trinity** *(tel 01223 338400)* has a Wren-designed library by the river. Undergraduates try to race around Great Court while the clock strikes twelve. Other colleges not to miss are **Clare, Magdalene, St. John's, Jesus,** and **Emmanuel.** Visitors may walk into their courtyards and chapels, and sometimes their gardens, or take a guided tour. (Access may be restricted at certain times.)

■ **Punters take visitors down the Cam River in tranquil Cambridge.**

Ely & Peterborough

Both these cities in the flat fenlands north of Cambridge have magnificent Norman cathedrals. Ely's is famous for its lantern tower and stained glass, Peterborough's for its west front and painted ceiling. Ely *(tel 01353 662062)* is an unspoiled market town on the Great Ouse River about 15 miles (24 km) north of Cambridge; Peterborough *(tel 01733 452336)* lies 25 miles (40 km) northwest of Ely. ■

Cambridge

🅰 221 C3

Visitor Information

✉ Peas Hill

☎ 01223 791 500

visitcambridge.org

YORK & LEEDS

A three-hour train journey from London reaches the wild moors of Yorkshire in northern England. Here Romans, Saxons, Vikings, and Normans have all left their mark on York.

York

▲ 221 B5

Visitor Information

✉ 1 Museum St.

☎ 01904 550099

visityork.org

Visitors can walk the city walls, first built by the Romans, and explore the **Jorvik Viking Centre** (Coppergate, tel 01904 615505), where they travel back through the centuries in "time-cars." But it is **York Minster** (tel 01904 557200) that dominates the narrow streets. Begun in the 13th century, it is England's largest Gothic church.

Other attractions include the **York Castle Museum** (The Eye of York, tel 01904 687687) with re-created period rooms, the huge **National Railway Museum** (Leeman Rd., tel 03330 161010), **Merchant Adventurers' Hall**

(Fossgate, tel 01904 654818), built by York's medieval guilds, and the **City Art Gallery** (Exhibition Square, tel 01904 687687), with paintings spanning 600 years.

Leeds

Across the moors lies **Leeds** (visitor information, City Station, tel 113 3786977, visitleeds.co.uk), a handsome city whose markets and public buildings testify to centuries of wealth. In town, museums include the **City Art Gallery** (The Headrow, tel 0113 3785350), notable for 20th-century works, and the **Royal Armouries Museum** (Armouries Dr., tel 0113 2201999), where you can watch live displays of jousting and swordsmanship. The **Henry Moore Institute**—the sculptor studied in Leeds—puts on a variety of exhibitions. Three of Britain's national parks are within reach: the Yorkshire Dales, the North York Moors, and the Peak District, all glorious places for walking. ■

▪ York Minster stands tall over the city of York.

TRAVELWISE

Bicycles for rent in Hyde Park

TRAVELWISE

PLANNING YOUR TRIP
When to Go

London is what you make of it. There are, however, seasons that are particularly good for certain interests, such as traditional events, gardens, or church music.

January, February, and **March** are good months for getting into popular plays and operas and enjoying museums in relative peace. Even the top restaurants are easier to book; and shoppers can take advantage of the sales. On the last Sunday of January, the beheading of Charles I is commemorated; February traditions include Chinese New Year celebrations in Soho.

Easter, which may fall in March or April, brings exceptional music when the Easter Passions are sung in the cathedrals, churches, and concert halls. At this time of year, there is plenty of horse racing, and the Oxford versus Cambridge boat race takes place between Putney Bridge and Hammersmith. In the parks, daffodils carpet the lawns while trees burst into leaf. Hyde Park is the setting for the Easter Parade and the Harness Horse Parade.

April and **May** mark an increase in cultural events. Arts festivals, houses that open only for the summer months, and fashionable sports such as polo at Ascot and the Windsor Horse Trials gallop into action. A string of antiques fairs begins. There are flower shows at the Royal Horticultural Society's halls in Pimlico, culminating in the Chelsea Flower Show. The queen spends most of this time at Windsor, so the State Apartments may be closed.

Watch for special events on the first and last Mondays of May, both public holidays.

June brings hope for good weather. Arts festivals include Greenwich, Spitalfields, and the summer-long season of open-air concerts at Kenwood House and Marble Hill House. Traditional sporting events include The Derby at Epsom, Ascot Week, Henley Royal Regatta, the AEGON tournament at Queen's, and the All England Lawn Tennis championships at Wimbledon—all need advance reservations for good tickets. Traditional events peak with Beating the Retreat, the Garter Ceremony at Windsor, and Trooping the Colour. Again, the queen is often at Windsor, when State Apartments close.

July and **August** are months when offices go quiet and many Londoners leave town. But museums and theaters fill up with visitors. To June's arts festivals add the City of London Festival and the nightly Henry Wood Promenade ("Prom") concerts at the Royal Albert Hall. With Londoners back from the summer break, **September** and **October** mix festivals on the Thames and in Covent Garden with major art shows, operas, and plays. In the parks, summer blooms give way to fall color.

November and **December** are strong on tradition: the State Opening of Parliament (October or November), Guy Fawkes Day, the Lord Mayor's Show, and then the Christmas festivities. Shops and streets are decorated, theater tickets need to be reserved in advance, and an abundance of music is performed in cathedrals, churches, and concert halls.

Climate

British weather is a daily surprise for every British person. Anything can happen on this island at the mercy of its surrounding seas, Gulf Stream, and prevailing winds: hot sun in April, sleet in August. This has two results in London: Weather is a constant topic of conversation; and, since anything can happen, few people carry umbrellas or raincoats.

For visitors, the motto is "be prepared." Ignore Londoners' laid-back approach to equipment and carry a fold-up umbrella, a waterproof coat, and consider waterproof shoes. Finally, any day planned outside needs a fallback indoor plan in case it rains.

Passports & Visas

Nationals of the United States, Canada, Australia, and New Zealand can enter the United Kingdom with just a passport (no visa is required).

HOW TO GET TO CENTRAL LONDON
From the Airports

Gatwick (tel 0844 892 0322, gatwickairport.com) The airport lies 30 miles (48 km) south of central London; traveling to London by rail is faster and more reliable than by road. There are two services: The more expensive Gatwick Express (tel 0845 850 1530, gatwickexpress.com) to Victoria, a 30- to 35-minute ride, runs every 15 minutes by day and less frequently by night. Southern trains (southernrailway.com) on the same route take longer as they are not nonstop. Thameslink trains stop at London Bridge, Blackfriars, City Thameslink, Farringdon, and King's Cross Thameslink.

By road, the easy Bus (easybus .co.uk) takes around 65 minutes; departures every 15 to 20 minutes, 4:10 a.m. to 12:50 a.m. A taxi costs more than £60 ($90).

Heathrow (tel 0844 335 1801, heathrowairport.com) London's main airport is 15 miles (24 km) west of central London, so rail and road are both options. Rail is more dependable during rush hours. By rail, the Heathrow Express (tel 345 600 1515, heathrowexpress.com) to Paddington, a 15-minute ride to Terminals 1, 2, & 3 (20 minutes to Terminals 4 & 5), runs every 15 minutes between 5:10 a.m. and 11:25 p.m. By Tube train, the Piccadilly line trains, a 40- to 60-minute ride, run regularly 5:02 a.m. to 11:35 p.m. through central London. National Express (tel 0871 781 8181, national express.com) runs from Heathrow Central Bus Terminal to Victoria Coach station every 30 minutes and takes 60 to 90 minutes. A taxi costs £30 to £50 ($45–$75), depending upon destination, congestion, and resulting trip time.

London City Airport (tel 020 7646 0088, londoncityairport .com) This small airport lies on the Isle of Dogs in Docklands, 9 miles (14 km) east of central London. It has a DLR station with links to Canary Wharf and Bank, on or near the Tube. Services run every 8 to 15 minutes; journey time to Bank is 22 minutes. A pre-bookable bus shuttle (tel 902 334 633, shuttledirect.co.uk) runs to and from Canary Wharf and central London. A taxi takes 20 to 40 minutes and costs £20 to £25 ($30–$37).

Stansted (tel 0808 169 7032, stanstedairport.com) The city's newer airport is situated 35 miles (56 km) northeast of central London, so getting there by rail is much faster than by road. Stansted Express (stansted express.com) to Liverpool Street station takes 47 minutes, and runs every 15 minutes between 5:30 a.m. and 12:30 a.m. By road, a taxi costs more than £60 ($88).

By Train or Bus

Eurostar trains (tel 0343 218 6186, eurostar.com) arrive at St. Pancras International (tel 020 7843 7688, stpancras.com) from Paris, Disneyland Paris, Brussels, Amsterdam, and Lille.

National trains (tel 0345 748 4950, nationalrail.co.uk) arrive at Charing Cross, Euston, King's Cross, Liverpool Street, Paddington, Victoria, London Bridge, and Waterloo stations.

Long-distance bus services arrive at Victoria Coach station. National Express (tel 0871 781 8181, nationalexpress.com) is Britain's biggest company, Eurolines (tel 01582 404511) travels to the Continent.

GETTING AROUND
Public Transportation

Learning to enjoy London's public transportation system is the first step to enjoying exploring one of the world's great capitals. Taxis, although fun, are just one transportation experience, and when the traffic snarls the bills mount up very quickly, especially after 8 p.m., when much higher tariffs apply. Taking the Tube or a bus, as all Londoners do, saves time and can be great fun; and just ask for help if you are in doubt.

By Taxi

There are two kinds of taxi: the "black cab" and the minicab. Black cabs (some painted other colors) are a distinct shape and are restricted in numbers, and their drivers have all passed the tough "The Knowledge" exams and know their city extremely well. They also have full insurance and are reliable to use to deliver parcels. To use one, either go to a taxi stand, phone a company such as Radio Taxis (tel 020 7272 0272, gett.com/radiotaxis) or Dial a Cab (tel 020 7253 5000, dialacab.co.uk), or hail one on the street that is displaying an illuminated yellow "For Hire" sign on top. The fare rises according to distance and time; charges rise evenings and weekends. The driver is obliged to use the straightest route to your destination unless you instruct him to do otherwise. To complain, call the Transport for London Taxi and Private Hire Directorate (tel 0343 222 4000).

Minicabs often have untrained drivers and uninsured cars. Legally they may only be booked by phone and may not be picked up on the street—it is extremely unwise to do so. A minicab company should only be used by personal recommendation. An exception is Lady Cabs (tel 020 8888 9999, ladysandgentsmini cab.co.uk), which can supply women drivers on request and is preferred by some single women.

By Bus & Tube

Transport for London (tel 0343 222 1234, tfl.gov.uk) runs the Tube (also known as the Underground) and most of the buses. Fares for both methods of transportation are structured according to nine concentric zones—zones 1 and 2 cover most of central London. Tickets can be bought individually for each trip, but the easiest, quickest, and most economical way to buy tickets is to choose a prepaid Oyster card. An Oyster card can be bought online (see below) or at any Tube/DLR station for a refundable deposit of £5 ($7.50). It is also sold in some stores. You load money onto the card, either with cash and credit/debit cards at the ticket office, or using credit or debit cards at touch-screen machines. You then swipe the card on the round yellow disks at ticket barriers (and swipe again on exiting at the conclusion of your journey). Cards can also be used on all buses, but need only be swiped on entry. Oyster card fares are significantly less than ordinary single-ticket fares, and less than most Travelcards.

A Travelcard can be used on the Tube and bus system, plus the DLR and some rail services. There are various kinds of Travelcards, including the One Day Travelcard (1 day), the Weekly Travelcard (7 days), and the Monthly Travelcard (1 month). Each card can be bought for some or all of the zones. Once bought, you simply use it or show it on demand.

Both Oyster cards and Travelcards can be bought online before you travel to the U.K. (visitorshop.tfl.gov.uk).

London's Bus System

There is nothing quite like rumbling through London on a bus, looking at the people, buildings, advertisements, and street art. To catch a bus, first find a bus stop, indicated by a pole with a red sign. This will list the bus numbers that stop there, together with their routes. Either pay with an Oyster card, Travelcard, or buy an individual ticket in advance.

The Tube (Underground)

This huge system of a dozen lines with about 300 stations snakes all over London and carries 2.5 million people a day. London's Tube (subway) is well lit, easy to use, and safe. First, plot your route on the Tube map. Then, buy a Travelcard, Oyster card, or individual ticket. Use this to pass through the automatic barriers, get on the right color-coded line, and ensure you are traveling in the right direction.

London Overground (LO)

(tel 0343 222 1234, tfl.gov.uk) Opened in 2007, this dense surface network covers a large part of Greater London and its suburbs, with 9 lines.

Docklands Light Railway (DLR)

(tel 0843 222 1234, tfl.gov.uk) This high-level railway runs from Bank and Tower Gateway stations, both connected to the Tube network, and on through Docklands.

Organized Sightseeing

Even the most independent traveler may find it helpful to take a tour sometimes. Bus tours give an overview of the city; walking tours open your eyes to a street's history and monuments; river tours provide a new perspective on London; and some tours simply get you into places usually closed to the public. Here is a selection; local tourist information centers will carry information on others, and *Time Out* lists several in its "Around Town" section. Most telephone numbers provide detailed recorded information.

Bus Tours

Big Bus Company (tel 020 7808 6753, bigbustours.com)
Original London Sightseeing Tour (tel 020 8877 1722, theoriginaltour.com)

River Tours

The website for all boat tours is tfl.gov.uk. See also sidebar p. 53.

Walking Tours

London Walks (tel 020 7624 3978, walks.com) has a huge variety of walks led by professionals and enthusiasts.

Tailor-Made Tours

To employ a guide with the highest qualifications, the Blue Badge, contact Tour Guides (tourguides.co.uk).

Tours From the Air

Adventure Balloons (tel 0125 284 4222, adventureballoons.co.uk)

Specialist Tours

The many available include Super Tours of Westminster Abbey and St. Paul's Cathedral, tours of the Royal National Theatre, and tours of special houses such as Linley Sambourne House or Dennis Severs's House.

London Pass

A bargain way of visiting several fee-paying attractions (tel 020 7293 0972, londonpass.com).

PRACTICAL ADVICE

Electricity

The supply is 230V, with a permitted range of 216.2–253V, and 50 cycles per second (kHz). Plugs are three-pin.

U.S. appliances need a voltage transformer and an adapter.

Money Matters

Sterling currency is used throughout Britain: 100 pence make 1 pound. Coins are in denominations of 1p, 2p, 5p, 10p, 20p, 50p, £1, and £2. Notes are in £5, £10, £20, and £50. A new 12-edged £1 coin was introduced in 2017.

What's Going On?

Time Out (timeout.com), published on Tuesdays, provides exhaustive lists of London activities, together with reliable reviews and previews. Quality newspapers include *The Financial Times, Daily Telegraph, Independent,* and *The Guardian;* London's only evening paper is the *Evening Standard,* published daily, Monday to Friday. It has a large entertainment section. *Metro* is a free morning tabloid, widely available from dispensers and many Tube stations. See also websites, this page.

Opening Hours

Major attractions are open seven days a week, though some open late on Sunday. Shops are open six days a week, but many open on Sundays at noon in key shopping areas. Late-night shopping takes place on Wednesday (Knightsbridge) and Thursday (Oxford Street, Regent Street, and Covent Garden).

Banks are open Monday to Friday from 9:30 a.m. to 5 p.m. Some branches also open 9:30 a.m. to 3:30 p.m. on Saturday.

Post Offices

Stamps can be bought at post offices and some newsstands and shops; Trafalgar Square Post Office, on William IV Street, stays open late. Mailboxes are red.

Public Holidays

January 1, Good Friday, Easter Monday, first Monday in May, last Monday in May, last Monday in August, December 25 and 26.

Restrooms

Otherwise known as toilets, lavatories, WCs (water closets), conveniences, ladies, and gents. If the public restrooms are unsavory, slip into the nearest large department store or hotel. In theaters, there are often few restrooms and long lines for them.

Smoking

Smoking is now banned in all bars, pubs, restaurants, and other public places.

Telephones

The traditional British Telecom red boxes have been largely removed. (They survive only in central areas as "monuments.") The city code for London is 020 (0044 UK code). To call a land-line number in London from the U.K., dial 020 + the rest of the eight-digit number.

For local calls omit the 020 city code and just dial the eight-digit number. Outside London numbers usually have a three- or five-digit code and a six-figure number. Evenly spaced beeps mean the number is busy; a solid sound means the number is unobtainable.

To make an international call, an international, prepaid phone card is the best value, on sale at newsstands and other shops. Before using the phone in your hotel room, check the mark-up charges with the receptionist, including for toll-free phone numbers; they may be substantial.

Directory assistance (118 500; fee payable) gives a list of services. Also, ukphonebook.com. For operator help, dial 100.

Time Differences

GMT (Greenwich Mean Time) is standard time; BST (British summer time) is one hour ahead of GMT and runs from late March to late October. GMT is five hours ahead of U.S. eastern standard time.

Tourist Information
Visit Britain Offices Abroad

In the United States
Los Angeles
tel 310/481-2989
New York tel 1-800/462-2748

In Canada
Toronto tel 416/646-6674

Online Information
visitbritain.com

Useful Websites
az.co.uk
  for useful maps
bbc.co.uk/london
  for news, travel, weather, entertainment, and sports
culture24.org.uk
  includes most London museum information
london.gov.uk
  the Greater London Authority
londonnet.co.uk
  information on restaurants, bars, nightlife, and more
londontown.com
  basic information on top sights, hotels, etc.
officiallondontheatre.co.uk
  the nonprofit organization gives on-the-day information on half-price theater tickets
pubs.com
riverthames.co.uk &
visitthames.co.uk
  places and events along the river
streetmap.co.uk
  plan your day, then print out the street plan
tfl.gov.uk
  for all transportation from buses and DLR to river services, plus journey planning help
ticketmaster.co.uk
  for tickets to shows and events
timeout.com
  for all London events
tiredoflondontiredoflife.com
  quirky site with something new

to do in London every day of the year

trailfinders.com
for all travel reservations

uktravel.com
click on a Tube station to be shown nearby attractions

visitbritain.com
the British Tourist Board

visitlondon.com
the official visitor site

Visitors With Disabilities

Facilities are generally good for visitors with disabilities. Artsline (artsline.org.uk) has advice on access to arts and entertainment venues; its publication is *Disability Arts in London*. The visitor site visitlondon.com has advice and information, with several links, including disabledgo.com for accessible places to visit.

EMERGENCIES
Police, Fire, & Ambulance

To summon any of these services, dial 999 from any telephone, free of charge. It is important that you tell the emergency services operator the address where the incident has taken place and the nearest landmark, crossroads, or house number; also, tell precisely where you are. Stay by the telephone until the service arrives.

Lost Property

Always inform the police, to validate insurance claims. Report a lost passport to your embassy (and carry a separate photocopy of the information pages so another can be prepared quickly).

For lost property on the Tube, DLR, buses, black taxi cabs, and London Overground: Transport for London Lost Property Office

(200 Baker St., NW1 5R2, tel 0343 222 1234, Mon.–Fri. 8:30 a.m.–4 p.m., tfl.gov.uk).

Lost Credit Cards

Report any loss immediately to the credit card company, so credit can be stopped, and to the local police station; also telephone your bank.

Health Precautions

If you need a doctor or a dentist, ask your hotel reception for advice about local medical services. If the problem is minor, go to the nearest chemist (pharmacy) and speak to the pharmacist. To claim insurance, be sure to keep receipts for all treatments and medicines. To call an ambulance, dial 999 (see Emergencies, this page).

National Health Service (N.H.S.) Hospitals

Hospitals with 24-hour emergency departments include:
University College Hospital, 235 Euston Rd., NW1, tel 0845 155 5000 or 020 3456 7890
Chelsea and Westminster Hospital, 369 Fulham Rd., SW10, tel 020 3315 8000

Other Facilities

Private hospitals (no emergency unit) include the **Cromwell Hospital,** Cromwell Rd., SW5, tel 020 7560 5700.

Great Chapel Street Medical Centre (13 Great Chapel St., W1, tel 020 7437 9360) is an N.H.S. surgery (doctor's office) open to all, but patients without the N.H.S. reciprocal agreement must pay.

For an optician and on-site workshop, visit danda.co.uk for a selection of London opticians. Those with more serious eye problems should seek help at **Moorfields Eye Hospital** (City Rd., EC1, tel 020 7253 3411).

For homeopathic practitioners and chemists, contact the **British Homeopathic Association** (Hahnemann House, 29 Park St. West, Luton, LU1 3BE, tel 01582 408675, britishhomeopathic.org).

Chemists (Pharmacies)

Many drugs freely available in the U.S. cannot be bought over the counter in the U.K. Be sure to bring sufficient supplies of medicines from home. If more are needed, take the wrapping with full printed description of its contents to the chemist or advice on buying the nearest equivalent on the market.

Chemists open from 9 a.m. until midnight include **Bliss Chemist** (5–6 Marble Arch, W1H, tel 020 7723 6116). Visit boots.com for other late-opening chemists.

Sensible Precautions

Keep valuables locked in your hotel safe. Note, and preferably photocopy, any important information on passports, tickets, and credit cards, and keep this information in a separate place.

Keep only a small amount of money with you; put the rest in the hotel safe. Keep documents and money in a closed bag when you carry them. Do not leave your bag unattended, or on the floor of a restaurant, theater, or cinema. Do not travel alone at night, unless in a "black cab" or along well-lit streets and in buses with other people. Avoid parks after dark.

Embassies & Consulates

High Commission of Canada, Canada House, Trafalgar Square, SW1Y, tel 020 7004 6000, canadainternational.gc.ca
Embassy of the United States, 33 Nine Elms Lane, SW11, 020 7499 9000, uk.usembassy.gov

HOTELS & RESTAURANTS

Location is the key to a successful London visit. There are hotels of every level of luxury, from simple to exotic, but their location is paramount: London is very big, and hours can be wasted moving around. It is wise to work out where you will be spending your days and evenings, then choose a well-placed hotel that suits your lifestyle, dreams, and budget.

London's hotels have undergone a revolution, especially at the top end. The emphasis is on design-led hotels, such as Kit Kemp's Firmdale hotels, including the Soho with its fashionable bar. Myhotel, which opened in Chelsea in late 1998, was Terence Conran's first hotel, planned with a feng shui expert as an "oasis of calm." Subsequently, he lavishly transformed the Great Eastern Hotel (now the Andaz Liverpool Street) in the City. Ian Schrager and Philippe Starck have brought New York panache and success to London with several new hotels, including the Sanderson and St. Martins Lane.

Boutique hotels have long been established in South Kensington with such successes as the sumptuous Blakes. Now the choice has spread right across central London—to Hazlitt's in Soho, Charlotte Street in Fitzrovia, The Rookery in Clerkenwell, and Threadneedles in the very heart of the City.

More traditional luxury hotels, such as the Ritz, Savoy, Berkeley, Claridge's, and Dorchester, are now joined by the Mandarin Oriental group's totally over-hauled Hyde Park Hotel and the Waldorf Hilton. Other refurbished hotels include Le Méridien Piccadilly and Marriott's Grosvenor House. Indeed, lavish refurbishments abound at all levels, while newly built hotels spanning all price brackets open monthly in the capital.

It is, nevertheless, important to make reservations well ahead. London hotels are some of the world's most expensive, so when reserving, ask about special deals. These may include weekends or the quiet month of February—you may find a better deal at a deluxe hotel than at a popular business hotel.

New hotels often offer discounts while they deal with early teething troubles. Some hotels have economic family rooms; others, such as the Citadines Trafalgar Square London, have a kitchen in each room. When reserving you may be asked for a deposit or for your credit card number. Check the room rate carefully: It should include the hefty 20 percent VAT, but occasionally prices are given without this.

If anything goes wrong, talk to the duty manager. If the problem is not solved, speak to the manager, then put it in writing.

Visit London has a hotel information and reservation section on its website (visitlondon.com) and publishes the reliable booklets "Where to Stay" and "Things to Do." It also handles serious complaints.

Some of the nicest hotels are in old buildings. If you have particular needs in comfort, services, or anything else, check that your hotel can provide them.

Visitors with disabilities can obtain information on suitable places to stay from **Tourism for All** (7A Pixell Mill, 44 Appleby Rd., Kendal, Cumbria LA9 6NES, tel 0153 972 6111 or 0845 124 9971, tourismforall.org.uk).

Apartments

Those visiting for longer periods may wish to rent a serviced apartment on a weekly basis. Rates can be very competitive even in the city center. Agencies specializing in vacation rentals include **CHS London Ltd** (tel 023 8355 3192, chslondon.com). **The King's Wardrobe** (1st Floor 8 Harewood Row, NW1, tel 020 7792 2222 or 800/278-7338 in North America, bridgestreet.com) has modest, well-priced apartments right near St. Paul's Cathedral. **No. 5 Maddox Street**, (5 Maddox St., W1, tel 020 7647 0200, living-rooms.co.uk) has contemporary suites equipped with workstations, balconies, and minimalist decor. **Citadines Prestige Trafalgar Square London** (18–21 Northumberland Ave., WC2, tel 0800 376 3898 or 020 7766 3700, citadines.com) has 189 simple studios and one- and two-bedroom apartments in an unbeatable location. Citadines also operates properties in Barbican, Holborn, City Road, and South Kensington.

Restaurants

London's food revolution began in the 1980s and continues today. In London, if you know where to go, you can find impressive cooking of almost every cuisine in the world, from Thai to modern Californian, from Indian to north Italian. The result is that the London restaurant world spins fast in an upward spiral. Chefs are the stars, emerging from the shadow of their mentors to open strings of their own restaurants, to write columns for newspapers, publish cookbooks, and star in television series.

A sous-chef of a major restaurant in January opens his own restaurant in March, a second, offbeat brasserie in June, and publishes his first book by the autumn. Sommeliers and front-of-house managers can also determine the success of a restaurant. High-fashion restaurants, mentioned in gossip columns and reviewed repeatedly, need to be reserved well in advance; even then, tables will be kept for regular favored clients. Certain tables may be unacceptable, such as ones beside the kitchen, near the restrooms, or by the drafty door; do not hesitate to refuse these. In summer, it requires luck or an early arrival to win a prized outdoor table on the sidewalk or in restaurant back gardens.

Prices are often high, so it is important to check such details as the existence of a cover charge per person. The service charge may or may not be included—if not, 10 percent should be added for a satisfactory meal, slightly more for exceptional service. If in doubt, ask. To eat some of London's finest food at a reasonable price, there is usually a good value set menu at lunchtime. As for the wine lists, if the restaurant is any good, its wine buyer will have chosen a good house wine. If you prefer tap water (quite safe to drink in London), be certain to ask for it specifically.

Few restaurants have a dress code, but in better restaurants, it is usual to dress up in keeping with glamorous surroundings and skillfully prepared food. Traditional restaurants such as the Savoy expect their patrons to dress in a jacket and tie. Smoking is now completely prohibited inside restaurants, bars, pubs, and public places throughout London. Visitors should also note that it is considered rude to use a cell phone at the table.

The increasing number of fashionable bars in central London demand nice dress, too. Some are in the deluxe hotels; others at the front of restaurants. Pubs, on the other hand, tolerate all forms of dress and often serve good food. A handful are included in the following pages.

Remarkable hotel restaurants and bars are noted within the following hotel entries. Beware: Some well-known chefs move locations regularly; if you want to enjoy a specific chef's creations, check that he or she is still working on-site. To be sure of a table at almost any of the restaurants listed below, a reservation is essential. If you have particular needs in cuisine or comfort, check that your chosen restaurant can provide them.

Apart from restaurants within hotels, closures for public holidays, Christmas, New Year's, and Easter may vary from year to year, so it is best to check.

Credit Cards

Most hotels and restaurants in London accept all major credit cards; if they don't, they will almost certainly say so when you make a reservation.

Virtually all U.K. credit and debit cards have a "chip and PIN" system, so check that you have a PIN for your card before you leave. Also increasingly widespread are cards with a "touch" facility that allows you to "swipe" and pay without a pin or signature.

LISTINGS

Hotels and restaurants are organized by chapter, then by price, then in alphabetical order, with hotels listed first.

Abbreviations:
L = lunch
D = dinner

PRICES

HOTELS
An indication of the cost of a double room in the high season is given by **$** signs.

$$$$$	Over $280
$$$$	$200–$280
$$$	$120–$200
$$	$80–$120
$	Under $80

RESTAURANTS
An indication of the cost of a three-course meal without drinks is given by **$** signs.

$$$$$	Over $80
$$$$	$50–$80
$$$	$35–$50
$$	$20–$35
$	Under $20

▶ **THE THAMES**

There is a limited number of rooms with good Thames views, so reservations are essential. (For a wider choice of Thames views, see South Bank, p. 249.) Riverside pubs are some of the best in London, and many serve excellent food; those listed here are near the main sights to visit.

HOTEL

🏨 **THE SAVOY**
🍴 **$$$$$**
STRAND, WC2
TEL 020 7836 4343
fairmont.com/savoy
This exclusive hotel is an ideal stylish location for mixing City with West End. The Savoy reopened in October 2010, after a major refurbishment. The 62 rooms have beautiful river views. The **American Bar, Pavilion Room** teas, and **River Room** restaurant are all top-notch.
ⓘ 268 🅿 Valet 🄲 🎮 🈁

📶 Free with some packages
🚇 Charing Cross

RESTAURANTS

🍴 TATE BRITAIN REX WHISTLER
$$$
TATE BRITAIN
MILLBANK, SW1
TEL 020 7887 8825
tate.org.uk
Sadly, there are no river views in this basement, but Rex Whistler's mural covers the walls, and there is breakfast, lunch, or tea to be had between picture-gazing sessions upstairs.
🚇 Pimlico

🍴 TATE MODERN RESTAURANT
$$$
BANKSIDE, LEVEL 7, SE1
TEL 020 7401 5108
tate.org.uk
Worth dressing up for breathtaking views of the City, the buzzy bar, and the good food; book to avoid standing in line.
🚇 Southwark, London Bridge

🍴 TATE MODERN CAFÉ 2
$$
BANKSIDE, LEVEL 1, SE1
TEL 020 7401 5014
tate.org.uk
This sleek but informal ground-floor Thameside café is ideal for simple, robust food pre- or post-museum exploration.
🚇 Southwark, London Bridge

WATERSIDE PUBS

🍴 THE BULL'S HEAD
$$
15 STRAND-ON-THE-GREEN
KEW, W4
TEL 020 8994 1204
pubs.com
A variety of beers, ideal before or after Kew Gardens. Food is served noon to 10 p.m. daily.
🚇 Kew Bridge, Gunnersbury

🍴 THE CUTTY SARK
$$
4–6 BALLAST QUAY, LASSELL ST., GREENWICH SE10
TEL 020 8858 3146
cuttysarkse10.co.uk
Delightful old village pub with open fire serving warming soups, whitebait, ribs, and steaks. Outside benches.
🚤 to Greenwich (5-minute walk along towpath)
🚇 Greenwich (DLR)

🍴 THE DOVE
$$
19 UPPER MALL, W6
TEL 020 8748 9474
dovehammersmith.co.uk
Just a short walk from Chiswick House along a pretty towpath. This simple, 300-year-old pub has a good atmosphere and plenty of rowing to watch while eating traditional bread and cheese or a Thai dish.
🚇 Ravenscourt Park, Hammersmith

🍴 LONDON APPRENTICE
$$
62 CHURCH ST., ISLEWORTH TW7
TEL 020 8560 1915
taylor-walker.co.uk/
This pub is just a few yards from the car entrance to Syon House. Good food and notable beers.
🚇 Hounslow East (then bus H37), Richmond/Overground Isleworth

🍴 MAYFLOWER
$$
117 ROTHERHITHE ST., SE16
TEL 020 7237 4088
pubs.com
Cozy pub close to the pier where the *Mayflower* was stocked for her historic voyage to America in 1620.
🚇 Rotherhithe (LO)

🍴 TOWN OF RAMSGATE
$$
62 WAPPING HIGH ST., E1
TEL 020 7481 8000
pubs.com
Traditional, possibly former smugglers' pub a short walk from the Tower of London.
🚇 Wapping (LO)

🍴 THE ANCHOR
$
34 PARK ST., SE1
TEL 020 7407 1577
greeneking-pubs.co.uk
A few yards from Clink Prison Museum, Southwark Cathedral and the Globe Theatre, this pub (a former brothel) is more than 800 years old: from here Samuel Pepys observed the Great Fire in 1666.
🚇 Monument

▶ THE CITY

Restaurants in the City are booming, and a short taxi ride reaches the impressive restaurants of Clerkenwell and Islington—useful for post-theater meals, too.

HOTELS

🏨 ANDAZ LIVERPOOL STREET
$$$$$
40 LIVERPOOL ST., EC2
TEL 020 7961 1234
london.liverpoolstreet.andaz.hyatt.com
Conran took a grand Victorian railway station and stylishly transformed it into a modern City hotel, though now renamed and run by Hyatt.
🛏 267 🅿 Valet 🔲 📺 📶 Free
🚇 Liverpool Street

🏨 THE ROOKERY
$$$$
12 PETER'S LANE

COWCROSS ST., EC1
TEL 020 7336 0931
rookeryhotel.com
Under the same management
as the successful Hazlitt's
(see p. 250), simple but
tasteful rooms in Georgian
row houses, and one
stunning suite.
🛏 33 🚗 📶 Free
🚇 Farringdon

🏨 THREADNEEDLES
$$$$
5 THREADNEEDLE ST., EC2
TEL 020 7657 8080
hotelthreadneedles.co.uk
The City's original boutique
hotel is inside a fine former
Midland Bank building,
equipped with plasma TVs
and other gadgets.
🛏 69 🚗 📶 Free
🚇 Bank

RESTAURANTS

🍴 ANGLER
$$$$
SOUTH PLACE HOTEL
3 SOUTH PLACE, EC2
TEL 020 3215 1260
anglerrestaurant.com
Set in London's financial
district, Angler serves a wide
array of fresh British seafood
on the top floor of the South
Place Hotel. The restaurant's
quality dishes have earned
it a Michelin star; its floor-
to-ceiling windows, specially
commissioned mirror ceiling,
outdoor dining terrace,
and surprisingly affordable
set menu makes this an
attractive choice for City
of London diners, expense
account or not.
🕐 Closed Sun. & L Sat.
🚇 Moorgate, Liverpool Street

🍴 CLUB GASCON
$$$$
57 WEST SMITHFIELD, EC1
TEL 020 7600 6144
www.clubgascon.com

Diners select three—four if
appetites are big—scrupu-
lously prepared Gascony
dishes; foie gras is almost
obligatory.
🕐 Closed Sat. L, Sun. L & D
🚇 Barbican, Farringdon

🍴 CAFÉ DU MARCHÉ
$$$
CHARTERHOUSE MEWS
22 CHARTERHOUSE SQUARE,
EC1
TEL 020 7608 1609
cafedumarche.co.uk
French brasserie dishes
include *daube en boeuf* and
tarte aux fruits in this relaxed,
informal escape from city
pressures.
🕐 Closed Sun. (Jan—Mar.)
🚇 Barbican, Farringdon

🍴 FREDERICK'S
$$$
106 CAMDEN PASSAGE, N1
TEL 020 7359 2888
fredericks.co.uk
One of Islington's oldest
restaurants, serving modern
European food in a double-
height conservatory. Confit
of lamb, roast salmon, and
beef Wellington are all good,
and there are plenty of vegetarian dishes.
🕐 Closed Sun. 🚇 Angel

🍴 MORO
$$$
34–36 EXMOUTH MARKET, EC1
TEL 020 7833 8336
moro.co.uk
Husband and wife Sam and
Sam Clark cook innovative
dishes, many influenced by
Spain. Try *cecina* (dry-cured
beef) with artichokes and
Spanish almond cake.
🚇 Farringdon

🍴 PATERNOSTER CHOP
HOUSE
$$$
1 WARWICK COURT
PATERNOSTER SQUARE, EC4

TEL 020 7029 9400
paternosterchophouse
.co.uk
Great location overlooking
the remodeled square and
St. Paul's Cathedral. Best at
lunchtime; serving reliable
British dishes.
🕐 Closed Sun. after 6 p.m.
🚇 St. Paul's

SOMETHING SPECIAL

🍴 ST. JOHN
$$$
26 ST. JOHN ST., EC1
TEL 020 7608 0848
stjohngroup.uk.com
In his fashionably spare
restaurant beside Smithfield
Meat Market, Fergus
Henderson has revived
British dishes that most
British people had forgot-
ten about. The emphasis is
on meat, of course: plenty
of offal, venison, pork, and
more usual meats; plus
homemade breads.
   Wickedly delicious old-
fashioned puddings and
English cheeses.
🕐 Closed Sat. L, Sun. D
🚇 Barbican, Farringdon

🍴 CICADA
$$
132–136 ST. JOHN ST., EC1
TEL 020 7608 1550
rickerrestaurants.com
Large, modern interior with
central bar and friendly
atmosphere with Asian food,
including seared salmon and
crab and ginger dumplings.
🕐 Closed Sat. D
🚇 Farringdon

🍴 THE EAGLE
$$
159 FARRINGDON RD., EC1
TEL 020 7837 1353
theeaglefarringdon.co.uk
Jolly atmosphere in this
converted pub. The short
daily menu written on a
blackboard might include

wholesome Italian sausages with butter beans or grilled swordfish.

🕐 Closed Sun. D
🚇 Farringdon

🍴 MODERN PANTRY
$$

47–48 ST. JOHN'S SQUARE, EC1
TEL 020 7553 9210
themodernpantry.co.uk
Two attractive Georgian town houses play host to a take-out service (the pantry); a bustling, informal café on the ground floor; and an equally informal restaurant spread across dining rooms on the floor above. Weekend brunch is especially good and popular, so be sure to make reservations.

🕐 Café open daily; restaurant closed Sun.–Mon.
🚇 Farringdon

🍴 SMITHS OF SMITHFIELD
$$

67–77 CHARTERHOUSE ST., EC1
TEL 020 7251 7950
smithsofsmithfield.co.uk
Head up past the noisy dining room to the fourth floor for a peaceful ambiance, splendid views across Smithfield to St. Paul's, and good food: tender steaks and desserts such as summer pudding and "British cheese from Neal's Yard with oatcakes."

🕐 Top floor closed Sun. after 6 p.m. 🚇 Farringdon

🍴 JERUSALEM TAVERN
$

55 BRITTON ST., EC1
TEL 020 7490 4281
stpetersbrewery.co.uk
The current building dates from 1720, but this tavern has traded since the 14th century. It sells hot food, coffee, and excellent craft ales from St. Peter's Brewery in Suffolk.

🕐 Closed Mon.–Tues.
🚇 Farringdon

▶ WESTMINSTER

At the heart of London, the capital's grandest hotels have exceptional restaurants and jolly bars, making for fine rendezvous spots.

HOTELS

🏨 THE ARCH
🍴 $$$$$

50 GREAT CUMBERLAND PLACE
MARBLE ARCH, W1
TEL 020 7724 4700
thearchlondon.com
Drawing their design inspiration from neighboring Marble Arch, the Arch's high-end guest rooms span seven Georgian town houses dating from the 18th century. Try the pizzas or the roasted meats in **Hunter 486.**

🛏 82 🅿 Valet 🌀 📺
📶 Free 🚇 Marble Arch

🏨 ATHENAEUM
🍴 $$$$$

116 PICCADILLY, W1
TEL 020 7499 3464
athenaeumhotel.com
The elegant comfort and high level of service draw guests back to Athenaeum's rooms and apartments, as do Windsor Lounge teas and the spa. Higher rooms have park views.

🛏 156 🌀 📺 📶 Free
🚇 Hyde Park Corner

🏨 BROWN'S
🍴 $$$$$

33 ALBEMARLE ST., W1
TEL 020 7493 6020
brownshotel.
grandluxuryhotels.com
Old-world English elegance in the heart of Mayfair. Totally refurbished. Roaring fires and creaking floorboards; an echo of Mayfair mansions. Especially good traditional tea.

🛏 117 🅿 Valet 🌀 📺
📶 Free 🚇 Green Park

🏨 THE CHILTERN
🍴 FIREHOUSE
$$$$$

1 CHILTERN ST., W1
TEL 020 7073 7690 (HOTEL)
TEL 020 7033 7676
(RESTAURANT)
andrebalazsproperties.com
Celebrities flocked to the latest London offering of André Balazs from the moment it opened in 2014. The intimate but expensive hotel and the attractive, airy setting of the bar and restaurant (part of a converted fire station) should ensure the establishment's continued success when the trendsetters move on.

🛏 26 🌀 📶 Free
🚇 Baker Street

SOMETHING SPECIAL

🏨 CLARIDGE'S
🍴 $$$$$

49 BROOK ST., W1
TEL 020 7629 8860
claridges.co.uk
State guests move here after Buckingham Palace to enjoy the huge corner suites and glorious public rooms—including the grand dining room—designed by Thierry Despont and Diane von Furstenberg, with food by Gordon Ramsay.

🛏 203 🌀 📺 📶 Free
🚇 Bond Street

🏨 THE CONNAUGHT
🍴 $$$$$

CARLOS PLACE, W1
TEL 020 7499 7070
the-connaught.co.uk
It is considered the most discreet of London hotels, where the famous can remain anonymous. Recently refurbished, this exclusive hotel boasts Michelin-starred food from Hélène Darroze and the fine Coburg and Connaught bars.

🛏 122 🌀 📺 🏊 📶 Free
🚇 Bond Street

🏨 **THE DORCHESTER**
🍽 **$$$$$**

53 PARK LANE, W1
TEL 020 7629 8888
thedorchester.com

Lavishly redone, including the rooftop Oliver Messel rooms and a luscious spa. Guests and visitors can enjoy fine Promenade teas, the zippy bar, and restaurants: the three-Michelin-star **Alain Ducasse**, and the opulent **China Tang** (Cantonese).

ⓘ 250 🅒 🅨 🛰 Free
🚇 Hyde Park Corner

🏨 **FOUR SEASONS**
🍽 **$$$$$**

HAMILTON PLACE
PARK LANE, W1
TEL 020 7499 0888
fourseasons.com/london

Refurbished in 2010, an intelligently designed hotel with excellently appointed rooms and suites, especially conservatory rooms; some of London's top chefs have worked in the Four Seasons restaurant (modern European). A second hotel is at Canary Wharf, Docklands.

ⓘ 192 🅒 🅟 Valet 🅨 🛰 Free
🚇 Hyde Park Corner

🏨 **LANDMARK HOTEL**
$$$$$

222 MARYLEBONE RD., NW1
TEL 020 7631 8000
landmarklondon.co.uk

The spectacular Winter Garden, a palm court that operates all day, sets the tone for this converted late-Victorian building. Large bedrooms with good bathrooms. The hotel is surprisingly well located.

ⓘ 300 🅒 🅨 🛰
🛰 Free for first two hours
🚇 Marylebone

🏨 **THE METROPOLITAN**
🍽 **$$$$$**

19 OLD PARK LANE, W1

TEL 020 7447 1000
www.comohotels.com

The Metropolitan has a reputation for cutting-edge cool design and matching guests, who book into its rooms and apartments. Getting a reservation at its **Nobu** restaurant (Japanese) is hard, though the once exclusive Met Bar is now less trendy than it was.

ⓘ 150 🅒 🅟 Valet 🅨 🛰
🛰 Free 🚇 Hyde Park Corner

🏨 **THE RITZ**
🍽 **$$$$$**

150 PICCADILLY, W1
TEL 020 7493 8181
theritzlondon.com

Exquisite hotel overlooking Green Park, whose painted and gilded dining room is London's most beautiful. Tea is disappointing but the bar is a promenade for the stylish. Note the formal dress code: no jeans or sneakers, and men must wear jacket and tie.

ⓘ 136 🅒 🅟 Valet 🅨
🛰 Free 🚇 Green Park

🏨 **THE STAFFORD**
🍽 **$$$$$**

16–18 ST. JAMES'S PLACE, SW1
TEL 020 7493 0111
thestafford.
grandluxuryhotels.com

One of London's most luxurious small hotels, tucked down an alley off St. James's Street. Delightful dining room, offering fine wines stored in 350-year-old cellars.

ⓘ 105 🅒 🅨 🛰 Free
🚇 Green Park

🏨 **LE MÉRIDIEN**
🍽 **PICCADILLY**
$$$$

21 PICCADILLY, W1
TEL 020 7734 8000
lemeridienpiccadilly.co.uk

Located at the crossroads of St. James's, Mayfair, and

theaterland. Guests enjoy fine rooms, a splendid health club and spa, stylish afternoon tea in the Oak Room, and of course excellent bars.

ⓘ 266 🅒 🅨 🚾 🛰 Charge
🚇 Piccadilly Circus

🏨 **TRAFALGAR**
🍽 **$$$$**

2 SPRING GARDENS, W1
TEL 020 7870 2900
thetrafalgarstjames.com

Designed to attract younger guests, this lifestyle hotel has sharp service, good design, and the popular Rockwell Bar and roof bar.

ⓘ 129 🅒 🅨 🚾 🛰 Free
🚇 Charing Cross

🏨 **DURRANTS**
$$$

26–32 GEORGE ST., W1
TEL 020 7935 8131
www.durrantshotel.co.uk

The hotel opened when its Georgian terrace was quite new, in 1790, and descendants of that family maintain its homey tone today.

📶 92 🛏 Some rooms 📶 Free 🚇 Bond Street

🏨 SUMNER
$$$
54 UPPER BERKELEY ST.
MARBLE ARCH, W1
TEL 020 7723 2244
thesumner.com

The excellent 5 Sumner Place hotel in South Kensington has morphed itself into a grander refurbished town house in Marylebone, installing its notably caring staff.

📶 20 🛏 📶 Free 🚇 Marble Arch

RESTAURANTS

🍴 LE GAVROCHE
$$$$$
43 UPPER BROOK ST., W1
TEL 020 7408 0881
le-gavroche.co.uk

Calm decor, perfect service, and an extensive wine list form the backdrop for Michel Roux's theater, which has been running for more than 25 years and is now directed by his son, Michel Roux Junior. Perfect French dishes include *darne de boeuf à l'ancienne.*

🕐 Closed Sat. L & Sun. 🚇 Marble Arch

🍴 GREENHOUSE
$$$$$
27A HAY'S MEWS, W1
TEL 020 7499 3331
greenhouserestaurant.co.uk

Michelin-starred chef Antonin Bonnet creates imaginative European fusions for his elegant, friendly dining room.

🕐 Closed Sat. L, Sun. 🚇 Green Park

🍴 BENARES
$$$$
12A BERKELEY SQUARE HOUSE

BERKELEY SQUARE, W1
TEL 020 7627 8886
benaresrestaurant.com

Atur Kocchar, who made **Tamarind** (see below) so special, focuses on the dishes of his native area of India, the ancient city of Benares and its surrounding area.

🚇 Green Park, Bond Street

🍴 LE CAPRICE
$$$$
25 ARLINGTON ST., SW1
TEL 020 7629 2239
le-caprice.co.uk

This and **The Ivy** (see p. 250, tables even more of a premium) are run with supreme efficiency by one team. Atmosphere is clublike, with chic customers greeting each other over champagne and *risotto nero,* all fashionably modern European.

🚇 Green Park

🍴 GINZA ONODERA
$$$$
15 BURY ST., SW1
TEL 020 7839 1101
www.ginzaonodera.uk

In this exclusive Japanese restaurant, food is a sensual, fulfilling experience. The restaurant has a main room and three private rooms devoted to specific cooking methods, such as *edomae sushi.*

🚇 Green Park

SOMETHING SPECIAL

🍴 LOCANDA LOCATELLI
$$$$
8 SEYMOUR ST., W1
TEL 020 7935 9088
locandalocatelli.com

One of the recent stars of London's dining scene (2019). The modish and understated contemporary dining rooms are a celebrity favorite, but the style and sleek service are underpinned by superb Italian cooking. The seasonal meat, fish, and

pasta dishes are often winningly straightforward—*minestrone di verdura* (vegetable soup), *tortellini in brodo* (meat parcels in broth), or *sgombro alla griglia in crosta di erbe* (grilled mackerel in a light herb crust).

🚇 Marble Arch

🍴 QUILON
$$$$
41 BUCKINGHAM GATE, SW1E
TEL 020 7821 1899
quilon.co.uk

This was the first southern Indian restaurant to win a Michelin Star. Chef Sriram creates a unique blend of ethnic dishes featuring fish, game, and vegetarian options.

🚇 St. James's Park, Victoria Station

🍴 QUIRINALE
$$$$
NORTH COURT 1–GREAT PETER ST., SW1P
TEL. 020 7222 7080
quirinale.co.uk

This quiet Italian restaurant set in a basement is a real culinary attraction near Westminster Palace (the clientele also includes members of parliament and senior officials). High-end classic food combined with an interesting wine list.

🕐 Closed Sat. L & Sun. 🚇 St. James's Park

🍴 SKETCH: THE LECTURE ROOM
$$$$
9 CONDUIT ST., W1
TEL 020 7659 4500
http://sketch.london

A dizzy combination of Mourad Mazous, founder of nearby **Momo,** Parisian chef Pierre Gagnaire, and a grand Mayfair mansion decked in uncompromisingly contemporary design by Gabhan

O'Keefe. Great café and fine dining rooms.

Oxford Circus, Bond Street

THE SQUARE

$$$$

6–10 BRUTON ST.

MAYFAIR, W1

TEL 020 7495 7100

www.squarerestaurant.com

Philip Howard's modern European dishes, with a French emphasis, served in a high-ceilinged, large-windowed space. The terrine of foie gras and the guinea fowl and artichokes with cured ham are superb.

Closed Sun. Green Park

TAMARIND

$$$$

20 QUEEN ST., W1

TEL 020 7629 3561

tamarindrestaurant.com

Serious Indian cooking. Original recipes, often gleaned from traditional Indian homes, are cooked to conserve their distinctive spices and aromas, such as chicken marinated in green chili and mustard.

Green Park

THE AVENUE

$$$

7–9 ST. JAMES'S ST., SW1

TEL 020 7321 2111

avenue-restaurant.co.uk

Restrained, elegant design, plus good value wines complement British and European dishes such as chilled cucumber soup with Colchester crab.

Closed Sat. & Sun. Green Park

CAFFÉ CONCERTO

$$$

29-31 PICCADILLY, W1

TEL 020 7494 6844

caffeconcerto.co.uk/restaurant/piccadilly.html

This Italian restaurant, inspired by the refined art of pastry making, offers breakfast, lunch, and dinner with excellent service. Elegant and calm decor.

Piccadilly Circus

THE CINNAMON CLUB

$$$

THE OLD WESTMINSTER LIBRARY

30–32 GREAT SMITH ST., SW1

TEL 020 7222 2555

cinnamonclub.com

Spacious late-Victorian municipal grandeur sets the tone for a stylish marriage of Western and Indian cuisine—and pricey wines; try the Rajasthani roast saddle of venison, and be adventurous with dessert. Serves breakfast on weekdays.

Breakfast: Mon.–Fri. 7:30 a.m.–10 a.m. Westminster, St. James's Park

MAZE

$$$

MARRIOTT

10–13 GROSVENOR SQUARE, W1

TEL 020 7107 0000

gordonramsay.com/maze

Worth penetrating the lackluster hotel to eat Jason Atherton's stunning Spanish-inspired food in David Rockwell's room.

Bond Street

THE PROVIDORES & TAPA ROOM

$$$

109 MARYLEBONE HIGH ST., W1

TEL 020 7935 6175

theprovidores.co.uk

Peter Gordon's fresh combinations of Asian and Middle Eastern ingredients keep the ground-floor tapas bar and upstairs restaurant filled to the brim.

Closed Sat. L & Sun. D Baker Street, Bond Street

IL VICOLO

$$$

3 CROWN PASSAGE

KING ST., SW1

TEL 020 7839 3960

ilvicolorestaurant.co.uk

Seek out this hideaway to join local St. James's art dealers and Christie's experts for good value, home-style Italian food served with a smile.

Closed Sat., Sun. L St. James's Park, Green Park

THE WALLACE RESTAURANT

$$$

WALLACE COLLECTION

HERTFORD HOUSE

MANCHESTER SQUARE, W1

TEL 020 7563 9505

peytonandbyrne.co.uk/the-wallace-restaurant

Laze over late breakfast, a coffee, lunch, or afternoon tea in the covered courtyard of one of London's great mansions. The house is now home to the Wallace Collection, which includes the best private collection of French art outside Paris.

Bond Street, Marble Arch

BENTLEY'S OYSTER BAR & GRILL

$$–$$$$

11–15 SWALLOW ST., W1

TEL 020 7734 4756

bentleys.org

Bentley's opened in 1916 and still occupies the same beautiful neo-Gothic building almost a century later. Tucked away on a tiny side street, yet just moments from busy Piccadilly and Regent Street, this is an iconic London restaurant, revitalized this century by a superb update that has respected the beautiful arts and crafts–inspired interior. Eat fine fish and seafood either in the lively (and less expensive) Oyster & Champagne Bar downstairs

---

Hotel Restaurant No. of Guest Rooms Closed Parking Air-conditioning Gym

or in the more sedate dining rooms upstairs.

🚇 Piccadilly Circus

🍴 MASALA ZONE
$$

9 MARSHALL ST., W1
TEL 020 7287 9966
masalazone.com
Imaginative pan-Indian food at affordable prices. An ideal pause for shoppers. Six other central London locations.

🚇 Oxford Circus

🍴 THE GOLDEN HIND
$

73 MARYLEBONE LANE, W1
TEL 020 7486 3644
The Golden Hind is a classic London "chippie," or fish and chip shop. It has been in business since 1914, offering great-value fried fish, chips, and a limited selection of side dishes to go or to eat in the simple, traditional dining room.

🕐 Closed Sun. 🚇 Bond Street, Baker Street

▶ SOUTH BANK

The strip along the south bank of the Thames is now one of the city's most exciting and innovative areas.

HOTELS

🏨 LONDON MARRIOTT 🍴 COUNTY HALL
$$$$$

COUNTY HALL, WESTMINSTER BRIDGE RD., SE1
TEL 020 7928 5200
marriott.co.uk
This hotel occupies part of the London administrators' 1930s building. Some rooms have river views, and the leisure facilities are all first class. Dining choices include **Gillray's Steakhouse & Bar,** with its breathtaking views of Big Ben.

🍴 200 🛗 📶 🏊
📶 Free in public areas
🚇 Westminster, Waterloo

🏨 MAD HATTER
$$$

3–7 STAMFORD ST., SE1
TEL 020 7401 9222
madhatterhotel.co.uk
A welcome new arrival located behind South Bank theaters, near Blackfriars Bridge, a short walk to the City or taxi to the West End. No river views.

🍴 30 🛗 📶 Free
🚇 Blackfriars

🏨 LONDON BRIDGE
$$–$$$

8–18 LONDON BRIDGE ST., SE1
TEL 020 7855 2200
london-bridge-hotel.co.uk
This modern hotel, just south of London Bridge, is a short walk from the Borough Market and the City. No river views.

🍴 138 🛗 📶 Free
🚇 London Bridge

🏨 PREMIER INN
$$

COUNTY HALL
BELVEDERE RD., SE1
TEL 0871 527 8648
premierinn.com
Excellent location for this no-frills, good value hotel tucked behind the deluxe London Marriott. No river views.

🍴 313 📶 Free for 30 minutes per day 🚇 Westminster, Waterloo

RESTAURANTS

🍴 ANCHOR & HOPE
$$$

36 THE CUT, SE1
TEL 020 7928 9898
anchorandhopepub.co.uk
A great gastropub in a useful location, serving bold British food. Take note: no reservations, and you may

have a long wait at busy times. The best dishes are the simple ones such as duck heart, beef rump, and Tamworth pork.

🕐 Closed Sun. L
🚇 Southwark, Waterloo

🍴 THE GREEN ROOM
$$$

101 UPPER GROUND, SE1
TEL. 020 7452 3630
greenroom.london
The Green Room is a project run by the National Theatre with the local association Coin Street Community Builders: an airy neighborhood restaurant, bar, and garden dedicated to British cuisine with an ethnic twist, furnished with props and sets used in theater plays.

🚇 Southwark, Waterloo

🍴 BLUEPRINT CAFÉ
$$

THE DESIGN MUSEUM
28 SHAD THAMES ST., SE1
TEL 020 7378 7031
blueprintcafe.co.uk
This modern restaurant offers fine views of Tower Bridge and the nicest service; river-view tables a premium. Chef Jeremy Lee combines European culinary influences with those of his native Scotland.

🕐 Closed Sun. D
🚇 Tower Hill

🍴 THE GEORGE INN
$$

77 BOROUGH ST., SE1
TEL 020 7407 2056
nationaltrust.org.uk/george-inn
This historic pub, south of Southwark Cathedral, is London's last surviving two-story coaching inn, known for its gallery (balcony). The Tudor-era original burned down in 1676. Pub food and fine Greene King ales.

🚇 London Bridge

ROYAL OAK
$

44 TABARD ST., SE1

TEL 020 7357 7173

royaloaklondon.co.uk

This beautifully maintained pub is worth seeking out for its local friendliness and its beer from Harveys of Lewes.

🚇 Borough

▶ TRAFALGAR SQUARE & SOHO

HOTELS

SOHO HOTEL
$$$$$

4 RICHMOND MEWS

DEAN ST., W1

TEL 020 7559 3000

firmdale.com

Designer Kit Kemp's sixth London hotel mixes country style with urban simplicity in a bare brick building. Lovely bathrooms. Buzzing bar and restaurant.

ⓘ 91 🅿 🈺 📺 📶 Free
🚇 Tottenham Court Road

SOMETHING SPECIAL

HAZLITT'S
$$$$

6 FRITH ST., W1

TEL 020 7434 1771

hazlittshotel.com

Once the home of writer William Hazlitt (1778–1830), this gracious building is now a town-house hotel in the heart of Soho. There are antiques in the beautifully furnished rooms. Ideal for theater and museum visits. As this is a landmark hotel, there are no elevators.

ⓘ 30 🈺 📶 Free
🚇 Tottenham Court Road

ST. MARTINS LANE
$$$$

45 ST. MARTIN'S LANE, WC2

TEL 020 7300 5500

morganshotelgroup.com

Hovering between West End theaters and Covent Garden restaurants, Philippe Starck's dramatically minimalist rooms and extensive bars attract design-conscious clients.

ⓘ 204 🈺 📺 📶 Free
🚇 Covent Garden, Leicester Square

DEAN STREET
TOWNHOUSE
$$$

71 DEAN ST., W1

TEL 020 7434 1775

deanstreettownhouse.com

This chic Soho hotel opened in 2010 in a converted four-story Georgian house with a rich history. Public spaces are opulent, while the rooms have original features and a decorative palette of mostly soft browns and off-whites. The popular dining room (open to non-patrons) has a traditional, clublike feel and serves classic British food at breakfast, lunch, tea, and dinner.

ⓘ 39 🈺 📶 Free
🚇 Tottenham Court Road

RESTAURANTS

HAKKASAN
$$$$

8 HANWAY PLACE, W1

TEL 020 7927 7000

hakkasan.com

Dress up to fit in with the other stylish patrons at this large, sleek, and dimly lit restaurant, which serves excellent and sophisticated contemporary Asian food. Prices are high, but you can eat for less at lunch.

🚇 Tottenham Court Road

SOMETHING SPECIAL

THE IVY
$$$$

1–5 WEST ST.

COVENT GARDEN, WC2

TEL 020 7836 4751

the-ivy.co.uk

Getting a table is the hard part. That achieved, the sharp staff ensures a memorable meal in this old Soho eatery though the cooking can be erratic. Lunchtime clientele eat roast fish and irresistible puddings while enjoying Howard Hodgkins and Alan Jones art hung on the walls.

🚇 Leicester Square, Covent Garden

QUO VADIS
$$$$

26–29 DEAN ST., W1

TEL 020 7437 9585

quovadissoho.co.uk

This Soho restaurant boasts excellent service and a smart interior. The menu offers classic British and European meat, fish, and seafood dishes, plus good-value set lunch and pre-theater menus.

🕐 Closed Sun.
🚇 Leicester Square, Tottenham Court Road

🏨 Hotel 🍴 Restaurant ⓘ No. of Guest Rooms 🕐 Closed 🅿 Parking 🈺 Air-conditioning 📺 Gym

🍴 VASCO & PIERO'S PAVILION

$$$$

15 POLAND ST, W1

TEL 020 7437 8774

vascosfood.com

Delightfully sober, this Italian restaurant offers simple, genuine Umbrian cuisine. Homemade pasta is the trademark here, alongside the furniture coming directly from Umbria. The menu changes twice a day.

🕐 Closed Sat. L & Sun.
🚇 Tottenham Court Road

🍴 BARRAFINA

$$$

54 FRITH ST, W1

barrafina.co.uk

In 2007 Barrafina helped establish the current trend for tapas and other small-plate dining across the capital. The small, informal dining room and fine Spanish food continue to be popular (reservations are not taken), their success having spawned an equally acclaimed second outlet in Covent Garden (*10 Adelaide St., WC2*) that has adapted the same no reservation policy.

🚇 Tottenham Court Road

🍴 MON PLAISIR

$$$

21 MONMOUTH ST., WC2

TEL 020 7836 7243

monplaisir.co.uk

A long-established French bistro. Choose from a range of reliable main dishes, but end with the crème brûlée.

🕐 Closed Sun. 🚇 Covent Garden, Leicester Square

🍴 THE NATIONAL GALLERY DINING ROOMS

$$

NATIONAL GALLERY

TRAFALGAR SQUARE, WC2

TEL 020 7747 2525

nationalgallery.org.uk

If you need a break from the tip-top art, eat lunch overlooking Trafalgar Square; book early for the best views. There's also a café on the ground floor.

🚇 Charing Cross, Leicester Square

🍴 PIERRE VICTOIRE

$$

5 DEAN ST., W1

TEL 020 7287 4582

pierrevictoire.com

Find hearty-size portions of no-fuss French food and a bottle of wine enjoyed in a calm, unhurried, candlelit room; and do not miss out on the *tarte au citron*.

🚇 Tottenham Court Road

🍴 POLPO

$$

41 BEAK ST., W1

TEL 020 7734 4479

polpo.co.uk

Polpo is an intimate and attractive Venetian-style *bacaro*, or wine bar, that offers *cicheti*, the Italian equivalent of Spanish tapas, and a fine choice of wines from mainly small northern Italian producers. Appropriately, it occupies part of an 18th-century Soho building that was once home to the famous Venetian painter Canaletto. Reservations taken for lunch only.

🕐 Closed Sun. D
🚇 Oxford Circus, Piccadilly Circus

🍴 CAFÉ IN THE CRYPT

$

CRYPT OF ST. MARTIN-IN-THE-FIELDS, TRAFALGAR SQUARE, WC2

TEL 020 7766 1158

stmartin-in-the-fields.org

Ideal for a cheap, cheery, and peaceful pause. Delicious wholesome food at bargain prices includes casseroles

and, among the desserts, delicious apple pie and custard.

🚇 Charing Cross, Embankment

🍴 CANTON

$

11 NEWPORT PLACE, WC2

TEL 020 7437 6220

Discerning Chinese patrons come to this simple diner to pay fair prices for delicious roast duck and its fine sauces; crab and oysters are good here, too.

🚇 Leicester Square

🍴 MISATO

$

11 WARDOUR ST., W1

TEL 020 7734 0808

misato.has.restaurant

Worth standing in line for the delicious katsu, teriyaki, and dim sum in this popular, cramped café.

🚇 Leicester Square

▶ COVENT GARDEN TO LUDGATE HILL

Hotels range from grand to bargain in this superb location. There are many restaurants, but fewer of quality than might be expected: The area has been hit by the exit of Fleet Street's newspapers and the simultaneous rise of City restaurants to the east.

HOTELS

🏨 COVENT GARDEN

$$$$$

10 MONMOUTH ST., WC2

TEL 020 7806 1000

firmdale.com

The wood-paneled drawing room and atmospheric Tiffany library, together with the individualized, brightly colored rooms, make this hotel seem far from urban London's hub.

🛏 58 🅿 Valet ❄ 🏋 📶 Free
🚇 Covent Garden

🏨 HAYMARKET HOTEL
$$$$$
1 SUFFOLK PLACE, SW1
TEL 020 7470 4000
firmdale.com
One of the Firmdale group's
stable of excellent, intimate
hotels, with an ideal location—the Haymarket is at the
heart of the theater district.
Rooms are calm, quiet, and
very comfortable, and facilities include a gym and swimming pool.
🛏 50 ❄ 🏋 📶 📶 Free
🚇 Piccadilly Circus, Leicester
Square

SOMETHING SPECIAL

🏨 ONE ALDWYCH
🍴 $$$$$
1 ALDWYCH, WC2
TEL 020 7300 1000
onealdwych.com
One of London's most
dynamic contemporary
renovations. Built in 1907
for the *Morning Post* newspaper, now transformed
by Gordon Campbell-Gray
and Mary Fox Linton into a
state-of-the-art hotel. Serious
art on the walls, sumptuous
health spa. Dine at **Indigo**
eatery or the formal adjoining **Axis** restaurant.
🛏 105 🅿 Valet ❄ 🏋 📶
🚇 Covent Garden, Charing
Cross

🏨 CROWNE PLAZA
🍴 LONDON—THE CITY
$$$–$$$$$
19 NEW BRIDGE ST., EC4
TEL 0871 9429198
ichotelsgroup.com
Superbly located between
Ludgate Hill and Fleet Street,
and with a vibrant bar and
the excellent **Refettorio** res-
taurant, this is an ideal hotel
for mixing business with
pleasure.

🛏 203 ❄ 📶 📶 Free
🚇 Blackfriars

🏨 THE FIELDING HOTEL
$$$
4 BROAD CT., BOW ST., WC2
TEL 020 7836 8305
thefieldinghotel.co.uk
A quiet, simple accommoda-
tion in a pedestrian lane just
across from Covent Garden
Opera.
🛏 25 ❄ 🏋 📶 Free
🚇 Covent Garden

RESTAURANTS

🍴 CHRISTOPHER'S
$$$$
18 WELLINGTON ST., WC2
TEL 020 7240 4222
christophersgrill.com
A grand former casino houses
Christopher Gilmour's res-
taurant, just off Aldwych.
Quality American food in the
basement café and the beau-
tiful upstairs dining room.
🕐 Closed Sun. D 🚇 Covent
Garden

🍴 THE DELAUNAY
$$$$
55 ALDWYCH, WC2
TEL 020 7499 8558
thedelaunay.com
A more recent restaurant
from the owners of **The Wol-
seley** (see p. 254), but already
as successful and as popular as
its predecessor. Food, service,
and setting (wood-paneled
dining rooms) are traditional
but not stuffy. Breakfast,
lunch, afternoon tea, and dinner (plus food to go).
🚇 Temple, Covent Garden

🍴 J SHEEKEY
$$$$
28–34 ST. MARTIN'S COURT,
WC2
TEL 020 7240 2565
j-sheekey.co.uk
Modern lighting and a fresh
look contrast well with the

original 1890s wood paneling,
creating an individual style.
The menu, with a strong
emphasis on traditional British
seafood dishes, also includes
modern dishes. Try the
oak-smoked eel or Cornish
cock-crab.
🚇 Leicester Square

🍴 MURANO
$$$$
20 QUEEN ST., W1
TEL 020 7495 1127
muranolondon.com
Gordon Ramsay protégé and
TV chef Angela Hartnett
opened this refined Italian
Mayfair restaurant as chef-
patron to acclaim in 2008,
and it continues to excel. A
three-course set lunch might
include a salad of wood
pigeon with a citrus fruit
sherry vinaigrette. Dress code
is "smart," but a jacket and tie
are not required.
🕐 Closed Sun. 🚇 Green Park

🍴 RULES
$$$$
35 MAIDEN LANE, WC2
TEL 020 7836 5314
rules.co.uk
Established in 1798, this
art-filled, quality traditional
English restaurant is the
place to eat such dishes as
potted duck, Highland deer,
and steak, kidney, and oyster
pudding.
🚇 Covent Garden

SOMETHING SPECIAL

🍴 BLEEDING HEART
$$$
BLEEDING HEART YARD, OFF
GREVILLE ST., EC1
TEL 020 7242 8238
bleedingheart.co.uk
A little off the beaten path,
but well worth seeking out.
The bar, bistro, and restaurant
in a warren of rooms off Hol-
born offer the perfect combi-
nation of good atmosphere,

a wide choice of wines, and authentic French food.

🕐 Closed Sat.–Sun.
🚇 Farringdon

🍴 JOE ALLEN
$$$
2, BURLEIGH ST. WC2
TEL 020 7836 0651
joeallen.co.uk
Comfortingly American menu served in a continuously buzzy basement. Reliable Caesar salad, clam chowder, ribs, and pecan pie. American cocktails.
🚇 Covent Garden

🍴 THE PORTRAIT
$$$
NATL. PORTRAIT GALLERY, WC2
TEL 020 7312 2490
npg.org.uk
Perched on top of the galleries, this is an ideal place to pause between portraits. Stunning views and efficient food, but can be noisy sometimes.
🕐 Closed Sun.–Wed. D. Reservation at least 6 weeks in advance. 🚇 Leicester Square

🍴 SIMPSONS-IN-THE-STRAND
$$$
100 STRAND, WC2
TEL 020 7420 2111
simpsonsinthestrand.co.uk
Almost a caricature of a traditional English restaurant, Simpsons was founded in 1828 as a coffeehouse. A full English breakfast is the best meal to eat here in the Grand Divan dining hall.
🕐 Closed 8 p.m. Sun.
🚇 Charing Cross, Covent Garden

🍴 THE SEVEN STARS
$$
53 CAREY ST., WC2
TEL 020 7242 8521
pubs.com

This pub dates from 1604 and offers good food as well as fine real ales.
🚇 Chancery Lane

🍴 THE LAMB & FLAG
$
33 ROSE ST., WC2
TEL 020 7497 9504
lambandflagcoventgarden.co.uk
A Convent Garden location close to the theater district makes this historic pub from 1772 a good, if often busy, place for a drink or light meal before or after a show; it is also celebrated for its extensive collection of whiskies.
🚇 Leicester Square, Covent Garden

▶ BLOOMSBURY
This area has a full range of good hotels, all within walking distance of the Bloomsbury museums, Covent Garden, and West End theaters.

HOTELS

🏨 CHARLOTTE STREET
🍴 HOTEL
$$$$$
15–17 CHARLOTTE ST., WC1
TEL 020 7806 2000
firmdalehotels.com
Smart yet friendly and relaxed hotel inside a period building, with a small gym and reliable **Oscar** restaurant.
🛏 52 🅿 Valet 🔆 📺 📶 Free
🚇 Tottenham Court Road, Goodge Street

🏨 ACADEMY
$$$$
21 GOWER ST., WC1
TEL 020 7631 4115
theacademyhotel.co.uk
Set in five Georgian row houses, with opulent furnishings and discreet art, this professionally run fairy-tale

view of English interiors works well.
🛏 49 🔆 📶 Free
🚇 Goodge Street

🏨 THE MONTAGUE ON THE GARDENS
$$$$
15 MONTAGUE ST., WC1
TEL 020 7637 1001
montaguehotel.com
Centrally located, this stylish hotel is imaginatively decorated, with attention to detail. Bedrooms offer bold decor and quality furnishings.
🛏 100 🔆 📺 📶 Free
🚇 Russel Square, Holborn

🏨 SANDERSON
$$$$
50 BERNERS ST., W1
TEL 020 7300 1400
morganshotelgroup.com
As with its sister hotel, **St. Martin's Lane**, the Schrager-Starck partnership creates minimalist rooms but crowded public spaces; try the **Long Bar** and the spa.
🛏 150 🔆 📺 📶 Free
🚇 Oxford Circus

🏨 HARLINGFORD HOTEL
$$$
61–63 CARTWRIGHT GARDENS, WC1
TEL 020 7387 1551
harlingfordhotel.com
Despite the budget rates, all guests enjoy en suite bathrooms, contemporary decoration, friendly management, and adjacent garden and tennis court.
🛏 44 📶 Free 🚇 Russell Square, Euston

🏨 MORGAN HOTEL
$$$
24 BLOOMSBURY, WC1
TEL 020 7636 3735
morganhotel.co.uk
Superbly located, this modest and good-value family-run hotel by the British

Museum has both rooms and small apartments.

🛏 21 ❄ Except apartments 📶 Free 🚇 Tottenham Court Road

🏨 GENERATOR HOSTEL
$
37 TAVISTOCK PLACE, WC1
TEL 020 7388 7666
generatorhostels.com/destinations/london
Steel, chrome, and exposed pipes plus its jolly bar and Internet room keep the setting sleek, the prices low, and the guests happy. Mostly shared dorm-style rooms.

🛏 848 beds 📶 Free 🚇 Russell Square

RESTAURANTS

🍴 ASK
$$
48 GRAFTON WAY, W1
TEL 020 7388 8108
askitalian.co.uk
Arguably the best of London's pizza chain restaurant groups; this branch has the usual wide variety of pizzas and other good dishes, plus sharp service.

🚇 Warren Street

🍴 FIVE GUYS
$
266 TOTTENHAM COURT ROAD, W1T
TEL 020 7637 2242
fiveguys.co.uk
The ultimate "high-end" fast food experience in a chain restaurant that is spreading fast in London. Good hamburgers with a good variety of flavors and ingredients.

🚇 Tottenham Court Road

▶ REGENCY LONDON & NORTH
For ease of use, restaurants covering this long strip are listed south to north.

HOTELS

🏨 DORSET SQUARE
$$$$
39 DORSET SQUARE, NW1
TEL 020 7723 7874
dorsetsquare.co.uk
Tim and Kit Kemp's first London hotel boasts their trademark professionalism, individual attention, and relaxed British atmosphere.

🛏 37 🅿 Valet ❄ 📶 Free 🚇 Marylebone

🏨🍴 GREAT NORTHERN HOTEL
$$$$
PANCRAS RD., N1C
TEL 020 3388 0800
gnhlondon.com
The restoration of Victoria railroad station at St. Pancras, the departure point for Eurostar trains to mainland Europe via the Channel Tunnel, has been a resounding success; and this associated hotel is great as a base before or after a train journey, or for a drink or meal. The Great Northern Hotel, right by St. Pancras and the adjacent King's Cross station, has won deserved plaudits since it opened in 2013. There are three cozy bars and the soothing **Plum + Split Milk** restaurant (open to non-residents) for classic English cooking from breakfast through to midnight snacks.

🛏 91 ❄ 📶 Free 🚇 King's Cross St. Pancras

🏨 TEN MANCHESTER STREET
$$$
10 MANCHESTER ST., MARYLEBONE, W1U
TEL 020 7317 5900
tenmanchesterstreethotel.com
This boutique hotel, centrally located on a quiet street north of Oxford Street in the heart of Marylebone, features fine guest rooms and suites in a handsome Edwardian building. The all-weather cigar terrace is the ideal place to indulge in a stogie from the well-stocked walk-in humidor.

🛏 45 ❄ 📶 Free 🚇 Marylebone, Baker Street, Bond Street

RESTAURANTS
PICCADILLY

SOMETHING SPECIAL

🍴 THE WOLSELEY
$$$$
160 PICCADILLY, W1
TEL 020 7499 6996
thewolseley.com
See and be seen for lunch in the magnificent 1921 former car showroom, enjoying a glass of champagne and then steak *frites* and fish. Book well ahead. Also open for stylish breakfast, tea, and dinner.

🚇 Green Park

PRICES

HOTELS
An indication of the cost of a double room in the high season is given by **$** signs.

$$$$$	Over $280
$$$$	$200–$280
$$$	$120–$200
$$	$80–$120
$	Under $80

RESTAURANTS
An indication of the cost of a three-course meal without drinks is given by **$** signs.

$$$$$	Over $80
$$$$	$50–$80
$$$	$35–$50
$$	$20–$35
$	Under $20

🏨 Hotel 🍴 Restaurant 🛏 No. of Guest Rooms ❄ Closed 🅿 Parking ❄ Air-conditioning 🏋 Gym

🍴 SAVINI CRITERION
$$$
224 PICCADILLY, W1
TEL 020 7930 1459
criterionrestaurant.com
Standing right beside the Eros statue at Piccadilly Circus, with marble walls and mosaic ceiling, it offers modern European food and live music Friday and Saturday from 7 p.m.
🕐 Closed Sun. L
🚇 Piccadilly Circus

REGENT STREET

🍴 NATHALIE
$$$
7 HANOVER SQUARE, W1
TEL. 020 3146 0663
nathaliemayfair.london
With a keen eye for nutritional values and sustainability, this restaurant offers balanced and delicious meals. Healthy food never tasted–nor looked–so good.
🕐 Closed Sun. L
🚇 Oxford Circus

🍴 RIBA CAFÉ AND BAR
$
ROYAL INSTITUTION OF BRITISH ARCHITECTS
66 PORTLAND PLACE, W1
TEL 020 7631 0467
architecture.com
Find the sleek 1930s building among Adam's grand mansions, check out the events program, and then head upstairs for a stylish breakfast or light lunch–on the roof terrace in summer.
🕐 Closed Sun. 🚇 Great Portland Street

PRIMROSE HILL

🍴 LEMONIA
$$
89 REGENT'S PARK RD., NW1
TEL 020 7586 7454
lemonia.co.uk
Near Primrose Hill, this local favorite serves traditional Greek Cypriot dishes such as *louvia* (black-eyed beans and spinach), squid, and delicious pudding of Greek yogurt, honey, and nuts.
🕐 Closed Sun. D
🚇 Chalk Farm

HAMPSTEAD

🍴 HIGHGATE BULL
$$
13 NORTH HILL, N6
TEL 020 8341 0510
thebullhighgate.co.uk
Among the many pubs here, the Highgate Bull wins for its historic building, outdoor terrace, quality beers, good service, and excellent food–from steaks to afternoon tea.
🚇 Highgate

🍴 JIN KICHI
$$
73 HEATH ST., NW3
TEL 020 7794 6158
jinkichi.com
Well-established Japanese izakaya-style restaurant, with loyal local clientele. Delicate dishes include chicken and shiso leaf.
🕐 Closed Mon.
🚇 Hampstead

🍴 LOUIS PATISSERIE
$
32 HEATH ST., NW3
TEL 020 7435 9908
louis-patisserie.com
Ideal stop during a visit to Hampstead or after a walk on the heath. Good apple danish pastries compete with interesting Hungarian ones such as cinnamon pretzels.
🕐 Closed 6 p.m.
🚇 Hampstead

▶ KENSINGTON & SOUTH KENSINGTON

There are several town-house hotels in this elegant residential area on the west side of central London, plus good restaurants patronized for dinner by local residents.

HOTELS

🏨 BAGLIONI
$$$$$
60 HYDE PARK GATE, SW7
TEL 020 7368 5700
baglionihotels.com
Inside a Victorian mansion opposite Kensington Palace, the atmosphere is easy, the decor chic modern, the rooms equipped with everything including espresso machines. With a serious spa.
🛏 68 🅿 📺 📶 Free
🚇 High Street Kensington

🏨 ASTER HOUSE
$$$
3 SUMNER PLACE, SW7
TEL 020 7581 5888
asterhouse.com
Welcoming and relaxed, and part of a fine, white stucco South Kensington terrace. Excellent service and a delightful, plant-filled conservatory for breakfast.
🛏 13 🅿 📶 Free 🚇 South Kensington

🏨 THE GORE
$$$
190 QUEEN'S GATE, SW7
TEL 020 7584 6601
gorehotel.com
Opened more than a century ago, the Gore carefully preserves its Victorian details with paneled rooms, potted ferns, rugs, and stained-glass windows. The building houses the fine quality **Bar One Ninety** and **Bistro One Ninety**. 🛏 50 🅿 📶 Free
🚇 South Kensington

🏨 KENSINGTON PRIME HOTEL
$$$
7 RUSSELL RD, KENSINGTON, W14
TEL 020 3911 9336

🏊 Indoor pool 📶 Wi-Fi 🚤 Boat 🚇 Tube/Rail/London Overground (LO)/Docklands Light Railway (DLR)

Former Thames Hotel, this luxurious boutique hotel opened in 2017 as a family business. The elegant building dates back to the 1930s.

🛈 19 🚇 Shepherd's Bush, Kensington Olympia

🏨 MAYFLOWER

$$$

26–28 TREBOVIR RD., SW5

TEL 020 7370 0991

mayflowerhotel.co.uk

Modern, well-appointed rooms of character with a touch of the exotic, such as colonial ceiling fans; plus adjoining apartments. There are two sister hotels nearby.

🛈 48 🚇 Free 🚇 Earl's Court

🏨 XENIA HOTEL

🍴 $$$

160 CROMWELL RD., SW5

TEL 020 7442 4242

hotelxenia.co.uk

This Victorian building down Cromwell Road from South Kensington's big museums offers compact but well-appointed guest rooms; the **Evoluzione** restaurant serves innovative modern Italian cuisine. Excellent customer service from a friendly staff.

🛈 99 ❄ 🚇 Free 🚇 Gloucester Road, Earl's Court

🏨 RUSHMORE

$

11 TREBOVIR RD., SW5

TEL 020 7370 3839

rushmore-hotel.co.uk

Frescoed wall, draped beds, an elegant breakfast room, and good service make this a bargain deal.

🛈 22 🚇 Free 🚇 Earl's Court

RESTAURANTS

🍴 CLARKE'S

$$$

124 KENSINGTON CHURCH ST., W8

TEL 020 7221 9225

sallyclarke.com

In the late 1970s, Sally Clarke's Cal-Ital food introduced new ideas to many young chefs. Fresh juices, home-baked breads, char-grilled duck, and perfect cheeses are all part of a good meal here. Brunch on Saturday mornings.

🕒 Closed Sun. D

🚇 Notting Hill Gate

🍴 HEREFORD ROAD

$$$

3 HEREFORD RD., W2

TEL 020 7727 1144

herefordroad.org

Despite a slightly austere dining room, it has been a success since it opened in 2007. Part of an increasingly trendy neighborhood, it serves unfussy and perfectly prepared classic British food—braised beef, roast calf's kidney, potted crab—at prices that are more than fair.

🚇 Bayswater

🍴 KENSINGTON PLACE

$$$

201–209 KENSINGTON CHURCH ST., W8

TEL 020 7727 3184

kensingtonplace-restaurant.co.uk

Plate-glass public eating in a loud, big room. Modern food includes grilled scallops with pea puree and mint vinaigrette—and don't miss the breads.

🚇 Notting Hill Gate

🍴 LAUNCESTON PLACE

$$$

1A LAUNCESTON PLACE, W8

TEL 020 7937 6912

launcestonplace-restaurant.co.uk

A sophisticated setting suits this restaurant's modern British dishes, such as Denham Castle lamb, Tamworth sucking pig, or West Coast scallops.

🕒 Closed Mon. 🚇 Gloucester Road, High Street Kensington

🍴 THE SCARSDALE

$$$

23A EDWARDES SQ, W8

TEL 020 7937 1811

scarsdaletavern.co.uk

Lovely tavern with a small garden in Kensington: great food and great beer.

🚇 Earl's Court

🍴 ABINGDON

$$

54 ABINGDON RD., W8

TEL 020 7937 3339

theabingdon.co.uk

Great atmosphere at this modern bistro in a converted corner pub. Try tuna, grilled steak with *pommes frites,* or duck leg confit.

🚇 High Street Kensington

🍴 THE CHURCHILL ARMS

$$

119 KENSINGTON CHURCH ST., W8

TEL. 020 7792 1246

churchillarmskensington.co.uk

Built in the 1750s, it was patronized by Churchill's grandparents. Today it is known for its original setting and Churchill's collection of memorabilia. Beer and authentic Thai cuisine.

🚇 Notting Hill Gate, High Street Kensington

▶ CHELSEA, BELGRAVIA, & KNIGHTSBRIDGE

Smart Londoners and foreign diplomats set the tone for elegant hotels and upmarket eating.

HOTELS

🏨 THE BERKELEY

🍴 $$$$$

WILTON PLACE, SW1

TEL 020 7235 6000

the-berkeley.co.uk

Now part of the Maybourne Hotel Group (which also owns **Claridge's** and **The Connaught**), the emphasis is on super-luxury all the way. The Berkeley is a modern hotel run on traditional lines: open fire in the lobby, lavish flower arrangements, spacious rooms, valet service. Excellent top-floor health club and swimming pool, equaled by the bar and restaurants that include Marcus Wareing's **Pétrus**.

ⓘ 214 🅢 🍴 🏊 📶 Free 🚇 Hyde Park Corner

🏨 COMO THE HALKIN
🍴 $$$$$
5-6 HALKIN ST., SW1
TEL 020 7333 1000
comohotels.com
The innovator: London's first design-aware hotel. Inspired by classic Italian style, notably the good air-conditioning and lighting control, staff dressed in Armani, and a Michelin-starred contemporary Thai restaurant called **Nahm.**

ⓘ 41 🅿 Valet 🅢 🍴
📶 Free 🚇 Hyde Park Corner

🏨 GORING
🍴 $$$$$
BEESTON PLACE
GROSVENOR GARDENS, SW1
TEL 020 7396 9000
thegoring.com
Run by the Goring family since 1910, this hotel promises excellent hospitality and service, and each room is individually designed and decorated. The excellent restaurant serves both traditional and contemporary British cuisine. The clublike bar is also first-rate.

ⓘ 71 🅢 📶 Free
🚇 Victoria

🏨 JUMEIRAH CARLTON
🍴 TOWER
$$$$$
CADOGAN PLACE, SW1
TEL 020 7235 1234
jumeirah.com
Impressive modern hotel, whose sky-high swimming pool and health club offer top-quality services at all levels; **Chinoiserie Lounge** for tea, **Rib Room** and **Oyster Bar** for traditional food. Convenient for Harrods and shopping.

ⓘ 220 🅿 Valet 🅢 🍴
🏊 📶 Free 🚇 Knightsbridge

🏨 THE LANESBOROUGH
🍴 $$$$$
HYDE PARK CORNER, SW1
TEL 020 7259 5599
lanesborough.com
Located on Hyde Park Corner, this modern hotel created inside a 19th-century neoclassical building offers lavish furnishings and extremely comfortable bedrooms. The **Conservatory** restaurant, with its palms and fountains, serves international cuisine.

ⓘ 95 🅢 🍴 📶 Free 🚇 Hyde Park Corner

🏨 MANDARIN ORIENTAL
🍴 HYDE PARK
$$$$$
66 KNIGHTSBRIDGE, SW1
TEL 020 7235 2000
mandarinoriental.com
/london
A splendid Edwardian landmark, extravagantly refurbished. Large rooms (request a park view), lavish bathrooms, and many Hyde Park views. Two outstanding restaurants are the **French Bar Boulud**, overseen by Daniel Boulud, and **Dinner by Heston Blumenthal**, the first London venture from Britain's own three-star chef.

ⓘ 198 🅿 🅢 🍴 🏊 📶 Free
🚇 Knightsbridge

🏨 THE CAPITAL
🍴 $$$$
22 BASIL ST.
KNIGHTSBRIDGE, SW3
TEL 020 7589 5171
www.capitalhotel.co.uk
Egyptian cotton sheets cover the beds in this immaculate, design-aware hotel that has both rooms and apartments. Eric Chavot cooks notably in the **Capital** restaurant.

ⓘ 49 🅢 📶 Free
🚇 Knightsbridge

🏨 KNIGHTSBRIDGE
HOTEL
$$$$
10 BEAUFORT GARDENS, SW3
TEL 020 7584 6300
firmdale.com
Good location for Knightsbridge shopping, and smart rooms to match. No bar, restaurant, or gym, but great room-service menu.

ⓘ 44 🅿 Valet 🅢
📶 Free 🚇 Knightsbridge

🏨 B&B BELGRAVIA
$$
64–66 EBURY ST., SW1
TEL 020 7259 8570
bb-belgravia.com
Away from chintz, the B&B Belgravia has a freshness and contemporary quality that gives a whole new understanding of a "B&B," from the quality bed linen and power showers to the fresh breakfast ingredients.

ⓘ 17 📶 Free 🚇 Victoria

RESTAURANTS

🍴 GORDON RAMSAY
$$$$
68 ROYAL HOSPITAL RD., SW3
TEL 020 7352 4441
gordonramsay.com/
royalhospitalroad
Celebrated chef Gordon Ramsay swears by his modern French dishes created in this small, intimate restaurant.

🏊 Indoor pool 📶 Wi-Fi 🚢 Boat 🚇 Tube/Rail/London Overground (LO)/Docklands Light Railway (DLR)

Dishes might include delicious lobster ravioli or langoustine and salmon poached in light bisque. Good value three-course set lunch.

🕐 Closed Sun. & Mon.
🚇 Sloane Square, then ten-minute walk

🍴 NO. 11 PIMLICO ROAD
$$$
11 PIMLICO RD., SW1
TEL 020 7730 6784
no11pimlicoroad.co.uk
Worth the detour to enjoy one of London's top gastropubs with bar, brasserie, and upstairs restaurant; great decor, charming staff, and accomplished European dishes. Leave room for the desserts, each matched with a dessert wine.

🕐 Closed Mon.–Sat. D
🚇 Sloane Square, Victoria

🍴 SALLOOS
$$$
62–64 KINNERTON ST., SW1
TEL 020 7235 4444
salloos.co.uk
Mr. Salahuddin's classy Pakistani restaurant, founded in 1979, serves family recipes. The focus is meat, including marinated lamb chops and chicken shish kebab, with warm naan breads.

🕐 Closed Sun.
🚇 Knightsbridge

🍴 TOM'S KITCHEN
$$$
27 CALE ST., SW3
TEL 020 7349 0202
tomskitchen.co.uk
Tom Aitken's modern bistro is busy and bustling, with an open kitchen, wood-fired oven, and spit-roast and grill. It offers classic modern British cooking, with hints of Italian, French, and American cuisine. Breakfasts are particularly good (especially the pancakes),

and there's an appealing bar on the upper floor.
🚇 Sloane Square, South Kensington

🍴 WULF & LAMB
$$$
243 PAVILION RD., SW1
TEL 020 3948 5999
wulfandlamb.com
This vegan restaurant offers surprising ingredients and flavors.

🚇 Sloane Square

🍴 THE THOMAS CUBITT
$–$$
44 ELIZABETH ST., SW1
TEL 020 7730 6060
thethomascubitt.co.uk
This airy and tastefully decorated contemporary pub with food sits well on Elizabeth Street, which is full of similarly chic and perfectly pitched outlets. Eat casually downstairs from the bar menu or in the small, more formal dining rooms upstairs.

🚇 Sloane Square, Victoria

▶ WEST LONDON

Some special hotels and some good restaurants to combine with sightseeing.

HOTELS

🏨 THE PORTOBELLO HOTEL
$$$$
22 STANLEY GARDENS, W1
TEL 020 7727 2777
portobellohotel.com
Town-house hotel tucked away in the leafy and exclusive residential area of Notting Hill. Its stuccoed Victorian facade belies a delightfully idiosyncratic and high-quality interior much loved by guests.

🛏 21 🌀 📶 Free 🚇 Holland Park, Notting Hill Gate

🏨 THE ROCKWELL
$$$$
181–183 CROMWELL RD., SW5
TEL 020 7244 2000
therockwell.com
One of London's best recent openings occupies a listed historic building. Rooms are all different, though all share elegant and understated contemporary styling. Triple-glazing blocks the noise from busy Cromwell Road. The location is good for Gloucester Road and the stores of Kensington High Street.

🛏 40 🌀 📶 Free 🚇 Earl's Court

🏨 ABBEY COURT NOTTING HILL
$$$
20 PEMBRIDGE GARDENS, W2
TEL 020 7221 7518
abbeycourthotel.co.uk
Designers Guild fabrics are used in the individually decorated rooms of this friendly town-house hotel. All rooms have plenty of books and a relaxing Jacuzzi bath.

🛏 22 📶 Free 🚇 Notting Hill Gate

🏨 COLONNADE
$$$
2 WARRINGTON CRESCENT
LITTLE VENICE, W9
TEL 020 7286 1052
thecolonnadehotel.co.uk
Leafy, romantic Little Venice is the rural setting for the sumptuous Victorian hotel with classically decorated rooms; worth the edge-of-town location.

🛏 43 🅿 🌀 📶 Free 🚇 Warwick Avenue

RESTAURANTS

🍴 THE LEDBURY
$$$$
127 LEDBURY RD., W11
TEL 020 7792 9090
theledbury.com

🏨 Hotel 🍴 Restaurant 🛏 No. of Guest Rooms 🕐 Closed 🅿 Parking 🌀 Air-conditioning 🏋 Gym

Moments from the chic Notting Hill shopping enclave of Westbourne Grove, The Ledbury has built a reputation over several years as one of the best restaurants in Britain, never mind London. Michelin has awarded the food one and two stars over a long period, but the rarefied culinary creations are combined with a pleasantly relaxed dining experience.

🕐 Closed L Mon.–Tues.
🚇 Notting Hill, Westbourne Park

🍴 THE RIVER CAFE

$$$$

THAMES WHARF
RAINVILLE RD., W6
TEL 020 7386 4200
rivercafe.co.uk

Famous across the world for inspirational cookbooks bearing its name, the fountainhead of Ruth Rogers's and the late Rose Gray's success is worth the effort of reserving well in advance and dedicating time to reach the offbeat location.

🚇 Hammersmith, then taxi or 20-minute walk

🍴 LA TROMPETTE

$$$$

5–7 DEVONSHIRE RD., W4
TEL 020 8747 1836
latrompette.co.uk

Worth the journey out (combine with Kew, Chiswick, or Syon, perhaps) to enjoy the impressive French dishes of James Bennington, together with his well-chosen wines and charming staff; a memorable and good-value treat.

🚇 Turnham Green

SOMETHING SPECIAL

🍴 THE BELVEDERE

$$$

ABBOTSBURY RD.
HOLLAND PARK, W8
TEL 020 7602 1238

belvedererestaurant.co.uk

A quality restaurant set in one of London's beautiful parks. The Belvedere was formerly the summer ballroom of the Jacobean mansion Holland House. Now it is one of London's most romantic settings, serving reliable, not exceptional, French cuisine. Best for lunch, when there is a good-value set menu.

🚇 Holland Park

🍴 THE FIFTH FLOOR

$$$

HARVEY NICHOLS
KNIGHTSBRIDGE, SW1
TEL 020 7235 5250
harveynichols.com

This is the ultimate shopping dream: four floors of Harvey Nichols fashion sandwiched between chic restaurants. The Fifth Floor is the smartest, serving dishes such as quail with pumpkin ravioli and creamy risotto. Also open for breakfast and tea. There is a trendy bar next door, a simpler café, and also a sublime food store nearby.

🚇 Knightsbridge

🍴 JULIE'S

$$$

135 PORTLAND RD., W11
TEL 020 7229 8331
juliesrestaurant.com

Julie's has been a chic and romantic fixture for West Londoners in the know since 1969, its main lure an eclectic maze of homey dining rooms and alcoves with a distinctly bohemian air. Tucked away in an enclave of prime real estate, it is perfect for a quiet drink at the bar or a full meal of mostly British-influenced dishes. Get a table in the wine bar—the food is the same but the setting more appealing.

🚇 Holland Park

🍴 RIVA

$$$

169 CHURCH RD., SW13
TEL 020 8748 0434
rivarestaurants.com

Enjoy Francesco Zanchetta's almost perfect rustic Italian food. Classic regional dishes, such as *frittelle*, *osso buco alla milanese* with saffron risotto, more than merit the long journey from the center of town.

🕐 Closed Sat. L & period in Aug. 🚇 Hammersmith, then bus 33, 72, 209, or 283. Train: Barnes Bridge

▶ EAST LONDON

The recent revitalization of East London, from the Tower of London to Canary Wharf, has included the birth of its own bar and restaurant scene.

HOTEL

🏨 CANARY RIVERSIDE PLAZA HOTEL

$$$$$

46 WESTFERRY CIRCUS, E14
TEL 020 7510 1999
www.canaryriversideplaza.com

This is Canary Wharf's only five star independent hotel, a stunning building that pampers guests with all modern conveniences including pool, health club & spa, three floors of fitness facilities, and tennis courts.

🛏 142 🅿 Valet 🕐 📶 🛁 🚇 Free 🚇 Canary Wharf

🏨 TOWN HALL

🍴 HOTEL

$$$$

PATRIOT SQUARE, E2
TEL 020 7871 0460
townhallhotel.com

The influx of artists, writers, and creative and tech businesses into parts of the East End meant that it was only a matter of time before the area acquired its first upscale hotel. The Town Hall Hotel occupies the grand old City Hall of Bethnal Green, combining its original Edwardian art deco flourishes with more pared-down contemporary features. Apartments and studios with kitchens are also available for longer or self-catering stays.

 98 🅟 💺 🚗 🛜 Free
🚇 Bethnal Green

RESTAURANTS

🍴 THE GUN

$$$$

27 COLDHARBOUR, E1

TEL 020 7515 5222

thegundocklands.com

This restaurant in the Docklands delivers a special gastronomic experience with a splendid view of the Thames and the O$_2$ Arena. Away from the hustle and bustle, it is the perfect place to relax with excellent fresh food and extraordinary wines.

🚇 Canary Wharf

🍴 BISTROTHEQUE

$$$

23–27 WADESON ST., E2

TEL 020 8983 7900

bistrotheque.com

Find a great bar upstairs and a casual but notable French restaurant, both in a former warehouse.

🚇 Bethnal Green; Overground: Cambridge Heath

🍴 CAFÉ SPICE NAMASTE

$$$

16 PRESCOT ST., E1

TEL 020 7488 9242

cafespice.co.uk

Modern, inventive Indian cooking by Cyrus Todiwala. Try the tandoori duck, Goan seafood pilau, and whichever new dish he has created.

🕒 Closed Sun. 🚇 Tower Hill

🍴 LYLE'S

$$$

TEA BUILDING, 56 SHOREDITCH HIGH ST., E1

TEL 020 3011 5911

lyleslondon.com

Sophisticated modern British cooking in a bright, clean-lined semi-industrial space. Menus change daily, with an emphasis on fine, regionally sourced ingredients such as Maldon oysters and Neal's Yard cheeses.

🕒 Closed Sun. & bank holidays 🚇 Old Street, Liverpool Street

🍴 PLATEAU

$$$

CANADA PLACE

CANADA SQUARE, E14

TEL 020 7715 7100

plateau-restaurant.co.uk

Suitably dramatic glass building on this superb waterside site. Bar, grill, and restaurant all good.

🕒 Closed Sat. L, Sun., & bank holidays 🚇 Canary Wharf (DLR)

🍴 DISHOOM

$$

7 BOUNDARY ST., E2

TEL 020 7420 9324

dishoom.com

East London's Brick Lane was for a long time the traditional place to find authentic curry in the capital, but these days the menu touts and falling standards have encouraged Londoners to look farther afield to places such as Dishoom, which affects the relaxed style of a Mumbai café, with all-day Indian dishes paired with English staples such as bacon and sausage with an Indian twist. Dishoom has two equally appealing central outlets in Covent Garden (*12 Upper St. Martin's Lane, tel 020 7420 9320, WC2*) and King's Cross (*5 Stable St., N1, tel 020 7420 9321*).

🚇 Shoreditch High Street (LO)

🍴 TAYYABS

$$

83–89 FIELDGATE ST., E1

TEL 020 7247 6400

tayyabs.co.uk

This is an East London institution, founded in 1972, specializing in Punjabi cuisine, with grilled dishes among the highlights. It is very popular, so make a reservation in advance (even then you may wait in line). When you get there, be prepared for brisk service and a bustling, hectic atmosphere.

🚇 Aldgate East, Whitechapel (LO)

🍴 BRICK LANE BEIGEL BAKE

$

159 BRICK LANE, E1

TEL 020 7729 0616

The fact that more than 7,000 bagels leave this tiny, unremarkable café on a Saturday night confirms its status as the best in town. Quality smoked salmon, cream cheese, and breads.

🕒 Open 24 hours
🚇 Liverpool Street

🍴 F. COOKE

$

150 HOXTON ST., N1

TEL 020 7729 7718

Pie, "mash" (mashed potato), and eels were once cheap, dietary staples of London's working families, but today only a handful of the capital's traditional "pie and mash" shops and dining rooms survive, most in the east of the city. This shop has been in the same family since 1862, and it offers a truly warm welcome and an authentic experience.

🕒 Closed Sun.
🚇 Hoxton (LO)

🏨 Hotel 🍴 Restaurant ⓘ No. of Guest Rooms 🕒 Closed 🅟 Parking ❄ Air-conditioning 🏋 Gym

SHOPPING

There are various ways of shopping in London. You may come with a specific shopping list, you may want to see the latest fashions, or you may simply wish to window-shop with the possibility of a purchase. Whichever it is, London has several shopping centers and offers several ways of shopping.

Although shops are traditionally open between 9 a.m. and 5 p.m., opening hours are no longer fixed times. Many Oxford Street, Regent Street, and High Street Kensington shops remain open until 7 or 8 p.m. on Thursday; most Knightsbridge and Chelsea shops do the same on Friday; and most stores in key shopping areas, including those on Tottenham Court Road, are open on Sunday. Seasonal sales take place in January, extending into February, and July, extending into August.

Most shops accept the major credit cards. There is often a fee for using travelers' checks.

The VAT, currently 20 percent, is payable on almost everything (exceptions include books, food, and children's clothes) but is almost always included in the product's given price. All non-U.K. passport holders and those officially resident outside the U.K. are exempt from the VAT if they are taking the goods out of the U.K. within three months. The tax must be paid, then reclaimed. There is one system for those living in EC countries, another for those living outside the EC. Shopkeepers are usually good at helping customers complete the necessary forms.

London shoppers are well protected by the law. For instance, a shopkeeper displaying a credit card sign is obliged to accept that card; goods in sales should be perfect unless they are labeled otherwise; and if an object fails to perform its job, there should be a full refund.

Department Stores

The one-stop shopping that department stores offer has advantages. Some well-known stores:

Fenwick, 63 New Bond St., tel 020 7629 9161. Fashion, cosmetics, and fabrics.

Fortnum & Mason, 181 Piccadilly, tel 020 7734 8040. High prices, but the own-brand goods make perfect presents.

Harrods, 87-135 Brompton Rd., tel 020 7730 1234. The epitome of these grand, multi-floored shops. It is often derided by Londoners who then admit they go there for one department.

Harvey Nichols, 109–25 Knightsbridge, tel 020 7235 5000. Classy clothes for women.

John Lewis, 300 Oxford St., tel 020 7629 7711. Good for reasonably priced, sensible homeware.

Liberty, Regent St., tel 020 7734 1234. Goods range from sumptuous fabrics to the best china and glass.

Marks & Spencer, 458 Oxford St., tel 020 7935 7954. An obligatory visit to M&S for underwear the world wears.

Peter Jones, Sloane Square, tel 020 7730 3434. John Lewis's slightly more stylish sister.

Selfridges, 400 Oxford St., tel 800 123 400. Vast store with notable food and cosmetics. Currently considered by shopaholics to rival Harrods.

Souvenirs

Museum and gallery shops have quality goods ranging from desk diaries featuring their treasures to full sets of tableware and related toys. Examples of these can be found at:

British Museum, Great Russell St., tel 020 7323 8299. Three shops plus an interesting children's shop.

London Transport Museum, Covent Garden Piazza, tel 020 7565 7298. An amazing selection of items that pays tribute to the city's public transport.

Natural History Museum, Cromwell Rd., tel 020 7942 5000. Thousands of dinosaur-themed souvenirs.

Queen's Gallery, Buckingham Palace Rd., tel 303 123 7301. Quality goods, often bearing the royal stamp of authenticity.

Science Museum, Exhibition Rd., tel 020 7942 4000. Projects for budding scientists.

Tate Britain, Millbank, tel 020 7887 8888.

Tate Modern, Bankside, tel 7401 5167 8000. Both Tates have excellent stocks of books and designer gifts.

Victoria and Albert Museum, Cromwell Rd., tel 020 7492 2000. Collection-inspired goods.

Specialty Shops

This is where the fun lies, although some homework with a map may be needed to avoid crisscrossing London. Certain kinds of shops tend to group together, such as in Bond Street or Sloane Street for fashion, Brompton Cross, Soho, and Clerkenwell for contemporary design and jewelers, and St. James's and Mayfair for upscale art. Here are some ideas:

Accessories

James Smith & Sons, 53 New Oxford St., tel 020 7836 4731. Every kind of umbrella and walking stick.

Swaine Adeney Brigg & Sons and **Herbert Johnson,** 7 Piccadilly Arcade, Jermyn St., tel 020 7409 7277. For classic accessories including umbrellas and hats.

Tiffany & Co., 25 Bond St., tel 0800 160 1114. For total extravagance.

Art at Auction

The two top auction houses are:

Christie's, 8 King St., St. James's, tel 020 7839 9060.

Sotheby's, 34–35 New Bond St., Mayfair, tel 020 7293 5000. It is also well worth visiting:

Bonhams, 101 New Bond St., tel 020 7447 7447.

Phillips, 30 Berkeley Square, tel 020 7318 4010.

Decor and Designs

Designers Guild, 267-277 King's Rd., tel 020 7351 5775.

Divertimenti, 227-229 Brompton Road, tel 020 7581 8065.

Heal's, 196 Tottenham Court Rd., tel 020 7636 1666.

Designer Fashion

Top designers, such as Vivienne Westwood and Burberry, have their flagship stores in or near New Bond Street, in Mayfair. Branches are usually in Knightsbridge (Sloane Street, Brompton Road), Kensington, and/or Covent Garden. Large department stores such as Harvey Nichols and Selfridges also house top designer lines (see p. 261). Other names to seek out:

Agnès B, 35-36 Floral St., tel 020 7379 1992.

Betty Jackson, 311 Brompton Rd., tel 020 7589 7884.

Issey Miyake, 10 Brook St., tel 020 7851 4620.

Paul Smith, 40-44 Floral St. and 122 Kensington Park Rd., tel 020 7379 7133.

Stella McCartney, 23, Old Bond Street, tel 020 7518 3100.

Gifts

Alessi Oggetti, 22 Brook St., tel 020 7518 9090. Chic designer objects.

Asprey, 167 New Bond St., tel 020 7493 6767. Ultimate deluxe gifts, but for most people just ultimate window-shopping.

Bibendum, 113 Regent's Park Rd., tel 0845 263 6924. Fine selection of wines.

Carluccio's, 1 Old Brompton Road, tel 020 7581 8101. Designer delicatessen with cheeses, herbs, and cosmetics.

Paxton & Whitfield, 93 Jermyn St., tel 020 7930 0259. Cheeses.

Shoes

Emma Hope, 207 Westbourne Grove, tel 020 7313 7493.

Irregular Choice, 35 Carnaby St., tel 020 7494 4811.

Manolo Blahnik, 49–51 Old Church St., Chelsea, tel 020 7352 8622.

Sports Equipment

Lillywhites, 24–36 Lower Regent St., tel 344 332 5602. Whatever the sport, this shop has the equipment and outfit that you need.

Specialty Bookstores

Books for Cooks, 4 Blenheim Crescent, tel 020 7221 1992. Possibly the world's best for cookware and cuisine.

Daunt Books, 83 Marylebone High St., tel 020 7224 2295. Travel specialist and general bookshop with seven London stores.

Henry Sotheran, 2–5 Sackville St., tel 020 7439 6151. Antique books and prints.

London Review Bookshop, 14 Bury Place, tel 020 7269 9030.

Just around the corner from the British Museum, bookworms should browse one of London's great independent bookstores.

Maggs Brothers, 46 Curzon St., tel 020 3005 6740. Locate that out-of-print, first edition, or rare antiquarian book.

Toys & Games

Hamleys, 188 Regent St., tel 371 704 1977. A seven-floor wonderland for kids and adults, but it's more congenial to go to the fourth floor of Harrods, where they take orders.

Unusual Sizes

Base, 55 Monmouth St., tel 020 7240 8914.

Evans, 529–533 Oxford St., tel 020 7495 3776. Stocks fashionable clothes in sizes 14 to 32, plus the French & Teague 1647 range and clothes for petite women.

Street Markets

Market goods range from fine antiques, as at Camden Passage, to fruits and vegetables, as in Berwick Street, Soho (see p. 165).

Camden Market, Camden High St. This and its adjoining markets provide a huge sprawl of stalls, street culture, and bargain shopping of all kinds.

Greenwich Market, King William Walk. This covered weekend market provides visitors with a lively and colorful destination at the end of a Thames boat ride. If you enjoy browsing through an exotic array of clothes, antiques, books, and prints, this is one of the capital's more enticing markets.

Portobello Road Market, Portobello Rd. More than a mile (1.6 km) long, selling quality antiques and fruits and vegetables (see p. 164). Main antiques market Saturday only.

ENTERTAINMENT

One of the most exciting, if frustrating, things about London is that there is so much theater, music, cinema, and other entertainment that it is impossible to see everything you would like to see. The range is wide, too, from serious opera, cinema, and sacred music to jazz restaurants, spectator sports, and extravagant musicals. And that does not include the plays and musicals, often the biggest draw for visitors. It would be impossible to list every entertainment venue in London. But here are some tips and essential information to help you find the right entertainment for your taste.

Information

Time Out, published free every Tuesday, has impressively comprehensive entertainment listings. Its often acerbic reviews should not be taken too seriously. The free *London Evening Standard*, published daily Monday through Friday, is London's monopoly evening newspaper, featuring day-after reviews, plus plenty of listings.

The Guardian newspaper publishes a detailed listings magazine free with its Saturday edition. See also websites pp. 239–240.

Cinema

London's cinema is not as good as some other European cities such as Paris. That said, there is a good mix of Hollywood, independent, European (subtitled, not dubbed), and oldies.

Large-Screen Theaters

The best places to see commercial first runs include:

BFI London IMAX Cinema, 1 Charlie Chaplin Walk, South Bank. Britain's largest cinema screen.

British Film Institute, South Bank, tel 020 7928 3232. Independent theater with four screens showing a mixed program.

Empire, 5–6 Leicester Square, tel 871 2002000.

Everyman, Hampstead, tel 0871 906 9060. Shows fine films, old and new in repertory.

Odeon West End, 40 Leicester Square, tel 333 014 4501.

Clubbing

London has arguably the most dynamic and varied nightlife in the world. The most exciting nights are weekdays, not weekends. Many clubs operate one night a week and have specific dress codes. To find your way, consult *Time Out*. As a start, check out Bar Rumba, Fabric, Egg, and Ministry of Sound.

Comedy

Comedy Café, 66–68 Rivington St., tel 020 7739 5706.

The Comedy Store, 1a Oxendon St., thecomedystore.co.uk. Budding comics face an unforgiving audience.

Dance

Bhavan Centre, 4a Castletown Rd., tel 020 7381 3086. Quality, traditional Indian dance.

The Coliseum, St. Martin's Lane, tel 020 7845 9300 (reservations). Major world dance companies in summer and at Christmas; otherwise, opera.

Dance Umbrella, 1 Brewery Square, tel 020 7407 1200. Offers an annual festival of dance and performances at nine major venues around the city.

The Place, 17 Dukes Rd., tel 020 7121 1100.

Royal Opera House, Covent Garden, tel 020 7304 4000. Home to the Royal Ballet, sharing time with the Royal Opera.

Sadler's Wells Theatre, Rosebery Ave., tel 020 7863 8016.

South Bank, the **Royal Opera House,** and the **Barbican Centre** (see Theater section) are also major dance venues.

Festivals

Major festivals include the Hampton Court Palace Festival, the City of London Festival, the Henry Wood Promenade Concerts (BBC "Proms"), the Spitalfields Festival, and the Almeida Festival. Jazz festivals include Ealing Jazz Festival (tel 020 8825 6640), Europe's largest, and the London Jazz Festival (tel 020 7324 1880).

Jazz

Find some of the best jazz in town at:

Bull's Head, 373 Lonsdale Rd., Barnes, tel 020 8876 5241. Good jazz in a friendly riverside pub.

Jazz Café, 5 Parkway, tel 020 7485 6834. Favorite among the young.

Pizza Express Jazz Club, 10 Dean St., tel 020 7437 9595. Quality pizzas and mainstream jazz.

Ronnie Scott's, 47 Frith St., tel 020 7439 0747. Run by jazz musicians for jazz lovers.

Music

Classical

It is said that there are a thousand concerts given across London each week. The capital has four world-class orchestras, many small ensembles, and countless venues. Major venues include:

Barbican Centre, Silk St., EC2, tel 020 7638 4141 (information),

020 7638 8891 (box office).

Royal Albert Hall, Kensington Gore, tel 020 7589 8212 or 0845 401 5045. London's circular concert hall and venue for the Proms.

Royal Festival Hall, Queen Elizabeth Hall, and **Purcell Room** on the south bank, tel 0844 875 0073.

Wigmore Hall, 36 Wigmore St., tel 020 7935 2141.

Contemporary

Big stars play venues such as:

Hackney Empire, 291 Mare St., tel 020 8985 2424.

O₂ Academy Brixton, 211 Stockwell Rd., tel 0844 477 2000 (box office; fee for call); 020 7771 3000 (information). The lesser, or newer, ones play here.

O₂ Arena, North Greenwich, tel 020 8463 3359 (Ticketmaster). Formerly the Millennium Dome, now an extremely popular music and events venue.

Wembley SSE Arena and Stadium, tel 844 980 8001 (stadium), 0844 8150815 (arena).

Music & Dance With Food

London is less good at upscale restaurants with dancing—the **Savoy's River Room** (see p. 242) is an exception—than it is at more modest places such as **Salsa!,** 96 Charing Cross Rd., tel 020 7379 3277, and **Sarastro,** 126 Drury Lane, tel 020 7836 0101, where budding opera singers entertain (usually Sun. & Mon.).

Musicals

London offers first-rate musicals, surpassed only by those of New York. The main long-running shows are:

The Lion King (Lyceum Theatre), **Phantom of The Opera** (Her Majesty Theatre), **Les Miserables** (Queens Theatre), **Mamma mia** (Novello Theatre).

Opera

The Coliseum (see Dance). English National Opera performs in English for seasons alternating with dance.

Royal Opera House (see Dance). Home to the Royal Opera and the Royal Ballet.

Sadler's Wells (see Dance) and **Opera Holland Park** (tel 020 7361 3570 or box office 0300 999 1000) also host opera.

Theater

Theater Information & Tickets

Tickets for almost any show can be bought legally. It is extremely unwise to buy from a ticket tout. Ticketmaster (tel 333 321 9999) is a reliable agency, with a reservation fee. Beware: Theaters taking phone reservations may also charge a fee.

Artsline (tel 020 7388 2227, artsline.org.uk) gives free advice on London arts for visitors with disabilities.

Ideally, either go to the theater (where there are seating plans) or go to the half-price ticket booth, called **TKTS** (Leicester Square, WC2, officiallondontheatre.co.uk or tkts.co.uk). Here you can save up to 50 percent on seat prices. It is open Monday through Saturday from 10 a.m. to 7 p.m., Sunday 11 a.m. to 4 p.m., selling tickets for that day's performance only. One person may buy up to four tickets (credit cards accepted; £3 service charge per ticket). Beware imitators around the square.

Commercial Theaters

The commercial theaters of the West End stage plays with broad appeal. Here are a few:

Almeida, Almeida St., tel 020 7359 4404. Lures top actors to perform highbrow plays.

Barbican Centre, Silk St., EC2, tel 020 7638 8891. Regional and foreign theater companies.

Donmar Warehouse, 41 Earlham St., tel 020 3282 3808.

The Gate, 11 Pembridge Rd., tel 020 7229 0706.

Hampstead Theatre, Eton Ave., Swiss Cottage, tel 020 7722 9301.

The Kings Head, 115 Upper St., tel 020 7226 4443.

Old Vic, The Cut, tel 0844 8717628. Shakespeare and classics.

Royal Court, Sloane Square, Chelsea, tel 020 7565 5000. Known for new writing.

Theatre Royal Stratford East, tel 020 8534 0310.

Young Vic, The Cut, tel 020 7922 2922.

"The Fringe"

The Fringe consists of many little theaters scattered across London, the venues often small and basic, many of them in pubs, often promoting young people and new ideas. Try these:

Etcetera Theatre, Oxford Arms Pub, 265 Camden High St., tel 020 7482 4857.

The Finborough, 118 Finborough Rd., tel 020 7244 7439.

Other Theaters

Regent's Park (see p. 147)
Shakespeare's Globe (see p. 103)

State-Supported Theater

The state supports the Royal National Theatre, which has three stages, each with several plays in production concurrently. Plays range from Greek to contemporary first runs.

National Theatre, South Bank, tel 020 7452 3400, tickets 020 7452 3000. Three theaters under one roof.

Royal Shakespeare Company, Stratford-upon-Avon, tel box office 017 8933 1111. The company's home is at the Royal Shakespeare Theatre, Waterside, Stratford-upon-Avon, Warwickshire.

INDEX

ILLUSTRATIONS CREDITS

4, Dean and Chapter of Westminster; 8, The Royal Collection; 13, dwphotos/Shutterstock; 21, The British Library Board; 25, akva/Shutterstock; 27, National Archives photo 306-NT-901C-11 (New York Times Paris Bureau Collection); 29, Press Association via AP Images; 31, Peter Smith/St. Paul's Cathedral; 32, Natasha Scripture; 39, Colin Streater; 40, The National Gallery, London; 42, National Portrait Gallery, London; 44-5, theatrepix/ Alamy; 50, Bridgeman Art Library London & New York/Roundnice Lobkowicz Coll., Nelahozeves Castle, Czech Republic; 68, © Guy Bell, 07771 786236, guy@gbphotos.com. All rights reserved.; 74, Dean and Chapter of Westminster; 86, Her Majesty Queen Elizabeth II (Photographer: Derry Moore); 88, Albert Philip Van Der Werf/dpa/Corbis; 89, Pres Panayotov/Shutterstock; 92, Jeff Gilbert/Alamy; 93, "Grosvenor House, A JW Marriott Hotel"—Anna's Afternoon Tea; 101, Richard Ash/IWM; 103, John Tramper; 104, © Tate, London 2014; 112, The National Gallery, London; 115, National Portrait Gallery, London; 117, National Portrait Gallery, London; 130, Courtesy Sir John Soane's Museum; 149, Ben A. Pruchnie/Getty Images; 158, Peter Scholey/Alamy; 171, Victoria and Albert Museum, London; 172, London Science Museum; 177, Lawrence M. Porges; 194, John Freeman; 197, St. Nick/Shutterstock; 208, SOPA/eStock Photo; 211, Tony Taylor/Alamy; 214, Museum of London; 215, Piero Cruciatti/Alamy; 222, Her Majesty Queen Elizabeth II (Photographer: Peter Smith); 224, Andrei Nekrassov/Shutterstock; 234, ronfromyork/Shutterstock.

National Geographic

TRAVELER

London

FIFTH EDITION

Since 1888, the National Geographic Society has funded more than 14,000 research, exploration, and preservation projects around the world. National Geographic Partners distributes a portion of the funds it receives from your purchase to National Geographic Society to support programs including the conservation of animals and their habitats.

National Geographic Partners, LLC
1145 17th Street NW
Washington, DC 20036-4688 USA

Get closer to National Geographic explorers and photographers, and connect with our global community. Join us today at nationalgeographic.org/joinus

For rights or permissions inquiries, please contact National Geographic Books Subsidiary Rights: bookrights@natgeo.com

Drive maps drawn by Chris Orr Associates, Southampton, England
Cutaway illustrations drawn by Maltings Partnership, Derby, England

Fifth edition edited by White Star s.r.l. Licensee of National Geographic Partners, LLC. Update by Iceigeo, Milan (Ilaria Ghisletti, Cynthia Anne Koeppe, Renata Grilli)

The information in this book has been carefully checked and to the best of our knowledge is accurate. However, details are subject to change, and the publisher cannot be responsible for such changes, or for errors or omissions. Assessments of sites, hotels, and restaurants are based on the author's subjective opinions, which do not necessarily reflect the publisher's opinion.

ISBN: 978-88-544-1677-2

Printed in China

MIX
Paper from responsible sources
FSC® C178000
www.fsc.org

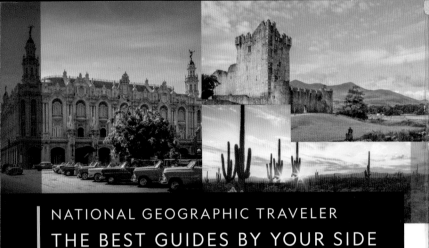